BLUELINE OF LIFE &

DEATH

STUART CANNOLD

DEDICATION

I dedicate this novel to Randy Narramore, whom I met while in the police academy. Randy Narramore became Chief of the Huntington Park, California Police Department, as I tested for various departments. It was Chief Narramore who pinned that badge to my uniform in 1996. I handled traffic enforcement. My call sign was 5 TOM. Thank you, sir. Those 15 years were the most productive, the happiest years of my working life. I will never forget those Level 1 Reserve years or the "shot" you gave me.

I also dedicate this novel to my wife Jo, who would ride with me often in that black and white and who observed her first two dead bodies just outside that unit. Jo became an HPPD volunteer. Jo persuaded me to chase my dream of publishing a novel. We are slowly approaching ten years of wedded bliss. We have yet to have an argument; no easy task being married to me! Thank you, angel!

My parents, long gone, are up above looking over me and keeping me on the straight and narrow. I know I was a tough bullet to bite, but you never gave up on your son. Thank you! I know we'll meet again!

In 1964, Mom, you wrote in my high school yearbook: We have a wonderful boy, and I say to him, "Son, be fair and square in the race you must run. Be brave if you lose, be meek if you win, be better and nobler than we've ever been. Be honest and noble in all that you do. And honor the name we've given to you." I can only hope I measured up.

To my editor Dr. Myles Bader, who gently prodded me into fulfilling a lifelong goal? The future's not ours to see. One can only hope. Thank you, Myles!

Last, but certainly at the top of my list is the fallen Officer who owned serial # 5172. I never thought I could miss anyone as much as I miss you. Thank you for seeing to it that I got home in one piece after my shift even though I smelled from cigarette smoke. RIP, friend. We'll meet again. I'm looking forward to it.

Once again, faith has conquered fear in favor of my Higher Power. I did the footwork. The rest is out of my hands!

5 TOM

ABOUT THE AUTHOR

The author was born in Brooklyn in 1946. He grew up on the streets of New York and New Jersey and created his own chaos   early on and damn near didn't graduate high school. At age 28, Stu started to turn his life around with the help of some amazing people who refused to throw in Stu's cards.

Stu earned a BA from Franconia College in New Hampshire. While attending Franconia College, Stu, a journalism major, spent a semester as an intern for a southern California newspaper. Although he turned down an offer to work for the newspaper, he returned to California years later and made it his home. He went on to earn a Master's degree in education, attending Oakland University, which was then affiliated with Michigan State.

He earned his administrative credential from Pepperdine University and his Doctorate in Educational Administration from United States International University in San Diego. He graduated from the Cerro Coso Police Academy in 1996.

Stu taught classes for many years for the University of Redlands and Phoenix University. He spent 33 plus years as a teacher and school administrator in Detroit and California.

Stu and his wife Jo, who reside in southern Arizona (and love it), collect classic cars. Three of their vehicles are in the Riverside Resort and Casino's car museum in Laughlin, Nevada. As you might have guessed, one of those cars is a 1930 Ford Model A, police car. Another is an authentic 1978 Harley Davidson Police Motorcycle with Sidecar, and the third is a 1957 Ford Thunderbird E Bird with overdrive, a rare bird, and a Gold Medallion winner in the 2019 Thunderbird Concours in Flagstaff.

The Camaro B4C CHP car pictured at the beginning of this novel belongs to Jo and Stu. Stu and Jo's 1974 Cadillac Miller-Meteor Criterion ambulance is a rolling memorial for September 11, 2001. **WE MUST NEVER FORGET!**

Stu is terrified of heights. Second, to publishing a novel, Stu wants to overcome the fear of heights and jump out of a plane. Years ago, Stu attempted this feat in California but chickened out. Stu doesn't know the meaning of the word quit and one day promises to make a second attempt at skydiving, this time with a jumpmaster.

Stu and Jo share their house with Princess and LT or Lieutenant, two Norwegian Elkhounds. It's actually their house. Princess and LT rent space to Jo and Stu. Years ago, a female friend gave Stu a piece of advice that he swallowed and digested: *you never fail until you quit trying.* From an unhappy kid growing up on the streets of New York and New Jersey to a young adult battling the "elements," in California, Stu's skin fits today. He and Jo couldn't be happier; life is great. Stu is *Happy, Joyous, and Free.*

SPECIAL NOTE:

Some of what you are about to read is absolutely true, I kid you not.
Some of it is pure unadulterated bullshit. You can decide for
yourself what is real and what is bullshit!

For obvious reasons, I can't let you in on that secret. You see, the
actual fact of the matter is that at one time I did work in Amity where
this series of adventures played out. Yes, I carried a badge; it was
number 108. I also carry a Glock and well…sometimes truth really
is much stranger than that which the mind can create!

When an officer leaves the station, they have no idea whether they
will live through their shift or not. In recent years times have
changed, and dangers that were not that prevalent years ago are now
everywhere and threaten an officer everyday they go to work. While
the majority of an officer's time is spent on mediocre calls, they
never know if one of those calls will escalate into a life and death
situation.

TABLE OF CONTENTS

CHAPTER 1

THE BLUE AND THE BADGE

L ife couldn't have been better. I had my hand on the throttle of life. I was in high gear. I was living the American dream. I felt so good there were days I felt guilty. I was in my thirties. I had money in the bank, not a hell of a lot to some, but a helluva' lot more than many others. The bills were paid, and my social life was about as good as I wanted it to be. I was dating several women and wasn't serious with any of them. I didn't want to get serious, not quite yet.

I had my dream job. I wore a blue suit almost every day. I was given a city car to drive, and I had a gas card. The car was black and white. The gun was a Glock, and the badge was number 108. I was an Amity Police Officer (APD). Amity is southeast of downtown Los Angeles. It is a city of 75,000 people, most of whom are Hispanic. The city is only 3.5 square miles. Most of the people in the city played by the rules and were law-abiding. The lawns were manicured and green. Most of the homes were clean, freshly painted. Then there were the assholes, the punks of Amity. These were the gangs of Amity who only wanted to deal in drugs and gang bang. They were the ones who wanted to terrorize the city.

When the dealers and bangers went to work, so did I. My partner had been my third and final field training officer and the finest of the three. Rocky Calhoun and I had become friends, good friends, in fact, very good friends. We lived in adjacent towns seventy-five miles from APD, so we took turns driving. Rocky was easy going, a perfectionist, had a sick sense of humor like mine and smoked like a summer forest fire.

Rocky married his high school sweetheart after they each married others, then divorced years later. When I drove the black and white, Rocky spent most of the time talking to Paula on his cell phone and smiling. I had a good idea of what she was saying to Rocky on the other end of the line that made Rocky smile. Paula, five one, a hundred ten pounds of tight, well-sculptured body, also had a sense of humor. Paula did not like the fact that I was single. She was forever attempting to find Miss Right. Paula was yet to be successful, although some of the women she introduced me to were winners.

It was Friday, and it was hot and muggy. It was late afternoon, and Rocky and I were enjoying the short skirts and short shorts on Pan Am Boulevard, the main shopping street in Amity. We were working morning watch, 0800 hours to 1800 hours, a ten-hour shift. It was a shift that could be graveyard dead or crazy as hell, there was no telling. If the natives weren't restless, we pulled traffic, wrote a few citations, and made a few bucks for the city.

If it was busy, we handled calls, backed fellow officers, and tried to steal time to write a report or two, so we didn't have to pull overtime. It was Rocky's turn to drive. Actually, since Rocky was the senior officer, it was always Rocky's turn to drive unless he wanted to flirt with Paula on the phone. I sat and eyed the pedestrians walking on the sidewalk. It was clear, sunny, and not too warm. I observed a "clown" driving northbound on southbound Rita Avenue, which meant the lone occupant was driving the wrong way.

I turned to Rocky and said, "I guess that guy didn't see the signs or the damn arrows. He probably didn't even see the Indians."

"Not funny, Tonto," Rocky replied.

I answered, "Get him before he rides off into the sunset."

Rocky was already on the guy's ass. He lit him up like a Christmas tree.

"13 Adam, show us 1038 on northbound Rita north of Western on three Victor William Victor 747. We'll be in the parking lot on the west side of the street," I said as I took a breath. "We'll advise on a back."

I switched to the loudspeaker. "Sir, pull into the parking lot on your left."

I eyed the vehicle carefully. The driver nodded and followed my instructions. We followed him into the parking lot. I approached the driver's side of the red Toyota. Rocky covered me from the passenger side.

"Good afternoon, sir. I stopped you because you're driving the wrong way on a one-way street."

I scanned the car, it appeared clean. I asked, "Can I see your driver's license, registration, and proof of insurance, please?"

The young Hispanic man took his hands off the steering wheel. "My license is in my pocket. The registration and insurance papers are in the glove compartment."

Contrary to certain thinking, if a police officer stops you for a traffic violation, if he hasn't already made up his mind to "write you," cooperation can increase your odds of getting off with a warning.

I nodded, "Go ahead, get them for me, please."

He fumbled in his pocket, then pulled out his wallet. He found his license and handed it to me. He opened the glove compartment, fumbled through papers, finally finding the registration and proof of insurance. The traffic violator handed them to me.

"I'll be right back," I said.

Rocky stayed in position watching the driver as I walked back to the unit and radioed dispatch. "13 Adam, I'll take an L1 status and a want 9 on one, your convenience, please."

An L1 is a license status check. A want 9 is a database check to see if there is a warrant out for the subject's arrest.

"Stand by 13 Adam." Half a minute later, dispatch responded. "No hits on the L1 and no wants or outstanding warrants."

I responded, "Copy that, thanks."

I walked back to the subject's Toyota, "Any reason you're driving northbound on a southbound one-way street, sir?"

He shrugged and was visibly embarrassed. "It's my birthday. I'm on my way to what's supposed to be a surprise party. I'm excited, I guess."

I looked at his license. I hadn't noticed it really was his birthday. "I can't write you on your birthday," I handed his papers back to him. "Happy birthday." Then I said, "Be more careful behind the wheel, sir. We'd like to see you around for many more birthdays." For good measure, I added, "When you exit the parking lot, make sure you go the right way." I walked back to the unit.

"You're getting soft at a tender age," Rocky said. "What's going to happen when you get my age?"

"How do you give a guy a ticket on his birthday?" I got back in the unit. Before I could shut the unit door, dispatch made contact.

"13 Adam, see the woman, 1811 Fish Street, a barking dog complaint."

"Copy that." I looked at Rocky. "Danger lurks."

Sometimes I'd rather handle a 417 than a barking dog. You can reason with a guy with a weapon, but a vicious dog only wants a piece of your cop ass.

"I have dog biscuits in my war bag," I said to Rocky.

"I thought those were for the women you've been dating?" Rocky responded and added a "Woof."

We drove to the northeast corner of the city. People had a misconception about a noise complaint. Most thought it had to be early in the morning or late at night for you to complain. Actually, loud noise is a loud noise; you can complain to the police about it at any time. It's up to cops to determine if the noise is causing a problem, then to work out the solution. Most noise complaints dealt with party calls, loud music, and drinking. Many of these calls occurred during late evening or early morning hours. Some of those calls could be dangerous.

Give an already intoxicated group of party-goers a reason to argue with the uniform, and sometimes tempers flare-up. Unfortunately, more frequently than not, empty beer bottles get tossed at cops, and fights break out. It wasn't unusual to see an airship overhead during late-night party calls. We had one call recently where a backyard party of over one-hundred resulted in rocks and bottles being tossed at officers to the extent that we had to call for mutual assistance from adjoining departments.

When the dust settled, three officers were transported to the hospital with cuts and bruises. One cop ended up with eight stitches over his eye. Eight suspects were transported to nearby hospitals. Eighteen party-goers were arrested. All this because the homeowner was asked to turn down the music, not turn it off, just lower it. Alcohol does crazy things to the mind and body. And we were afraid the state was going to legalize marijuana. This call seemed run of the mill.

Rocky pulled to the curb in front of the house. "13 Adam, show us 97."

"Copy that," dispatch responded.

We walked up to the front door. I knocked then stepped to the side. The door was immediately opened by a woman in her sixties, dressed in white slacks and blue button-down blouse.

"Morning ma'am, you called about a barking dog?" I asked.

"Would you officer's like to come in?" she politely replied.

"No ma'am, but thank you. Can you tell us about the barking dog?"

She pulled at her ear lobe, then said, "It's the Elephant next door," as she pointed east.

"It's the Elephant?" I asked, a bit surprised, wondering if she had all her marbles. A barking elephant?

"It's a boxer," she said, "They call him Elephant. I wish it was an elephant; it would make less noise. It barks all hours of the day and night."

"What is her name?"

She answered, "Juanita Dominguez."

"Have you tried talking with her?"

"Several times. She's nice enough, but she's hard of hearing. I don't think she hears Elephant barking half the time."

Rocky, who looked bored, then piped in, "Is your neighbor home now?"

"I think so," she responded.

"Okay, thank you, ma'am. We're going to have a chat with her. We'll come back and let you know what we can do about Elephant."

We walked next door and knocked. Ms. Dominguez came to the door. She was five four and probably 170 pounds. Her hair was grey, and her face was round. She was wearing an apron over a pair of jeans and a pullover top.

She smiled and asked, "Is something wrong, officer?"

I introduced Rocky, then I said, "We had a complaint from a couple of your neighbors."

I lied so she wouldn't have a clue who called the police. "Several of the neighbors are saying your dog barks constantly that he's causing a disturbance."

"No, no, no," she replied, looking puzzled. "My neighbors aren't disturbing me. You have that all wrong."

I took a breath. Rocky decided to try his luck. He spoke slowly, clearly, loudly, "Do you have a dog named Elephant?"

She waved her hand. "Here, Elephant. Why didn't you say that in the first place?" She turned then said, "Elephant, come here, boy."

The boxer ran to the door its short, brown tail wagging. "Do you need to see his license?" She asked.

"No, ma'am, we're not with animal control. We're with the police department. We got a call about the dog barking."

With a puzzled look again, she asked, "I don't understand. I don't have a car. How can I have double-parked?"

It was my turn. I took out my note pad. I scrawled the words Elephant, barking, and noise disturbance on the paper then handed it to Elephant's owner. She took a pair of glasses out of her apron. She read the note then waved her hand in the air.

"Well, why didn't you just say that instead of beating around the bush? "If Elephant is barking too much, I'll talk with him. He'll stop if I tell him to."

She turned to Elephant, who was now seated at her feet. She patted him on the head, and said, "Isn't that right, Elephant. You listen to Mommy, don't you?"

We put closure on the call and walked back to the unit.

"Coffee? Let's clear the call."

I decided to punch the narrative of the call into the computer. I wrote, "Contacted RP (reporting party). Met with Elephant's owner, the elephant is a boxer who promised not to bark if we brought him peanuts. Suggest units that might follow up bring unsalted peanuts as Elephant does not include salt in his diet. 10-8!"

"You did such a creative job on that call, coffee is on me." The Rock, as he was sometimes called by the troops, was being funny.

Coffee at the 7-11 was free. The owner and staff liked it when APD's finest stopped by. The 7-11 hadn't been hit in years.

"Sounds good to me," Rocky said as he turned the Crown Victoria north, heading in the direction of the 7-11. It wasn't meant to happen!

"13 Adam, a possible 459 residential."

I jotted down the address as Rocky again made a U-turn. I hit the lights, Rocky hit the gas, and we were five short blocks from the burglary call. It was more common for houses to be burglarized during the day than at night. School-aged kids committed most burglaries. When the kids cut classes, they often committed crimes. A common crime among the ditchers was home burglaries. I killed the flashing lights. Rocky slid the Ford to a smooth stop several houses east of the location. We would make a covert approach on foot.

I put out our arrival on the scene. "13 Adam, we're 97 Filbert."

"Copy that 13 Adam." Dispatch responded, then added, "There is no available unit to back."

"Copy that. We'll keep you posted."

"Take the rear. Be damn careful, it's just the two of us. Turn your radio down," Rocky said.

I had already turned the volume low. Being partners, we often reminded one another of the routine actions of our job. Sometimes you can forget the obvious. Officers died that way.

My Glock was out of its holster at the low ready. I wasn't familiar with the condo complex. I was checking numbers and located unit D. I slowed, looked left, right, and behind me. There wasn't a human in sight. The only living thing I observed was a kitten playing on a porch several units beyond the target.

"Rocky, what is your 20?" I asked in a low voice. "Where are you?"

"I'm at the front door, stand by," a faint voice answered.

I located a tree with good visibility of the rear door, and I used it for cover. There was no visible activity at the rear of the unit. Two weeks ago, a sheriff attempting to serve a warrant in the Antelope Valley on a subject who failed to appear in court on a suspended license charge, knocked at the subject's door. The response was immediate. The suspect fired three blasts from an AK 47 through the door. The sheriff made one mistake; he stood in front of the door. Our brother was DOA at the hospital. The suspect later surrendered without a struggle.

I heard Rocky on the radio. "13 Adam, we're code 4. The alarm was set off accidentally by the owner/occupant. Copy a CDL, please."

"Go with your CDL, 13 Adam."

I holstered my weapon and walked around the complex. I met Rocky at the front door. A little old Hispanic lady who looked to be about 215 years old said she accidentally hit the wrong keys on the pad when she reentered the house from shopping. She couldn't stop apologizing. Rocky and I assured the apologetic lady that this was part of our job; we were only too pleased to help. I handed her a business card.

I had her promise that she would call if she needed any other assistance. Hell, public service is what we're all about. Besides, good public relations, especially these days, never hurt any PD. We got back in the unit.

"Coffee?" I nodded.

"You're buying this time."

"My pleasure."

We made it to the 7-11 parking lot.

"13 Adam, see the man, 1726 Cadillac Court, a possible 459 from the vehicle."

I keyed the mic, "Copy that." I looked at Rocky, "Are we the only unit working?"

He replied, "Sounds like it."

The address was on the east end of Amity and in a lower-class part of town. The bangers congregated in this area, as did the dealers and carjackers.

It was common for the vehicle's owner to wake up in the morning, walk to his car, and not find it. In this case, the suspect may have only stolen shit from the vehicle. I put us out. Rocky and I walked to the door. I knocked. A thirtyish, male Hispanic, wearing a white tee-shirt and black jeans answered the door. He had almost as many tatts as the tattooed man at the circus. He needed a shave, badly.

I started to say, "We're here about….."

"It took you long enough," was my greeting by the RP.

Rocky glared at him. He didn't say a word. I did. "Can I get your license for the report, please? We're going to need to see the car. We can talk as we walk. The reason we're late is that we're busy as hell this morning. We have a rash of burglary calls. But what really put us behind was we had to get a cat down from a tree. The fire department was too busy."

The guy looked at me with a screwed-up face. He didn't know whether or not to take me seriously.

"Here's my license," he said as he scratched his underarm.

We continued to walk to his car, a seriously beaten up Chevy Impala with more cancer than a stage 4 patient. He continued to scratch.

"Who else has keys to your car?" I asked. I was careful not to touch the vehicle. I didn't think we'd bother with prints, but I hadn't determined that yet.

He replied, "No one, I'm divorced, and live by myself."

This time he scratched his other underarm. I wasn't taking prints since I wanted to get the hell out of there and have coffee. I know Rocky wanted out.

Rocky walked around to the passenger side of the Chevy and peered inside. "Nothing looks disturbed. The radio appears intact, the glove compartment is closed, and the seats are present." Rocky seeing that everything looked intact, asked, "What's missing?"

Now the guy was scratching both armpits. We kept our distance thinking he had some disease we could catch.

Then he says, "Step back detective and see if you can nail it down."

I knew the clown's tone was going to piss Rocky off. He grew irritated, real irritated. "You need to understand, sir, that the first test a police officer has to pass to become a detective, is what's called a 459 from the vehicle or a burglary. If we can nail down what's missing without the victim telling us, then we move on to how to get along with an uncooperative victim." Rocky walked back around to the driver's side of the cancer car. He got within a few inches of the victim.

Rocky looked him in the eyes and said in a serious tone, "We've gotta' get another cat out of another tree. So why don't you save us both sometime and tell us what the hell was stolen."

He stopped scratching long enough to answer, "There's a hubcap missing from the right rear."

"It's only one hub cap?" Rocky asked.

"That's right, is that a problem for you?" the RP spat back aggressively.

Rocky was trying to keep his cool. "Any idea who might want one hub cap from your car?"

"That's your department, Dick Tracy," the RP snapped back at Rocky.

14

I contacted dispatch on my cell. I wanted to get the hell out of there before this became an IA investigation. Rocky looked like he was going to put the jerk through the windshield.

Rocky took a cigarette out of its pack. He fingered it. I could feel his anger building. "My partner is going to give you a business card with a computer-generated report number on the card. If you are going to submit this to your insurance company, use that report number. If the insurance company has any questions, they can call the department and refer to that number. If you happen to find the hub cap or discover anything else that might be missing, call my partner."

I handed itchy the department business card.

"Aren't you going to dust for prints?" itchy asked.

I didn't have a chance to answer before Rocky said sarcastically as hell, "A team of detectives who passed the hub cap test will be out to do that. Besides, we have to save a cat."

As we both walked back to the unit, Rocky asked, "7-11 partner? Coffee? I'm buying."

We were less than a mile from the 7-11.

"13 Adam, suspicious circs. RP reports a light brown Honda Civic, no plates, has been parked in the alley to the rear of 2242 Wilbur for the last two hours. RP thinks the vehicle may be occupied twice."

"I didn't want any damn coffee, anyway," Rocky said.

The alley to the rear of Wilbur was minutes from our twenty. We approached the alley from the north. We spotted the Honda immediately. As we drove closer, we observed the figure of one subject in the vehicle. We pulled up behind the Honda, which had no rear plates. You needn't have been "Columbo" to piece this one together. Two people were having sex on the rear seat of the vehicle.

I approached the Honda on the passenger side, Rocky, from the driver's side. Either we were quiet enough, or they were engaged to the degree that neither heard us approach (police work at its finest)! She was on top and had absolutely nothing on but two hard nipples on her "D" cup boobs. They were bouncing up and down with each up and down motion on her partner's nozzle. Her hair was long, blonde, clean, and covered half her face. She was in silent ecstasy.

His eyes were closed. He appeared to be in his late twenties, maybe a couple of years older than his rider. He was wearing a green polo shirt, brown socks, and a smile. "Ride 'em cowgirl!"

I recognized him from a wanted bulletin distributed during a recent briefing. The underling was wanted for burglary, possession of burglary tools, and FTA (failure to appear) on traffic warrants.

The warrant was a no-bail warrant out of Amity, which meant he was about to be knocked out of the saddle.

Rocky tapped on the window with his nightstick, no response. He tapped again, longer harder, nothing. I walked to the front of the car and located the VIN.

"13 Adam, clear for a 28, 29?" I asked dispatch for information on the vehicle.

"Go with your VIN check, 13 Adam."

"1 George, 3 Adam, Robert 4, 7 Adam, 6 Edward, Robert 3, 27, 99, 1, any repeats?"

Dispatch responded immediately, "Your vehicle comes back no hits to an O.J. FLON, 10/10/94, out of Downey. No wants, no warrants."

"Copy, we'll be out with two. We're code 4," I told dispatch.

Rocky said, "Both of you, put your underwear on and hand my partner and me the rest of your clothes, then stay put for a minute."

We searched the clothing and handed them back their clothing through the Honda's window.

"Get dressed and get out of the car. Party's over," Rocky said.

The warrant suspect looked at me and crooked his head. He looked like a dog pleading for a cookie. He asked, "Just one more ride. I didn't get to finish."

Rocky answered with, "Hold that thought. We just might accommodate you."

I was starting to enjoy this. It was almost better than 7-11 coffee. She wasn't wearing a bra. No complaint here, she was kind of cute; at least her breasts were something to look at. Her nipples pointed straight out like a number two pencil eraser.

I checked the female's ID. It came back to O.J. Flon. "Are your parent's fans of OJ?" I asked.

She looked at me as if I was from the planet, Pluto. She was stoned. Ricardo Juan Gomez Flores did not yet know we recognized him as being a warrant suspect. He too was stoned. In his condition, I was certain he didn't recognize much.

Rocky gave me the OK, and I said, "Today's your lucky day. Since OJ here is also warrant free, we're going to let you finish what you started in the back of the unit." I paused so OJ and Ricardo could swallow and digest what I had said.

"Are you for real man? We can screw in the police car?" Ricardo replied with a look of surprise.

I clarified my statement, "Only on one condition amigo; you have to have your hands cuffed behind your back."

Slowly he digested what I told him. "I'm going to be handcuffed, and then she and I can f**k in the back of your car?"

"I bet you were an A student before you started using," I said.

I walked toward Ricardo. Rocky was shaking his head. He said, "Turn around, put your hands behind your back, palms together."

He cuffed him, shook him down, and tossed the nonthreatening contents of his pockets on the hood of the unit. Rocky locked the Honda. I opened the back door of the unit. Ricardo slid in.

"This isn't the first time I've had sex with handcuffs on," Ricardo said as if it was a big deal.

Yeah, I thought, but this time it won't be up the ass. I slammed the door.

Through the partially opened window, Ricardo yelled, "Let OJ in."

"Sorry, Ricardo, not today. "OJ's got football practice," I said.

"But you promised we could have sex. You promised!"

"And you did, you just got f****d by Amity's finest."

We drove back to the barn, booked Ricardo, hammered out the paperwork, put ourselves 10-8, back in service, then hit the streets.

"I want that mother f*****g coffee!"

CHAPTER 2

VERY BAD GUYS ON THE LOOSE

Rocky activated the overheads. We drove code 2 to the 7-11. Lights were OK, sirens going code 3 might be a little much! We made it to the front door of the 7-11. My cell phone started to play the theme from Dragnet. That meant the watch commander was calling.

I looked at Rocky, then grabbed the phone. I listened intently. "Yes sir, ASAP, sir. We're five minutes out."

"What's up?" Rocky asked when I hung up.

"WC wants us in his office last week."

The WC was Lieutenant Anthony Valdez. Valdez was a gung-ho former Marine who stood five foot nine inches tall if he was wearing elevator shoes. He was built solid, but no muscle man. Valdez thought his shit didn't stink, but everyone else's did. He was a prick, but he was a good cop. He had shot and killed three perps during three different stick-ups; everyone was ruled a good shoot.

To cancel the tickets of those three-armed assholes, took a total of six rounds. Valdez commented that he didn't want to waste tax payer's money on ammo. Rocky led the way into Valdez's office. Valdez was seated behind his glass-covered mahogany desk.

"Gentleman, be seated," he said.

We sat in silence. Valdez shuffled papers on his desk, ignoring us. Then he looked up. His smile was forced.

He nodded then said, "As you well know, three charming Blacks, excuse me, African Americans have been robbing jewelry stores all around APD. Their M.O. is pretty much the same each time. They park a dark-colored SUV with paper plates in front of the store. One sits behind the wheel of the vehicle, the other two make an entrance. The two are dressed in all black, including black ski masks.

"They smash display cases and take jewelry in a pillowcase then, apparently for kicks, pistol whip the manager, owner, and/or employees. If there are customers in the store, they place them in a prone position on the floor. No one has been killed, *yet!* A couple of hours ago, right next door to us in Trenton, our three heroes hit the Garcia/Dominguez jewelry store on Atlantic.

"The place was empty except for the owner and his twelve-year-old daughter, who was helping dad in the store, so she could raise money to give to a neighbor who had extensive fire damage to their house and not enough insurance to cover it. These two *African Americans*," Valdez began as if it was a dirty word, (and in this case, it was a filthy word) shook his head. He let his sentence hang. He gave us a copy of the report.

Valdez was not going to wait for us to read it. He went into detail about what had recently occurred, adding his own personal narrative. "After the perps locked the door, they put the closed sign on the door and pulled the blinds. These black mother f*****s tied up dad and gagged him. They did the same to his daughter. One watched over both Dad and daughter in the backroom as the other systematically rifled the store for expensive jewelry. When he was finished cleaning out the jewelry, he went in the back.

"Right in front of dad, the nigger raped the twelve-year-old. When he finished, he pistol-whipped both of them. Both will survive, whatever survival means. Neither will ever be the same. The daughter was able to tell detectives that she thinks the bastard had a tattoo above his belly button. She thinks it said, '**F**k Your World.**' Each and every burglary, there's now been six these idiots have hit, has been on a Saturday. Every time they hit its early afternoon, late afternoon, or early evening, never when it's dark.

"You two, beginning tomorrow and every f*****g Saturday until Amos and Andy are caught or killed, will be on special duty in soft clothes and an unmarked. Saturday, you will work 1100 hours until 2100 hundred hours. Adjust your schedule accordingly. Also joining you will be Lyons and Holfe. They don't know this yet, but I'll catch up with them when they get back from code seven." Valdez concluded, "Any questions?"

"Not from me, sir," I said as I looked at Rocky.

"Do we get a bonus if we don't have to handcuff them?" Rocky asked.

Valdez quickly responded, "Dinner for four at the Ranchito. I'll make that dinner for four twice at the Ranchito if you don't have to book either of them. Take all three out, and I'll send the four of you to Vegas for the weekend; that is Cannoli, if you can come up with a date desperate enough to go out with you."

I wanted to say your daughter, sir. But I wanted to keep my job. Besides, a pissed off Valdez would shoot me without thinking twice. I didn't date Mexicunts. I dated real women.

Valdez barked, "Get out of here. When it quiets down, go home and get a good night's sleep so you can be fresh for tomorrow." Valdez looked at us. "Seriously, be careful, guys, the one place these sick pricks haven't hit is APD. It's going to happen, it's just a matter of when. When it does go down, these guys won't go easy. I don't want any dead cops. Do you understand me?"

I spoke for both of us. "Yes, sir. Has the sheriff been notified?"

Valdez continued, "They know we'll have undercover units in the area of Pan Am Boulevard. They'll be doing their own patrol south of the Boulevard. They have your special frequency, so they'll monitor your calls in case you need back up. But we're talking about LA County Sheriffs for backing. If they start shooting, the only thing they'll hit is their own unit, so be careful."

We worked closely with the County Sheriff. The north side of Florence belonged to us, south of Florence was patrolled by the sheriff. We often backed each other. There was good-natured ribbing, but in a clutch, we were brothers. My thinking was since the undoing of Lee Baca, the sheriff's stock has doubled in value.

We went back to work. It was thirty minutes before we got another call. It was an unknown trouble call, and the RPs were two different neighbors who reported loud noises from an adjacent house. We were one of two backing units. When we arrived, it looked like Christmas.

There were more unit lights blinking colors than Willie Nelson had sad country-western songs. Apparently, a couple of units who were in the vicinity decided to see what they could do to help, or they were bored. 17 Adam had the man, the owner of the small 1350 square foot home, inside his unit. 17 Adam was leaning against the black and white's open door. 17 Adam was talking to the guy, calmly, professionally.

I asked, "Anything I can do to help?"

17 Adam turned to us and said, "His wife is inside; you might want to get her story." I noticed the guy was not in handcuffs.

Rocky and I walked into the house. The noise had to be domestic violence. As we were walking into the house, 17 Adam put out a code 4. The wife was short, a bit on the heavy side, dressed in brown neatly pressed slacks and white blouse. She had obviously been crying. Her makeup was running down her face. She introduced herself. I pointed to a chair. She sat down.

"Have a seat, officers," she said.

The inside of the house looked like someone had participated in a demolition derby. Several holes were either kicked or punched into the wall. Pictures were on the floor, the television was smashed, a table leg was broken off the dining room table, causing it to tip at a dangerous angle. I wondered if the other rooms in the house looked the same.

"Thanks, ma'am, we've been sitting in the car. It's good to get out and stretch. Can you tell us what happened?"

"Is my husband going to jail?" she asked worriedly.

"What happened? It looks like there was a big fight."

She shook her head, and then said, "My husband was watching the ball game. The television went out for some reason. He has a bad temper. When he couldn't get it to go back on, he started throwing things and punching things."

"Has your husband been drinking?" I asked.

"Not even a beer," She replied.

"How about drug use?"

"No, he only takes a blood pressure pill once a day."

Adam 17 would know about that. "Is this the only room he busted up?"

She nodded, yes, still concerned. "Is he going to jail?"

I again ignored the question. "Has your husband done this before?"

"Once, a long, long time ago," she said.

"Who owns the house, ma'am?"

"It's our home. Actually, the bank, but our payments are up to date."

"Did your husband hit you?"

She quickly replied, "No, Jorge would never touch me."

I didn't believe her story. I left Rocky with the wife and walked out to 17 Adam. Paul stepped away from his unit after closing the door.

"We talked to the wife; she claims the guy's got a temper and smashed his house up because the TV went out while he was watching the game. She said neither alcohol nor drugs were involved. She told us he never laid a glove on her. She has no visible marks on her," I told Paul.

"He's clean and sober, no warrants or wants and no priors. My partner Max is checking with the neighbors. Jorge has cuts on his hands from punching the walls and breaking shit," Paul explained.

"There's got to be several thousand dollars' worth of damage in there, at least," I said.

"It's his house; the guy's got one helluva' temper. There's nothing to charge him with so far. There's no law against smashing your own property. We'll shoot some pictures for the report, and that'll do it," Paul concluded.

THE ADVENTURE CONTINUES

It was Saturday afternoon, early afternoon. Rocky and I were in street clothes. Rocky was driving a black Ford Mustang convertible that had once belonged to a drug-dealing Pimp. The pimp's ass was in jail. His car belonged to the City of Amity, thanks to the laws of the beautiful state of California. We monitored two frequencies, the primary frequency, and our special assigned frequency, which was to be used only by the two teams assigned to the rolling stakeout.

"Can you believe these sick mother f*****s doing that to a twelve-year-old?"

Rocky took his eyes off the road. "We've become a real whacked up society. It's easier to take what you want, especially when you know very little will happen to you if you get caught. If you're a minority, you get to play the race card. If you don't like the way you were arrested, you get an attorney, and you sue the city and the PD, tax-free money."

"These assholes better hope I don't get my hands on them. I'd love a weekend in Vegas on Valdez."

Rocky turned back to watch the road then continued, "They have the right to a jury trial just like any other f*****g criminal. Do you know these idiots have hit white-owned jewelry stores, Hispanic owned stores, Asian places but never a heist in a Black-owned store?"

"And if they hit APD, it won't be a Black jewelry store either because there aren't any Black jewelry shops in Amity. I don't think there is a single shop owned by Blacks in Amity."

I abruptly changed the subject. "Hey, check that out." I looked up at a black Ford Explorer in front of us driving northbound in the number one lane of Pan Am Boulevard. Inside the vehicle were three Blacks.

"That's interesting," I said. "Do you think they know we're behind them?"

"Are you kidding me?" In this thing, "Hell no, they'll never suspect. Run the plate."

I switched frequencies, so I could reach dispatch. "UC (undercover one)."

"Go, UC one."

"Twenty-eight, twenty-nine a plate."

"Go with your plate, UC one."

I gave dispatch the plate, and it came back clean to an address out of Compton. It was still a possibility. I switched back to our frequency.

"Let's stay with them and see where they go," Rocky said.

They continued northbound on Pan Am Blvd. then drove westbound on Almador.

"They're probably headed back to Compton. Maybe, they're looking for a hit. Make a note of that plate; I'm going to pull alongside them at the next light. Let's get a closer look."

We had a video of two of the three perps from cameras that were in the stores they hit. But it did little good. They were covered up better than an Arab in a desert sand storm. The best clue we had was the tattoo given to us by the pre-teenager the prick had repeatedly raped. That would make our case in court; if we had to make a court case. They caught the red light at Almador and Alameda. Rocky slid next to them. I turned up the radio, drummed my hands on the dash then gave them a quick glance. It appeared to be Dad driving, short-haired Mom was in the front passenger seat and their son in the back seat.

"Wanna' find a reason for a T-stop?" I asked Rocky.

"No, we've got the plate, but I think its code four." Saturday remained quiet.

ANOTHER DAY – BACK ON PATROL

The following Tuesday, we were back in uniform and back in a marked unit. It didn't take long to get a call.

"13 Adam, a possible 273.5 now, 6373 Acacia, apartment 27, RP is Roberto Morales resident in apartment 28. He states he can hear a woman screaming for help. You're clear code 3. 17 and 18 back 13 Adam."

I rolled my window up as Rocky hit the siren. We were a few blocks east of Acacia.

"13 Adam is rolling," I told dispatch.

You could smell the rubber burning as Rocky braked. I was first out of the unit. Rocky was a few feet behind me. I heard his boots closing fast. The gate in front of the faded brick apartment building was black wrought iron. It was unlocked. I swung the door open and held it for Rocky then took an APD business card, securing it between the gate lock and the spring so the gate would stay unlocked for the backing units. Rocky and I were up the stairs and headed down the hall.

We could hear screams from a female and loud cursing from a male. Then we heard the ugly sound of breaking glass and finally silence. We were in front of apartment 27. My Glock was in my right hand behind my right thigh. Rocky and I stood at opposite sides of the apartment 27's door.

Rocky nodded then shouted. "Amity Police Department open the door. Do it now!" Nothing. I inhaled.

"Open the f*****g door now," I yelled, "or we're going to kick the f*****g door down, and then we're going to kick your ass!"

A lock turned. Slowly the door opened a few inches. Rocky put his shoulder to the door. He pushed hard. A fat, short, Hispanic male in brown shorts and a tee shirt lost his balance, stumbling backward. Rocky was in the apartment and on the guy like a heavy 747 on a landing strip.

Rocky yelled, "Get against the wall. Do it now." Then I heard Rocky ask: "Any weapons on you? Are there any weapons in the apartment?"

I ran to the woman; she was sprawled on the couch, crying. I turned her over. Her face was bruised and swollen. She had been badly beaten.

I radioed dispatch. "13 Adam, roll paramedics. The victim is conscious and breathing, but she's been badly beaten." I heard footsteps from outside the apartment. Backup had arrived.

"One of you get a camera and photograph the Vic for me," Rocky said. "Someone else go next door and take a statement from the RP."

I wasn't about to get a statement from the victim now. I advised dispatch, "13 Adam, we're code 4, sufficient units."

Rocky took one look at the beaten female and slammed the suspect against the opposite wall. "Put your hands on the wall dirt bag, get your feet back, and spread 'em wide."

The guy did as he was ordered. When his feet were about two and a half feet from the wall, Rocky kicked them farther back and wider apart. He handcuffed the husband. Rocky searched him, not too gently. He pulled his wallet from his rear pocket, found his driver's license, and ran him for wants and warrants. He had a prior for assault.

Before fire rescue entered the dwelling, Senior Officer Wilson took a dozen pictures of the beaten victim's injuries and of the damage to the apartment. He also shot photos of the husband to prove he had no visible marks. Then Wilson pulled up the suspect's shirt and shot pictures of his torso and back, further proof that the beating he had administered was not in self-defense.

All this would be compiled later in a report that would be used to prosecute the husband. Four county medics and two ambulance attendees entered the apartment. The f*****g place wasn't large enough to accommodate us all.

They stood aside until Wilson finished his photographing. They treated the woman the best they could before loading her on a gurney. Under California law, a woman could refuse to testify or prosecute the husband for beating the shit out of her. Many beaten spouses opted not to prosecute, mainly because the woman was afraid she'd get worse when he was released from jail or because she was afraid she'd have no support for her and the kids.

That had changed. Under the current law, the decision was taken out of the victim's hands. If upon arrival, the police found evidence of injuries, the state made the arrest under penal code 273.5, spousal abuse, or domestic violence. Any signs of bruising, a cut, swelling, strangulation marks, and the suspect went to jail.

This guy, with or without a prior, was better than good to go! I followed paramedics to the ambulance and went to the hospital with the victim to get her statement. Rocky handed off the subject to one of the backing units for transportation to the Station. Rocky followed the ambulance to the hospital. I watched in disgust as the emergency room doctors stitched up the victim's wounds. It took eighty-five minutes for the doctors to perform their medical skills.

When they were finished, Maria Mendoza had sixteen stitches in her face. She also had gashes above both eyes. I interviewed Maria after the doctors cautioned me that I had ten minutes and not a minute more; that Maria would be admitted, overnight, for observation. I took fifteen minutes and copious notes, which would be included in my report. I would complete the report later at the Station.

Few things pissed me off more than a man beating a woman. For some reason, Hispanics thought a wife was chattel. Once you had a piece of paper stating you were husband and wife, the man owned the woman.

Our second most popular call was 273.5. I had gotten heavy-handed with more than one domestic violence suspect.

A LEARNING EXPERIENCE – REPORT WRITING

Next to filling out what's called a CHP 180, a long-form in triplicate filled out on the scene when a vehicle is impounded, I disliked report writing. One reason is that early on in my police career when I was in field training with Rocky, I was being taught the fine art of report writing. Following a simple warrant arrest during a traffic stop, Rocky instructed me to walk into the report writing room and complete the arrest report. I did so, or attempted to do so. After I completed what I thought was a good report, checked it for errors, ran spell check, then reported to Rocky with the report, I stood and waited.

Rocky made a couple of corrections then said, "You didn't **SEE** the vehicle, you **OBSERVED** the vehicle. Also, be specific about the vehicle. It was a 1992 red Toyota four-door with California license plates so and so. Make the necessary changes."

I nodded, swallowed, and went back to the computer room and re-constructed the report. I took it to Rocky again. He read it carefully, too carefully.

"Looks good to me, take it to the WC for approval," Rocky said.

The WC was about to go EOW (end of the watch). Hopefully, he'd read the report then sign off on it. It was "a go nowhere" report anyway, a simple warrant arrest. I stood in front of his desk as Sergeant Morelez read the report.

When Morelez finished, I heard, "Goddamn it, Cannoli.

"What is all this bullshit about my partner, and I was on patrol in a marked black and white police unit when I observed a red Toyota failing to stop for a stop sign……. I know, and the court knows you were in a cop car. Establish your PC (probable cause) for the traffic stop in one f*****g sentence then get on with it. This f*****g report isn't an armed robbery."

"Yes, sir, sorry, sir," I responded.

I took the report back to Rocky. He laughed then said, "Cut and paste." Rocky pointed to the computer room.

 I redid the report, cut out the bullshit. Sergeant Morelez was off duty Sergeant Paera was now the WC. I knocked on his door. Paera was the oldest of the cops at APD. He was a good guy with a hell of a sense of humor but a stickler for doing things correctly. Because he would write tickets for excessive speed, you wouldn't catch Paera speeding in his unit or in his private car. Paera not only went by the book, he wrote most of it. Paera read the report as I stood in front of his desk.

"Cannoli, Cannoli, Cannoli. I would have thought your FTO's would have trained you better than this. The court is going to want to know what you were doing when you observed the red Toyota. Were you on foot patrol, bicycle patrol, in an airship, or a black and white? Let's go back and write the full report. Let's be professional here, son." Sergeant Paera said, smiling.

"Yes, dad, sorry, dad," I responded, smiling as well.

Paera looked up at me. His smile broadened. "I didn't think you knew." He laughed then said, "Clean up that bullshit report so you can get back on the street where you belong, Cannoli."

Every third person called me Cannoli. I was from New York, I was Italian and I looked like a f*****g Mafiosi. So, it was Cannoli!

I trudged back to where Rocky was seated. "Are we good to go?" He asked.

"I gotta correct the mother f*****g report."

"What's wrong?"

"All the shit, Morelez said to me 86, Paera told me to revive it," I said.

Rocky laughed so hard he had to wipe tears from his face.

"With all due respect, sir, what the hell is so funny."

"That just goes to show you."

"Goes to show you what?"

"Goes to show you, you have to know who your watch commander is and what kind of paper he wants you to write." Rocky didn't want me to get discouraged. "It's not a big deal. It's a learning factor. Do it one more time, turn it in, get it approved, and let's go eat. I'm starved, and you're buying!"

I began the report. "On the above date and time, my partner Rocky Calhoun and I were on patrol in a marked police unit. We were patrolling in the vicinity of Rita and Western Avenues. We received a call dispatching us….." It took me an hour to complete the report, confer with the other officers at the scene, to review the pictures that were taken at the scene and booked into evidence by Rocky.

I had Rocky proofread the completed report, then I put it in the WC's mailbox for his stamp of approval. Rocky and I left the Station and went back out on patrol.

THAT WAS THE PAST – BACK TO THE PRESENT

"No," I said adamantly as Rocky talked with Paula on his cell. I repeated, "No more f*****g blind dates."

Rocky held his hand over the phone. He said to Paula, "Tony said he'd love to meet her." He also said dinner is on him. "Go ahead and set it up."

I shook my head. "C'mon Rocky, give me a break."

"What can I say? Paula thinks you need a woman in your life."

"What I need is to pull that vehicle over. She ran the red." I sped up and got behind a blue Honda Civic two-door. I didn't light her up.

Rocky ran the plate on the computer. It came back, "clean and current."

"F**k her," I said, "I'm pulling her over anyway. She really ran that light. It wasn't even close."

I lit her up, and I took point. Rocky approached the vehicle, occupied one time, on the passenger side. She was Caucasian in her twenties. Her eyes were blue, and her hair was blonde. She was well built. Her white blouse was buttoned up just enough so that when she leaned forward, I could see boobs sticking out from her white bra. Her blue skirt was hiked up to mid-thigh.

I scanned the car. It was clean. Rocky and I made eye contact. He shrugged, which was our signal for 'it's your call!' I hadn't decided if I'd write her up. It depended on her attitude and her prior record.

 "Ma'am, can I see your driver's license, registration, and your proof of insurance, please?"

She turned to look at me and batted her blue eyes. That was strike one.

She said, "Did I do something wrong, Officer?"

 "License, registration, and insurance papers, please," I responded.

"Can I get an answer to my question?" She replied.

Strike f*****g two! I looked through the driver's window, and across at Rocky. He was grinning.

 "You need to give me your license, your registration and your insurance, please miss. You need to do it now!"

She sighed. Her purse was on the passenger seat. She reached into the bag as Rocky, and I watched carefully. Out came her pocketbook. She fumbled through it.

"Here! The registration and insurance are in the glove compartment."

 "Get it for me, please." When I had all three in my hand, I examined them. They were valid. "Miss, you ran the red light on….."

"I did not." She raised her voice and ran out of strikes. The bitch was getting a ticket.

"Miss, both my partner and I observed you run the light. It wasn't even close."

"I'll fight it in court if you give me a ticket. I promise I will."

"Stand by, ma'am."

I walked back to the car to run her license for wants and warrants. I stood behind the door of the unit. She was clean, I scratched the citation.

I caught Rocky's eye before I approached her vehicle. Rocky was in a position to cover me from the passenger side of her vehicle. No traffic stop was ROUTINE. Routine stops got cops shot. Routine traffic stops got cops killed. I was prepared for a ration of bullshit from the bitch when I returned to her car. I was surprised.

"Officer," she said sweetly, "I want to apologize for my mouth. I'm really sorry." She smiled then added, "I understand you don't give tickets to pretty women with sweet smiles and blue eyes."

I nodded. My citation book was tucked neatly under my arm. "You're correct, ma'am. I have never written a ticket to a pretty woman with blue eyes and a cute smile. Never!" I held out the cite book and a pen. "Please sign in the red rectangular box. Signing is not an admission of guilt; it's a promise to take care of the ticket."

Her eyes wanted to slay me. She grabbed the pen out of my hand and started to sign the ticket while I held the cite book. "Press hard," I said to offset her hard look. "You're signing three copies."

When we were back in the unit, Rocky said, "You should have been a comedian instead of a cop."

"I don't like being played like an f*****g baby grand piano. Ask me to cut you slack and take responsibility for what you did, and chances are I'll cut you a break. But pull that shit, it's old, and game over."

Rocky said, "You know the CHP are notorious for stopping you and writing you. Rarely do you get a break from a Chippie even if you have a badge? Before I became a police officer, I got pulled over four times by the CHP. Each time I told the officer the truth that I was listening to the damn country western music on the radio and wasn't paying attention to my driving. Each of those four times I was cut a break, no cite."

"You're lucky," I said.

"Yeah, you can say that again. Now I listen to the news station."

CHAPTER 3

THE DANGERS OF THE JOB

The following Saturday, we were back in street clothes and back in the Mustang. This time I was behind the wheel. It was noon on the money. It was a balmy seventy-five degrees. I swore up, down, and sideways to Rocky and Paula that I wasn't going out on any more of her blind dates. Of course, those words fell on deaf ears. Rocky was bigger than I. I didn't like being the third wheel.

The first hour was quiet in Amity. A couple of loud music calls, a couple of laborers drinking in a parking lot, and one possible 415 verbal call. We listened to the radio calls but didn't respond. We were still looking for our Black friends. My mind couldn't wrap itself around the brutal rape of a twelve-year-old in front of her father. You had to be a real sick puke pot to do that. How the hell anyone could engage in any sex act with a twelve-year-old is beyond my comprehension.

I didn't believe in locking someone like that up for twenty-five years to life because after you served half your sentence and were eligible for parole, you came out sicker than you were when you went in. I also didn't believe in putting the cost of incarceration on the taxpayer.

Put a bullet in the asshole or a needle in his arm; just don't let him back on the street to offend again. These animals fooled the public and the parole board into believing they found God in prison.

They'd "buy" online degrees, read a few pages of the Bible, teach another prisoner to read before or after they had sex, and the rehabilitation process was complete. Growing up back east, my dad and I used to have loud arguments about capital punishment. He detested the death penalty.

He was a card-carrying member of the ACLU. He was also a man of the cloth. I wear a badge, and I certainly believe in upholding the law. But shit happens, just look at the OJ case. Shit happens!

I wanted to be the one to take these guys down. I don't think that in my police career, I ever wanted anything more. I criticized other officers for thinking the way I was now thinking, but this was different. If these assholes were arrested, they'd go to trial. They weren't about to cop a plea. Trial meant the family, the dad, and the twelve-year-old would again be dragged through reliving all the slime of the robbery and the rape.

After thinking about what they had done, I turned to Rocky, who was quietly driving and observing then said, "It's not fair, I know I'm not judge and jury, but I am a first responder, and I want a piece of those assholes if we ever find them. I really do! I could do the asshole who raped that preteen girl. I could do him and take you and Paula out to dinner and enjoy every bite of that succulent steak. Shit, I'd even buy you a bottle of their best booze."

"Tony, your career is not worth it," Rocky said. "If that doesn't sell you, you have a partner to consider, and I know you; you couldn't live with that. That's just your anger that's talking."

I looked at Rocky. "You'd be surprised. I keep seeing a picture of a twelve-year-old being raped by that piece of shit. I could do it and sleep really well."

"Don't! That's not a threat, its advice from a friend. Don't! I've seen shit go down out here, and years later, it comes back and f**k's you in the ass, so don't even think about it."

"Rock, if that twelve-year-old happened to be your daughter….."

I saw the black Ford Explorer first. It had paper plates and was parked at the west curb, one store north of a jewelry store.

"Check out the Explorer," I said as I reached for the radio and notified Lyons and Holfe. "There's a Black male behind the wheel. The engine is running."

Rocky passed the Explorer and made a U-turn further up the block. He asked, "Were you able to see inside the store?"

"Negative." I called dispatch on my cell in case the perps had a police radio, and I advised what we had observed. "Call the Pan Am Boulevard Jewelers, and if someone answers, ask them their hours. If someone answers, I want to know what they sound like, if it's a Hispanic voice or a Black. I'll hold on."

Rocky made another U-turn south of the Explorer and slid into a parking space several cars behind the Explorer. We watched and waited.

Cheryl, the dispatcher, came back on the line. "No answer, Tony."

"Copy." I called Lyons and Holfe.

"We've got a black Ford Explorer with one male Black behind the wheel. It's just north of the Pan Am Boulevard Jewelry Store. The Ford has paper plates and the engine's running. Dispatch called the store, and no one answered. I'm going to have two marked units cover the back door from the alley and from a distance. You guys take the car. Just sit on it. Rocky and I are going to attempt entry as Joe citizen. What's your ETA?"

"About six," Lyons responded.

Rocky advised dispatch of the need for two black and whites. He also asked dispatch to have a couple of units drive around the area a couple of blocks away but not on Pan Am.

"We're going in," Rocky said.

We each carried a small Sony handheld radio in our pocket. Before we exited the Mustang, we turned down the volume. Rocky carried his duty weapon and a backup. I carried my Glock, a baby Glock, and a "throwaway" 38 that was a gift from a fellow officer, just in case. Lyons and Holfe were at the opposite end of the city. They were at the Richmond strip. Although it was only three and a half miles, in Saturday afternoon traffic, with lights and siren, it could take time to weave in and out of traffic.

43

We exited the Mustang. We began walking toward the front door. The street was filled with shoppers. We were trying to be casual as if we were part of the throng of shoppers. We both had our hands in our windbreaker jacket pockets. Our hands were on our weapons. I stepped in front of Rocky. I reached for the door.

I pushed it opened and scanned the store, tightening my grip on my Glock. I knew Rocky was doing the same. There was an older male Hispanic behind the counter. Directly in front of the Hispanic male was a Black male. One word came to mind, **SHIT!** Was the guy buying a gift for his wife, or was he robbing the place.

If he was our guy, where the hell was the other one? If anyone tells you race does not enter into a situation like this, they're lying through their teeth. If this guy was an innocent shopper, and odds were he was, the newspapers would have a field day. I could picture the front page: **White cops arrest Black shopper**. On the other hand, there was a vehicle matching the perps' vehicle parked outside. There was a male Black "shopping."

The vehicle had paper plates. Coincidence? Cops shouldn't buy into coincidences; it could get them killed, someone said. "I'd rather be tried by twelve than carried by six."

"Can I help you?" The Hispanic clerk asked.

I thought I heard nervousness, tension in his voice. He looked worried.

I looked at Rocky. "We're looking for something for our wives. We'll look around."

The Black guy had his right hand in the pocket of his black pants. He was wearing a black watch cap, but it wasn't pulled down to hide his face. He had to be our guy. To my left was an archway, which I was sure, led to the backroom? I nodded to Rocky.

"Check this out. Monica might like this."

"I'm sure she would," Rocky answered.

As soon as Rocky was next to the Black man, I walked toward the archway. There was no door, just a curtain. I looked over my shoulder.

Rocky came out of his pocket with his Glock, then I heard him say, "Breathe hard, and it'll be your last breath. Take your hand out of your pocket slowly. If I even smell a gun, I'll kill you."

I pushed the curtain aside at the same time, taking cover behind the archway. The second Black man was holding a woman by the throat and had a gun to her head.

I looked him straight in the eyes and said, "Drop the gun, and we all walk out of here upright. Get froggy with that gun, and you die on the floor. You make the call."

"I'll kill her mother f*****r; I'll kill her," he yelled.

He jerked her backward but lost his balance. She pulled right. He stumbled left. I fired. My round caught him in his right shoulder. He grabbed for the shoulder and dropped the gun. She ran through the curtain to the front of the store. The scum bag bent and reached for his weapon. I took two steps and kicked him in the balls. He went down gagging. The gun was inches from his outstretched hand. I took two small steps forward.

I looked down and said, "Lift up your shirt." He spits blood on the floor.

"What?"

"You heard me, you Black mother f*****r. Lift up your goddamn shirt."

"Relax, man, relax." He said as he pulled the shirt out of his black pants.

"Higher," I said, and saw everything I wanted to see. The tattoo read, *"F**k Your World."* All at once, I did three things. I rolled up my jacket. I showed him the tattoo on my right forearm. "Read it out loud," I yelled at him.

"I Keep the Peace!" he muttered.

I heard Lyons and Holfe talking loudly as they entered the front of the store.

The second action I took was to kick the prick's gun closer to his right hand. Then I said, "Say hello to God for me." I leaned forward and put two rounds center mass.

We booked two at the Station, the driver that Holfe and Lyons took into custody without incident, and the asshole Rocky took into custody in front of the store. The third suspect, the child rapist, went for a ride in the coroner's wagon.

We walked out of the booking room. In the hallway, Rocky asked, "What happened back there?"

I smiled, and said, "The suspect reached, I double tapped, end of the story. We get dinner for four. I guarantee you I'll sleep very well tonight. *I Keep the Peace!*"

Rocky gave me a strange look but said nothing. We both drew ten days of desk duty. SOP (Standard Operating Procedure) at APD. APD and the Sheriff investigated the shooting. I came out as clean as purified water. Better, I was a hero at the Station. The Hispanic people of our great city said my name was now "*hero.*" I expected to have a nightmare or two over the shooting. I figured it might cost me sleep. Neither was the case.

The guy was a scum bucket. As far as I was concerned, they all should have died. People argue over the callousness of the death penalty, I support it! There is no such thing as LWOP (life without parole). A sentence can be commuted, a governor can grant a pardon, and the death penalty can be ruled unconstitutional. An attorney can file appeal after appeal until he gets lucky for his client.

The Manson gang was proof positive of that. Besides, the taxpayers shouldn't have to pay room and board to house and feed these animals.

Dead is dead. I did not second guess my actions, not for a New York minute. The one thing that did play hard in my mind is that I believed in karma. That was a chance I would have to take.

CHAPTER 4

COMPASSION ON THE JOB

The guy rolled past our unit in the slow lane. When he stopped at the light, I observed no brake lights. There was a male behind the wheel, a female in the passenger seat, and two young children under five in child safety seats in the rear of the black Ford.

"I'm going to pull him over just to let him know that his brake lights are out," I said.

Rocky nodded, "It's a fix-it ticket."

"I know. I'm just going to give him a warning. He needs to get the lights fixed."

Rocky put us out as I got out of the car. I walked slowly so Rocky could catch up to me to cover me from the passenger side of the Ford.

"Good evening, can I see your license, please?" The kids in the back were crying. I looked at the female, she was casually dressed. The foursome looked like most other Amity families. She started crying. I took his license from him. I asked him if everything was all right?

She took a tissue from her handbag. "We promised the kids ice cream, but the welfare check didn't come in. Things are tough for us, but I feel for the kids."

I checked the license. It was valid. "My insurance is in the glove compartment," he said.

"That's okay."

"I wanna' be police when I grow up," one of the kids said, through his tears.

The other youngster said, "Me too."

I thought about my own early days growing up. We were poor. My brother and I often went without ice cream when the ice cream man rolled around in his Good Humor truck. The other kids ran to the truck. Steve and I stayed back.

"I stopped you because your brake lights are out. I'm not going to give you a ticket," I said. "Maybe it's a loose wire. When you get home after having ice cream, check the wiring. Driving without brake lights is dangerous."

"I promise the minute we get home, I'll check it. Thank you for not giving me a ticket," he replied.

I handed him back his license. Underneath the license were two twenty-dollar bills. "Enjoy the ice cream," I said.

I looked at the kids. "When you're twenty-one, come down to the Station. APD needs real good police officers. I know both of you will make fine police officers."

The man looked at the two twenties and then showed them to his wife. More tears rolled down her cheeks. These were tears of joy. "Officer, can I see you name tag. I want your name."

"Let it go." If that story got around, I'd be the laughing stock of the Station. "That's okay, sir, it's our pleasure."

When we were back in the unit, Rocky cleared the call. He looked at me. I was waiting for some smart-ass remark. "What the hell did you do back there?"

I hesitated. "Gimme' a break. The kids were promised ice cream….."

"We're partners, right?"

"Correct."

Here's my half, partner." Rocky handed me two ten-dollar bills.

TIME OUT FOR FUN

The four of us ended up at the bowling alley. It was Paula and Rocky against Roni (my blind date) and me. Neither one of us were a threat to the pro bowlers tour. We decided to roll three games. The pair who won two out of three would eat breakfast compliments of the losers. We were all competitors, especially Rocky and me. Roni, about five foot seven with a tight 22-year-old bod, was an even match for Paula while Rocky and I averaged about one sixty-eight per game.

By eleven fifteen, each team had won one game. This was the rubber match. Rocky and Paula were thirteen pins up on us in the sixth frame. In the seventh frame, Rocky buried his ball in the pocket but left a ten pin, which he promptly missed. I threw a strike. Paula, working on a spare, left the three-ten (baby split). She converted it.

"Helluva' shot," I applauded then said, "Too bad you don't have a decent partner."

Roni, who struck in the sixth, doubled in the seventh. We not only closed the gap, but we were up. Roni was not only cute and well put together; she could also hold her own in a conversation, a rare commodity.

We took a short pause going into the tenth frame, for drinks. Then the action resumed. I had to admit I was having a ball.

"You know there is an indoor go-kart track in Burbank. Anyone interested in testing their behind the wheel skills on our next days off?" I asked.

"Let's beat you at one thing at a time," Rocky said.

Both Roni and Paula threw open frames. I left a damn five-pin on a light hit and somehow managed to miss it.

"Doors open," Rocky quipped.

"Somebody once said, if you can't do it with a pencil, you can't do it with a bowling ball. I think you're history."

Rocky looked at the scores. "Check your math. If I strike out, we win by one pin."

I had to put my two cents in. "If you strike out, I buy breakfast tonight and every shift next week."

That's all it took. Rocky lit up like the overheads on our unit. "Sounds like a bit of a 415 to me."

"Not a disturbance," I responded. "More like an ADW, assault with a dead weapon."

Rocky threw the ball deep in the pocket and had his first strike. I wasn't worried; no one had thrown three in a row tonight. Rocky's second shot clinched it. He crossed over to the Brooklyn side and just caught the headpin. When the pins stopped bouncing around, he somehow had his second strike.

"Open your eyes, man. If I ever observed a 211 in progress, that's it." A 211, I explained to Roni, is a robbery.

"I know Sergeant Friday. I watch Dragnet and Adam 12 reruns," she said.

I loved her sense of humor. "Cute. Didn't I give you your Miranda rights?"

Roni cocked her head, smiled, and gave me a stare with her warm blue eyes. I couldn't read the eyes.

"Take your pencil," Rocky said, grabbing his ball. "See if you can do it with the pencil cause I'm about to do it with the ball."

"Actions, my friend, speak volumes. BS will get you held in contempt."

I eyed Rocky. He stepped up to the lane with the ball in his left hand. He put his fingers in the hole, wiggled them to get a secure grip then inserted his thumb. He was concentrating like I had seen him do at the shooting range during qualifications. Like most everything else Rocky did, he was a crack shot, earning expert nearly every qualification. I watched Rocky's four-step approach, starting with his right foot.

He was smooth. On Rocky's third step, the ball arced high behind him. His fourth step brought him to the foul line. The ball rolled out of his hand and on its mark. He buried the f*****g ball in the one-three pocket. It was a clean strike. To loud cheers from Paula and Roni, Rocky took a long, prolonged bow. I broke the pencil.

 "I'm getting really hungry," Rocky said. "Who else is hungry?"

CHAPTER 5

A DANGEROUS PURSUIT

It was an absolutely gorgeous weekday afternoon in Amity. The temperature was in the mid-seventies. Most people were at work. Traffic was moderate. Rocky was smoking a cigarette in the unit. I was driving, checking out the asses on the shoppers walking in and out of the stores on Pan Am Boulevard. Roni and I had a budding relationship. Life was about as good as it gets.

Rocky disturbed my lady watching. He called dispatch on the radio. "13 Adam, are you clear for a roller?" The blue Honda Civic in front of us had expired tags.

"Go ahead 13 Adam."

"6 Paul Sam Union 425, that's 6 Paul Sam Union 425."

"13 Adam that vehicle comes back 1035. It's a stolen out of Compton earlier today. Is the vehicle occupied?"

"13 Adam is southbound Pan Am Blvd. south of Glaze. The vehicle is occupied one time by a twenty or so year old male Hispanic wearing a dark-colored ball cap and blue shirt. He hasn't observed us."

Rocky looked at me and smiled. Then he continued, "Vehicle is in the number two-lane. His speed is thirty miles per hour."

Pan Am Boulevard was crowded with shoppers. The street was wide with two northbound lanes and two southbound lanes. Speed was posted at 25 mph because of the heavy vehicle and pedestrian traffic.

"13 Adam, 22, 16, and 18 are rolling to assist. We have an airship en route."

"Copy that."

MY FIRST PURSUIT

My heart was pounding I had been in two previous pursuits but only as the passenger officer. This was my first pursuit as a driver. Rocky was on the radio and yelling shit at me at the same time. I had no f*****g idea of what he was yelling. If you've ever been in the family car with your teenage son or daughter who had the radio blasting while you're driving, you know what I heard from Rocky was about every third word, most of that was indistinguishable.

Pedestrians were all over the freakin' place. I was trying to watch people, traffic, lights, cars, peds and the asshole I was chasing all at the same time. I just knew I was going to crash the unit. The idea in a pursuit is to stay with the suspect until, hopefully, he stopped. If the chase became too dangerous, the officer or the watch commander could shut the pursuit down.

"13 Adam, Airship S-1 has been redirected to a more urgent call. No airship is available."

Rocky responded, "Copy that dispatch."

I followed the car southbound on Pan Am. I weaved in and out of traffic as he weaved in and out of traffic. I felt like I was playing follow the leader as we did on bicycles when we were kids, except this time, a mistake could cost someone his life. The light was red for southbound Pan Am Boulevard traffic, but this bozo didn't give a shit. He ran the light, nearly sideswiping a white, westbound pickup truck.

His tires squealed as he made a quick right turn, cutting off several more cars. He was now headed westbound on Western Avenue. My siren and lights warned drivers who were paying attention. Those who were on cell phones, or talking with passengers, damn near got clipped. I felt my adrenalin pumping, pumping, and pumping. It was a high I hadn't known. It was frightening but also exhilarating.

I could barely hear Rocky on the radio, but instinctively I knew he was giving DOT information to dispatch and to the units that had almost caught up with us. A glance in the rearview mirror told me we had three other units with us.

"Speed is now sixty-five," I told Rocky so he could relay that information to dispatch.

Western Avenue is the main street that runs east and west through Amity and into Compton on the west and Bell on the east. Each direction has two lanes. Traffic is never light on these streets. Today was no exception. The son of a bitch continued weaving between lanes and in and out of traffic. He damn near ran over a dog that ran across the street. I was an animal lover. This guy was mine.

The blue Honda made a hard northbound turn and hit seventy-two racing up Elm, a wide street that carried less traffic than Western Avenue. It was a mix of residential homes and businesses. If he continued north several miles, he'd hit the freeway. I wasn't about to let that happen. Rocky kept yelling at me. I still couldn't hear him. His words were muffled. He sounded like he was trying to talk through a mask.

The light was red at Glaze Avenue and Elm. Traffic was heavy east and westbound. The Honda slowed to forty. He took the light damn near catching the rear end of a tan Toyota driving westbound. I slammed on the brakes and went around the back of the Toyota.

Pursuit training was kicking in. I could feel the sweat stinging my left eye. I wasn't about to take either hand off the steering wheel to wipe away the sweat. The guy could drive; I had to give him that. He had probably been stealing cars since he was ten. Maybe he was an ex-cop. He was hitting speeds in the seventies and was crossing over into the wrong lane of traffic to avoid vehicles that were doing the speed limit.

I was within five or six car lengths. He approached Almador Avenue, an east-west major artery that consisted of stores, pedestrians, and traffic. He made a hard left and went westbound. I was staying with him but took my eyes off the road long enough to glance at Rocky. He gave me the thumbs up. I kept my hands on the wheel, nodded my head up and down. I grinned. I was tense, but the adrenalin rush damn near beat a great blow job.

My heart was pounding. Suddenly traffic came to a dead stop at Alameda and Almador. Asshole drove the Honda up on the curb and around three pedestrians, a cat, and a discarded baby carriage with no wheels. The policy was you don't go up on curbs during a pursuit, and you don't go the wrong way on a one-way street. I had two options. Sit in the gridlock until I could get around all this congested shit then probably lose the asshole or drive up on the curb and hear about it later from the watch commander.

I looked over at Rocky. Rocky shrugged as if to say, "You're driving." The siren was blaring. I went over the curb. He went around the

peds, I went around the peds. He missed the cat, which probably had nine lives anyway. The cat was nowhere in sight when I passed where the cat had been. He clipped the baby carriage sending it into the street and into the passenger door of a beat-up red Chevy step van. When asshole came off the curb and around the traffic, I was right behind him.

He headed southbound Alameda with four units in hot pursuit. I think I actually had a hard-on! The west side of Alameda is a sea of used car lots. Sandwiched in the middle of these lots was a new car dealership that added a touch of class to the less than attractive appearance of the dingy used car lots. People were looking at cars and talking with the salesman. They stopped their animated conversation long enough to turn toward the lights and the sirens.

The asshole was passing slower drivers. There were four lanes of moderate traffic, two in each direction. He was forcing cars into the number one lane to move to the number two-lane and was forcing cars in the number two lane to drive onto the shoulder. I was right behind him. I worried about hitting somebody or something. I was worried about smacking up the car. More importantly, I didn't want to lose the GTA suspect.

First off, he was driving a stolen. He could be a robbery suspect, a killer, a rapist, or a child molester. He could be armed. Most importantly, if I let this guy getaway, I'd be the laughing stock of the Station until the next officer lost a GTA suspect. I heard a familiar noise. Adjacent and running parallel to Alameda northbound is a train track. The distant sound I heard was the train's whistle.

When he intersected with Western Avenue, the light was red. Western was heavy with traffic. He ignored the light to a blast of blaring, angry horns. He made a U-turn heading back northbound Alameda. I stayed with him. People were gathered in the growing darkness watching the pursuit. They were yelling and screaming motivating him to keep going.

I didn't want to see anyone get hurt, at least no one but him. I chased him, with now four units behind me, back to Alameda and Almador, a good three miles.

He weaved in and out of traffic, across the solid double yellow line then into oncoming traffic. I still had no air support. Near Almador and Alameda, another major intersection with heavy traffic, he caught another red light. Traffic was heavy eastbound and westbound. He didn't seem to give a shit. He didn't even slow down. I watched a blue Ford pickup enter the intersection westbound. There was no way in hell he was going to avoid a collision. He didn't. He caught the pickup on the driver's side rear quarter panel spinning the heavier pickup one hundred eighty degrees.

The pickup slid into another car on its right. Smoke poured from both vehicles. Miraculously the son of bitch skidded across two lanes of congestion but didn't hit another car. The collision with the pickup only caused a busted headlight and fender damage to the passenger side of his stolen vehicle. Asshole regained control and kept driving. He had to run out of luck sooner or later. I hoped it would be sooner, however, it wasn't! My eyes darted in all directions.

I had one mindset, which was to stop the asshole. He was hitting speeds in access of sixty, which was crazy with this traffic. The crowd of onlookers on the west curb grew. To many, it was a game. They couldn't see or didn't care about the danger to innocent people. This wasn't going to end well. I heard the train whistle again. The train was crossing Western headed north. Asshole was in the southbound number one lane traveling sixty-seven miles an hour in what was now heavy traffic.

He was weaving in and around cars occasionally driving into northbound traffic, at times forcing oncoming cars to pull to the shoulder. I was more than six car lengths behind him closing fast. Pitting him was out of the question. I wasn't PIT certified, and his speed was above PIT standards. There was too damn much traffic. Rocky remained on the radio in constant touch with dispatch. We had a dedicated frequency. All other units were directed to tack two a secondary frequency.

I could hear Rocky's voice. I could feel his tension. I could still barely make out his words. Being the passenger officer in pursuit is more stressful than being the driver cop. I had eight hundred things going on at once, which kept my mind occupied. Rocky, on the other hand, had the radio, was watching the perp, and had to worry about my driving. Actually, I was doing enough worrying for both of us. There is a card casino on the west side of Alameda.

Apparently, without looking north, and without expecting a southbound vehicle to be in the northbound lanes, a gorgeous burnt orange Dodge Challenger pulled out of the casino parking lot. Asshole didn't see him. The Dodge veered up on the curb and around a tree, coming to a stop inches from a fence. Asshole never even swerved. He flipped the driver of the Dodge off and stepped his speed up to seventy, moving back into southbound traffic lanes.

The approaching train was two blocks away. I could hear its warning whistle. I was getting tired of chasing this asshole. It was going to end badly. He was going to hit something or somebody, or I was going to hit something or somebody. This clown was reckless and didn't seem to give a shit about anyone. He wasn't drunk, and he wasn't on anything. His motor skills were too sharp. We knew the vehicle was stolen, but he could have committed a crime or had serious warrants out for his arrest.

It was at times like these that I'd like to be able to throw a f*****g hand grenade at the vehicle. Do that once or twice, and the next time you light some asshole up, he'll pull over. Asshole made a sudden eastbound turn. He was heading directly into the path of the northbound train. I heard the whistle scream at the car. The guy accelerated. The wooden arms were blocking the street. This was going to be close. If it was going to be close to him, it was going to be closer to me. My chest was f*****g pounding.

It hurt as I watched the train, which was hauling ass. I watched the stolen vehicle. He wasn't slowing down. I accelerated. He weaved between the downed wooden warning arms that blocked the intersection. It was like a hard-hit ground ball that found its way between the third basement and the diving shortstop. The ball had eyes; this clown had balls. His balls were big and brassy. There was an uphill slope in the road a few feet before the tracks. The trains warning whistle blaring couldn't have missed the stolen by more than a few feet.

The car left the ground as it crossed the incline to the opposite side of the tracks. I could see sparks as the vehicle again made contact with cement. I was committed (maybe I should have been committed). Smoke and dust were all the bystanders could see. My unit skidded to a stop as the train raced by. I was out of the black and white pounding my fists on the hood of the car. A crowd formed out of nowhere. The idiots cheered for the asshole.

Rocky gave me several seconds to beat the shit out of the hood. Then he put his arm on my shoulder. "Enough. It's over. Tomorrow's another day."

"Too f*****g bad, the train didn't take him out." That was all I could say. I was pissed!

Rocky laughed. "Because he stole a car and got away? Do you know anyone who ever stole a car?"

I looked at Rocky. "Yeah, me!"

I walked into the WC's office, not knowing what to expect. Lieutenant Samuels was five-ten, 165, fifty years old, quiet and sharp. He had started his police career as a Reserve and worked his way up the cop ladder. He knew the streets.

Just because he had reached the rank of lieutenant didn't mean that he had lost touch with his men (and women) and didn't mean he had lost touch with the streets. He constantly found reasons to leave the Station and assist the troops. I liked the LT.

"Sit down. Take a load off." The LT. said as he got up from his desk and walked over to where I sat. "I know you're pissed at yourself.

"I followed the pursuit on the radio and talked to a couple of the secondary units and Rocky. Here's the bottom line. Had you attempted to beat that train, had you beaten it, there would be paper in your file right now. I swear there would be. Not much is worth risking your life or the life of your partner not to mention the lives of the passengers on that train.

"He got away this time. We'll get him eventually. He'll steal more cars, and you'll be in more pursuits. You'll catch some, you won't catch others. The bottom line is you and your partner get to go home, and so does everyone on that train. You can stew in your juices, Tony, for the rest of tonight and until you come to work tomorrow. After that, it's history. Is that clear?"

"Yes, sir, crystal clear, sir," I said.

"Great, Tony! Now, get out of here, find your partner, and hit the streets."

CHAPTER 6

ON PATROL, ONE-MAN UNIT

Rocky took Thursday night off. I didn't. Working a single man unit is obviously more dangerous than working a two-man unit. Tonight, I was not a two-man unit, an Adam unit. Working alone was also boring. I had only myself to talk with, that was scary. Rocky told me to be careful. Thursday evenings tended to be busy in APD. The later it got, more of the criminal element hit the streets. We had a rash of stolen cars, Thursdays, Fridays, and Saturdays.

The bangers were getting ready for robberies, burglaries, general criminal activities such as drive-by shootings, snatch and grabs, any illegal activity that could translate into quick cash. Lately, on Pan Am Boulevard a couple of these Hispanic bangers had teamed up, and where knocking off jewelry stores on the Boulevard. They were loud, they were quick, and they were organized. We weren't certain whether there were three or four. We had various descriptions from the victims and the wits.

What we thought we knew was that they were in their early to late twenties. At least one was armed with a handgun. He'd find a female employee, stick the gun under her nose, then tell her if she didn't want to get hurt to hand over the cash and any jewelry he pointed to in the display case. No one had been physically hurt to date. They came in the front door and exited the rear door to the parking lot to a waiting vehicle.

Different witnesses described the car as everything from a Ford Explorer to a Ford Focus to a Dodge Challenger. The cameras inside and outside of the store gave us little more to go on. These clowns were wearing hoodies, and ball caps pulled low to cover their faces.

Even if their faces were clearly depicted, most of the people wouldn't ID the perps either out of fear of retaliation or for the same reason cops won't normally rat out other cops. The only way we were going to get these idiots was to catch them in the act; that would take miraculous luck. I'd have a better chance of winning the Florida lottery. No one had been seriously hurt to date, although a non-cooperative male store manager had been pistol-whipped.

The take totaled approximately 133,000 dollars in cash and another hundred or so grand in heisted jewelry. In and around Amity, they had hit nine jewelry stores. Thursday, Friday, and Saturdays were strike days for these perps. It was still early in the shift. It was 2130 hours, and I was cruising northbound Acacia Avenue, a one-way street. I was thinking about Roni. We had gone out a few times, dinner and a movie, bowling, nothing heavy, but I was growing fond of Roni.

She had separated from her husband several months earlier. Roni had no kids. She was a teacher's aide in a public elementary school. She was stable, reasonably happy, and fun to be with. I was growing fond of her tight body, as well.

The car, which was headed eastbound on Glaze, made a right turn to go south on Acacia. I observed it and watched it. I continued northbound Acacia. The vehicle, still traveling southbound, was traveling the wrong way on Acacia. It continued coming toward me at 25 miles an hour. I lit him up. He didn't stop or slow down. I put my spotlight directly into his windshield. He slowed then pulled into a driveway on the west side of the street. I stopped. I couldn't read the plate. He was too far away.

He rolled down the driver's window and yelled to me to pull up. "I'll back up and pull in behind you."

F*****g idiot! There was no way in hell I was going to let him get behind me, especially when I was working a solo unit.

I yelled, "Pull the car out of the driveway, damn it! Pull up in front of me. Stop the damn car!"

He finally followed my instructions. When he stopped, I pulled up a few feet. I gave dispatch my twenty and read off the license plate. The asshole had his hands straight up in the air. That raised a flag. Normally when a cop pulls you over, your hands are on the steering wheel. Adam Henry's hands weren't where I wanted them.

"13, your plate comes back no record on file," dispatch said.

"Copy that."

I could have read the plate incorrectly. The dispatcher was new. He could have punched the wrong plate into the computer. The license plate had a frame around it. If the bottom of the 'I' in the plate was

67

covered by the license plate frame, I could have read it to dispatch as a 'T.'

I was cautious since his hands were not where they should be, and the plate coming back "no record on file." He was violating 21650 of the California Vehicle Code, driving the wrong way on a one-way street. I wasn't taking any chances. I exited the black and white. I stood behind the door until my flashlight was secure under my left arm. My Glock was out of its holster and hidden behind my right thigh. Rocky wasn't on the passenger side of the vehicle. I had no back.

Slowly, I made my approach. I reached the car's doorpost. I stood behind the post. He couldn't see me unless he turned his head; advantage: me! I moved the flashlight. I could see into the car. I observed the interior of the car slowly, carefully, never taking my eye off the driver's hands, which remained in the air.

He appeared as nervous as a groom on his wedding night. "Good evening. I stopped you because you are going the wrong way on a one-way street," I said.

He was Caucasian, about thirty-five years old, wearing black slacks, a black pullover shirt, and black tennis shoes. Criminals dressed this way to blend in with the night. "Is there anything in the car that doesn't belong in the car?"

He looked at me, then quickly looked down at his leg. Nervously he said, "I...I...I have a loaded gun under my right thigh."

My movement was automatic. "If you move," smoothly and quickly, I raised my Glock so that it was pointed squarely at his head, "I'll shoot."

"I'm…I'm…I'm an FBI agent," he said.

I nodded, not moving my gun. "I'm **F**ull **B**looded **I**talian, too." I took a breath. "Relax and take a couple of deep breaths. That's what the terrorists are saying."

He was looking straight at the barrel of my Glock and said, "Didn't your watch commander tell you we're out here tonight doing an operation?"

"My watch commander didn't tell me anything. Now, do exactly as I tell you and you won't get shot. Keep your hands in the air." I backed up less than a foot. "That's good, just like that."

He looked over his shoulder at me. "Holster the damn gun, I'm FBI!"

"I told you, shut the f**k up, and do as you're told." When he started to protest, I leveled my Glock at the back of his head. I was in control, and we both knew it. There was as much chance of his being FBI as there was of my being King Tut.

I called the WC on my cell. The WC's response was immediate and immediately clear. "Oh shit. I forgot to tell you guys at briefing the Feds are doing an operation."

If the WC could see my face, I would have drawn a suspension. I wanted to kick him in the crotch. "Copy that, Sir."

I kept my Glock aimed at his head and asked, "Where is your ID?"

"It's under my shirt." He was still nervous. I could see his hands shaking. His hands were still straight up in the air.

"With your left hand only, pull up your shirt." He did.

FBI ID. I holstered my weapon. I snapped two pictures of Mr. FBI with my Smartphone.

"Was all that shit necessary?" he asked.

"You're the freakin' FBI agent, you tell me."

I wasn't going to let the idiot off that easily. "I gotta' protect myself. And you're the one going the wrong way with a f*****g pistol under your thigh. Don't they teach driving skills in the FBI academy?"

"I was following someone. You screwed up the operation."

He tried unsuccessfully to hide his embarrassment. I was enjoying the hell out of it. "Do I look stupid to you?" I said, looking him straight in the eye.

"What does that mean?"

"If you were following someone, he would have been going the wrong way, and I would have pulled him over first. Now before I cite you for 21650 (A) of the vehicle code, I suggest you turn the vehicle around and head the right way, f***in' pronto!" End of conversation!

By 0200 hours, I had answered a few lightweight calls and backed a couple of disturbance calls but nothing of any consequence. I continued to patrol the streets of Amity. Good police work consisted of moving, moving, and moving. The burglar, who saw a black and white, would move on. The potential car thief, who observed a cop on patrol, would move on.

The 459 from the vehicle, the asshole looking to jack a radio from a car, would see the unit in motion and would be less likely to hit that car. Good police work meant driving around the city when calls were quiet and keeping your eyes and ears open. I knew cops who in the dead of winter drove with both windows open and the heater on so they could *hear* the sounds of the night.

I was cruising when I observed an older white Cadillac come out of the Chase Bank parking lot on Acacia and Western. The sole occupant made a southbound turn on a northbound one-way street. He drove west on Western. I let two cars get between us. I slid into his lane, followed, and observed. At this time of the morning, when the bars closed, the drunks flooded the streets. I watched the two white lines for signs that he was weaving. I watched his speed. He was on the money.

He may have been in a hurry, or maybe he didn't see the one-way street sign in the bank lot or the arrow indicating the one-way street. I made up my mind. I'll make the stop.

"13, I'll be traffic Western and Elm, on 4 Edward, Robert, Charles......."

"Copy that, 13."

I lit the Caddy up. The guy immediately pulled to the curb at the northeast corner of Western and Elm. I pulled in behind him, offsetting the black and white. I pointed my tires toward the street.

71

There were two reasons for pointing the unit's tires toward the street. If you had to get out in a hurry, you jumped in the unit, stepped on the gas and off you go. If you needed cover, the tires were a source of low cover; not much cover, but cover was cover. I was out of the car making my way toward the Cadillac's sole occupant.

The new dispatcher's voice was calm over the air. "13, your vehicle is 1035." It was stolen.

I should not have made my approach until dispatch came back with the information on my stop. I screwed up. Too late, I was committed. I was too damn close to the car to turn back. I kept walking, drew my Glock, and aimed it where it would do the most damage, at the driver's bald head.

The guy looked at me, looked at the gun and in a thick accent that obviously came from south of the border, he yelled, "Man, whassup? Put the gun away."

I responded, "Shut up, the car is stolen."

"My car, no stolen," he said in that thick Mexican accent.

"It's stolen, according to my dispatcher," I said.

Just then, dispatch interrupted my intelligent conversation with "Oops. I meant to say there is a 1035 attached to the vehicle."

Mother f*****r, I thought. But I said into the mic, "Copy."

A 1035 attached to the vehicle meant that somebody on the registration had a warrant for his or her arrest. I didn't put the Glock in its holster. I held it steady. It remained pointed at his head.

"What's your name?" I asked.

"Rodriguez, Juan Hernandez."

"Rodriguez, whose car is it?"

"It's my car," he said in a cooperative tone.

"I need to see your license, registration, and proof of insurance."

Three units had rolled up behind me, thinking I had a rollin' stolen. Baldy leaned over in the direction of the glove compartment. He extracted paperwork from the glove box. He also handed me his license. My back up was covering me from the passenger side of the car.

"Give your license to the officer on the passenger side of the car," I said. He immediately complied.

Officer Monahan ran the license. Baldy had a fifty thousand dollar outstanding warrant. I holstered my Glock.

"Please step out of the car. You're under arrest for an outstanding warrant. We'll discuss it further at the station."

Officer Monahan asked me if I was going to impound the car. I had options. Baldy could call someone to come get the car. If they lived close by, if I didn't have to wait half the night for the impound truck, that was an option. If I left the car on the street and it was stolen, or 459'd, the Department could be held liable.

"Do you have someone who can pick up your car?" I asked.

Baldy shook his head, no.

I wasn't going to allow him to park the car on the street. "The car is good to go," I told dispatch.

Monahan said he would do the CHP 180, the impound form. I pulled the DR, the report number, stuffed baldly in the back of my unit, and transported him to the station for booking on the outstanding warrant.

CHAPTER 7

SATURDAY NIGHT & WHEELCHAIR WILLIE

It was Saturday night in the fine city of Amity. Saturday night was hell night in APD. The bangers, the dealers, the hookers, the tranny's, and every other shade of grey were patrolling the streets of Amity for fun and profit. In the last six months, we hadn't had a Saturday night go by that there wasn't a shooting or stabbing.

Rocky was driving and smoking. I was talking to Roni on my cell. Life was good. Earlier in the evening, I had picked up a necklace with a heart attached for Roni. Nothing too elaborate just a little something to let her know I cared. I thought that had a nice romantic touch to it without overdoing it. Of course, I purchased the jewelry in Amity and in uniform. In return, I enjoyed a fat discount.

Almost every store owner in Amity showed "love" to their coppers. "Love" translated into deep discounts, which we were forbidden by the Chief from accepting; however, everybody accepted "love." 15 Adam caught a call of possible shots fired on the east side of Amity, the heaviest of the dealing and banging in the city.

I waited until I had radio silence then said, "13 Adam will also respond to back."

These gang punks got their hands on guns as easily as a child could buy candy. It was a nightmare for us. Couple that with the fact that many a politician, mainly those aligned with the left, wanted to make it harder for the average, law-abiding citizen to legally possess a weapon, and you have a dilemma. The punks know the average citizen is unarmed.

The punk is packing. My belief was if the punk believed Joe citizen might be armed, he wouldn't screw with Joe. When Bush was Governor in Florida, he proved that point. He made it relatively easy to get weapons permits if you were felony free. Many people said crime would go up. Crime plummeted. The reason "punks will be cowards!" Rocky made a hard U-turn and headed to the east side without lights and siren but with a heavy foot.

Dispatch updated us that they had received several calls. That meant the likelihood was it was a legit call. The speed limit on east Glaze Avenue was half of what Rocky was doing. Years ago, Rocky drove a truck for a living. Pushing a patrol car was child's play for the Rock. The guy who was headed northbound across Anne Avenue not only lacked driving skills but was also color blind.

He didn't see our red lights. I knew it was going to be close, too damn close. It was closer. Rocky tried to swerve left and around the guy. We damn near made it. Damn near doesn't cut it unless it's a hand grenade. The northbound vehicle clipped the passenger rear quarter panel of the unit, sending us spinning 360 degrees. Rocky's skill kept us from hitting anything else. Neither of us had on our seat belts, neither of us was injured.

I exited the unit and checked on the driver of the older red Chevy Nova that hit us. He wasn't hurt and didn't want medics. Rocky called for a supervisor on his cell phone. He didn't want to tie up the radio because of the shots fired call, and if he did use the radio to call for a supervisor, everyone and his Aunt Gloria would know we f*****d up. It took two hours to clear the street, get the necessary accident information, take measurements and statements from the drivers and the witnesses, and to get us back to the station after the tow trucks picked up the vehicles.

Now we had our notes to write and give to the accident investigator who was from Bell PD. It would be a conflict of interest for us to write our own accident report. The final problem was lack of units. There wasn't a marked unit left. Between the units in the field, the units out of service for maintenance, and our crashed unit, we were down to unmarked units.

"There's a dark blue Mustang in the lot," the Watch Commander said. "The keys are on the board. It has a radio in the glove compartment. Take that." Then he added, without a smile, "See if you can bring it back in one piece. As a matter of fact, Rocky, why don't you let Tony drive?"

We were on our way out of the WC's office but hadn't quite made it. The WC said, "You know what, as long as you're going to be in an unmarked unit, go downstairs and change into soft clothes. Tell dispatch you're only going to back calls, you will not be the primary unit. Go out there and see what shit you can stop before it starts."

Rolling around Amity from time to time, there was this sad yet comical story of a guy in a souped-up wheelchair who we knew was a drug dealer, but we couldn't nail him. As a matter of fact, he "nailed" us a couple of times. Wheelchair Willie Williams had someone build him a wheelchair complete with dual tailpipes, an Ahooga horn, mirrors, wire chrome-spoked wheels, and freakin' engine that would get that thing going up to a good twenty-five miles an hour.

A couple of rookies, who thought they had observed him making a drug sale, chased him on foot for half a mile, long enough for the local reporter to make it to the scene. When they caught Wheelchair

Willie, he was as clean as your freshly vacuumed living room carpet. The reporter had a field day with that story.

Letters to the editor were published for a week wanting to know if the cops had anything better to do than chase a poor guy in a wheelchair. Willie was a decorated combat Vet. He came back home to Amity and fell on hard times, so the story was told. I respected anyone who fought for our Flag. I didn't care if you were male, female, gay, straight, or somewhere in between; however, I had no love for Willie. I wanted a piece of Willie and his wheelchair, a big piece, a noticeably big piece.

He started drinking, drugging, and then dealing to support his habit. One night he passed out on the train tracks. A train came by, and Willie survived but lost both his legs. It was tragic. The guy gave his best for our country but couldn't get a break when he came home. That was the story that had been floating around Amity for about a year and a half. I was determined that I was going to be the cop who brought Willie down.

There was a bounty of sorts on Willie's head. The first cops who nailed Willie dead bang and got a conviction would get one meal a day paid for by each officer in the Station. That was almost three months of free meals. That made me more determined to get Willie's ass in handcuffs. The Rock and I first observed Willie rolling around in his wheelchair on Glaze and Lawrence Avenues. By night's end, the guy would travel over a good part of the eastern end of Amity. I swear he put more miles on that wheelchair some nights than we put on the unit. Amazingly, his tires still had tread.

Dispatch broke the monotony. "13 Adam, a possible 273.5 now……"

We "flipped a bitch," as Rocky liked to call it, heading toward the address dispatch gave us.

"I guess they ran short of units. So much for Willie," I said. "We'll have fun with him later, I'm sure."

"13 Adam, we're 97…."

Rocky and I walked to the back house and listened. We could hear yelling, cursing, and crying. It sounded like two adults, but it was difficult to hear through the door and the security door. Rocky took out his baton and rapped on the security door. He quickly stepped to the side away from the door. Silence from inside.

He rapped again, and we heard, "Open the f*****g door, numb nuts." Then we heard footsteps coming closer and "Bitch!"

The door opened, and a man about five-ten, at least at first look it appeared to be a man, dressed in a brown skirt, white blouse, wearing an obvious wig, blonde in color, too much makeup, flung the door open wide.

"Good day, officers." He turned to his partner as if to say, "Now see what you've done. I knew to move in with you was a mistake." Then he said, "Won't you come in."

We stepped cautiously, stopping just inside the threshold, and asked, "Is anyone else in the apartment?"

"Just the two of us, officers" he/she said in a weird tranny voice.

"Any weapons here or on you? Guns, knives, tanks, hand grenades?" I asked.

He/she or whatever the hell "it" was laughed then replied, "No."

Rocky did not like Amity's gay population. Rocky did not like gays. Amity had a gay bar. Rocky did not like taking calls that entailed entering that bar.

Rocky believed a marriage, a relationship was between two individuals; one had to be a man, one a woman. I, on the other hand, couldn't care less who did what to whom.

"Okay, folks," Rocky asked. "You called; now what is going on here?"

The "shemale" spoke up. "It was just a friendly argument, no harm, no foul."

"That's what you say. There was nothing friendly about it. If you can't have it your way, there is no discussion. Well, this time it is going to be different," the other "shemale" said.

"Who called?" Rocky persisted.

"I did." The 'male' half continued, "I want to get a tattoo, and 'she' doesn't want me to. I have the right to do what I want with my body, don't I?"

Rocky and I nodded at the same time. I took the male in female clothing or whatever, outside the apartment out of view of the shemale half. I had nothing against people who had different sexual preferences than I. What you did behind a closed door, as long as two adults consented, I could care less. Two guys, two women or half a woman and half a man, I didn't care. It beat the shit out of killing one another.

I asked, "Did 'he' put a hand on you?"

"No, sir. We yell a lot, but that's it."

I heard Rocky put out a code four.

"Did you touch him in any way?" I asked.

"No, he just told you….."

"I just want to be sure. Here's the deal. One of your neighbors called the station, thinking that there might have been a fight going on. Your neighbor meant well. My suggestion is to keep it down to a low roar in here. Talk over your tattoo dreams in reasonable tones and do what you need to do. If we have to come back today, one of you may go to jail. Any questions?"

I got a reply. "Do you think I should get a tattoo?"

"It's your body. Do what you want with it." I was wearing a long sleeve shirt.

He asked, "Do you like tattoos?"

"I have a couple of tattoos," I said. "I have one on my left lower arm and another on my upper right arm. As a kid, I was terribly short. I had a height complex, and to prove I was tough, I got a heart tattooed on my upper left arm. I was in my senior year of high school. When my Dad saw the tattoo, he told me if I got another tatt, he'd throw my ass out of the house. Of course, by the end of the weekend, I had another tattoo. He didn't throw me out."

"That settles it, I'm getting a tattoo," he/she said as we walked back into the apartment.

"Honey," she said. "I'm sorry; I think you should get a tattoo. This officer explained to me all about making your own decisions. Officer Calhoun has tattoos. He got them when he was in the army."

She walked over to him. They embraced, and said, "The other officer also has tattoos."

As we walked down the hall, Rocky muttered, "f*****g faggotts."

We didn't get another shot at Wheelchair Willie that night, but he and I had a date with destiny, only neither one of us knew it. It was late Saturday afternoon. We had left the "barn" as Rocky called it, a few minutes early. He was driving, and I was feeling sorry for myself. Rocky must have read my mind.

"How did your date go?" Rocky asked.

I hesitated.

"You're awfully quiet. That means one of two things. Either it went very well, and you don't want to share the details, or you got the door slammed in your face and went home and took a cold shower."

"The latter. Apparently she got a surprise call from her ex, or so she says. She's going back with him, and they're going to try to work it out." I glanced at the peds on the sidewalk and said, "Story of my life!"

Rocky didn't say anything. We drove in silence for several minutes until we observed Wheelchair Willie motoring toward the alley just west of Rita. That was just what I needed to cheer myself up, a shot at Wheelchair Willie.

"Get his mother f*****g ass," I said to Rocky. "I want the puke pot."

The wheelchair, with Willie in it, got to the alleyway ahead of us. The mouth of the alley split into three different directions. We had a one in three shot of catching his ugly ass. That meant he had a two out of three chance of losing us. Rocky hit the brakes before he entered the alley completely.

He looked at me and asked, "Which way did he go?"

"It beats the shit out of me." I shook my head. "I'll choke that mother f*****g dope dealer when I get him. This asshole is like a rabbit hiding in a hole."

"Tomorrow's another day," Rocky, sometimes the philosopher quipped. "Willie's day will come."

"Yeah, like Santa comes down the chimney, once a f*****g year."

It was quiet for the next couple of hours. We were dispatched to a few loud music calls and a call of a suspicious person in the area. The calls were handled quickly, quietly, and without an arrest. My thoughts bounced between Wheelchair Willie and Roni. The fact of the matter was that I had no control over either. Roni had made a decision to try to start anew with her ex. That was her decision. All I could do was wish her the very best.

The times we had gone out, I had grown to like Roni. I was disappointed but not heartbroken. As far as Wheelchair Willie, I really wanted his ass, and the bounty on his head. I liked to eat. I liked to win a challenge. This was a challenge.

Rocky's cell phone rang. It was Paula; he took the call while driving. Rocky had a badge. He could get away with that. They chatted for a few minutes; Rocky laughed, told Paula he loved her, then hung up. We continued patrol.

We finished backing a call of a possible 211, robbery in progress. It turned out, as most do, that an employee unwittingly and unknowingly hit a silent alarm. Do that three times, and you get a citation. In actuality, I had never known any business owner in Amity to get slapped with a cite for setting off an alarm three times.

Give a business owner a cite, you can say good-bye to *"love."* We cruised without a call for fifteen minutes. Rocky was driving so I could be the observer. I caught a few minutes of R and R. Two blocks east of where we lost sight of him, we observed Wheelchair Willie motoring eastbound on Almador enjoying the cool of the early evening breeze.

"Let me show you how this is done," Rocky said.

Rocky shot past Willie like a Kershaw fastball. He was inches in front of Willie and his motorized chair when he suddenly jerked the wheel of the Crown Vic and climbed the curb. I thought for sure Rocky was going to T-bone Willie and his ride. Rocky was first out of the car. He had Willie by the shirt, half out of his chair.

"You can hide puke pot, but you can't run. Where's the stash?"

"Where's your warrant, PIG? You ain't got shit. Go back to writing f*****g parking tickets," Willie yelled at Rocky.

"I'm not a meter maid, asshole." Rocky bitch slapped Willie.

"C'mon Rocky," I said, as I pulled him away from Willie.

I don't know why. I wanted that slime bucket more than any other cop in Amity, but for some reason, a piece of me felt Willie didn't deserve this treatment, at least not tonight. Maybe Rocky was right. Maybe I was getting soft in my old age.

I said, "Didn't you tell me earlier that tomorrow's another day? Let the asshole go."

Willie couldn't keep his mouth shut, "Your partner's got more smarts than you, pig. Go fix a parking meter." Rocky bitch slapped Willie again.

Somebody from the crowd that had gathered yelled something about the fuzz and the guy in the wheelchair. I expected we'd hear about this shit.

"C'mon Rocky, that's enough!"

CHAPTER 8

FELLOW OFFICER IN TROUBLE

Rocky's cell phone interrupted us. This time it was the WC. He instructed us to report to the Station NOW. Several minutes later we arrived at the Station. We were ushered up a set of marble stairs to the little Chief's office, a fond term for our ACOP, Assistant Chief of Police Juan Rolando. The "Little Chief" was a big Hispanic man in his early fifties. ACOP Rolando worked out regularly, and it showed.

His hair was jet black, combed back and full. He had a thick black mustache. His starched blue uniform was decorated with "salad." ACOP Rolando was jovial and willing to listen. He often gave the impression that he was more politician than cop. Rolando liked people. He loved his job; it showed. There was a scowl on his face tonight. He looked menacing.

"Close the door and sit down." He looked like he was ready to cry. "I need help. I don't know who to turn to. I'm turning to people within the ranks who I know I can trust." He ran his hand through his jet-black hair.

I was focusing on the picture on the wall behind the desk where ACOP Rolando sat. It was the APD Little League team that Rolando helped coach to a championship last year, the Southern California Cubs. I watched a couple of innings of a few of those games. Rolando put his heart not in winning but in teaching the kids teamwork, spirit, the meaning of winning gracefully and losing with class.

He said, "Some time ago we took some gang punks off the street who were dealing drugs and guns, heavy hitters, real heavy, dirty and ugly players.

"You may remember the name, Hernandez. We busted three of them dead bang. Two of them copped a plea, but the old man was unshakable. His trial is scheduled to start in two days. He has two smart mouth kids who are as vicious as they come. When the trio was busted, they swore that APD would feel the revenge they would extract."

"I remember reading several articles in the paper right after their father was busted," I said. "The assholes were flashing gang signs and swore up, down and sideways that they'd get even. If I remember correctly, both brothers were interviewed at car shows in Pomona. They have several classic cars. Probably all earned dirty, dealing. They're proud of the cars, and they're always looking to add to their collection. It's a clever way of washing their dirty money."

"Unfortunately, ACOP continued, "We can't get the Feds to go after them for tax evasion. But right now, none of that shit helps. These guys are sick puppies. The entire family is f****d up. More often than not, they're coked out."

Rocky spoke up, "What's the problem?"

Rolando folded his hands across his chest. "I was one of the arresting detectives, and I was the cop who cuffed the old man. The punk wants to make good on his promise. He's giving it his best shot." Rolando squeezed his lower lip.

"The old man is due in court the day after tomorrow. I received this message earlier today." Rolando reached for his phone. He hit the play button. The message began to play. "I don't talk with scum. In your case, I'll make an exception, pig. We got your grandkid, Lil Roberto. The kid is cute, really cute. One of the guys, who's babysitting him, likes cute kids, especially young, cute kids, the younger, the better!

"Guess what, PIG? You either tell the judge that you forgot to give the old man his Miranda, or we lock the fag and Roberto alone in a room for a couple of hours. If you have questions, PIG, call 1-800-Roberto."

The Mexican on the other end of the phone with the Spanish accent laughed. It was a sick laugh, and a very demented, menacing laugh.

Jesus Christ, I thought. "How ballsy can you get?"

"Shit, sir," Rocky said. "Whatever we can do? You know we'll do it."

"I don't know what you can do?" Rolando said.

"Do we know where these two are?" Rocky asked.

Rolando was visibly shaken and said, "We've got them under surveillance. We know Roberto isn't in their house. We're sure the two punks know where Roberto is being held, but we'll never get them to give him up."

"You might not be able to get them to give up an address, but I can," I said.

"You mean we can," Rocky added instantly.

"I can't ask you to do that. It can cost you both your career and criminal prosecution."

"Any port in a storm," Rocky said. "And right now, it's pouring. How much time do we have?"

"About eighteen hours, give or take." Rolando sighed, "I've got a team on the brothers. There's a car show going on near Dodger Stadium. It's the first of its kind. It's a 24-hour show that includes low riders. The cars and people come and go all night long. The Hernandez brothers have been there for about an hour."

Rocky and I huddled in the parking lot. This was unfathomable. These guys were desperate and were also into drugs, so anything was possible. We knew they had grabbed Roberto. What we didn't know was where they were keeping him and if they really had a fag child molester babysitting him.

I was first to say it. "I'll do whatever it takes to bring Roberto home safely. I don't give a shit what I have to do. These guys are mother f*****s to the extreme!"

"You get no argument from me," Rocky said as he lit a cigarette. "We've got free reign to do whatever it takes. Let's grab a seriously unmarked car and get to work, the clock's ticking."

Anything in our police lot was out of the question. We needed something concours, something flashy, something worth big bucks. I called in a favor. The car I commandeered was a "borrowed" black 1964 Impala Super Sport complete with hydraulics. Both Rocky and I could pass for at least part Hispanic in the dark, and the low rider would get us exactly where I planned to go.

I didn't know precisely where I was going, but in the few minutes it would take to drive from APD to Dodger Stadium, not far from the LAPD Academy, we'd come up with something. This was serious shit, and I did my best thinking either on the pot or under pressure.

"Where the f**k did you get that?" Rocky asked more than a bit surprised.

"What difference does it make? It may be our ticket to the brothers. Smoke another cigarette. I'm going upstairs and borrow a cold license plate from the gang unit, one that won't come back to the PD. In the meantime, take a dime out of your pocket and unscrew the rear plate on the SS. These punk ass mother f*****s have a date with Starsky and Hutch."

Rocky put his cigarette between his lips and saluted me. "Yes, sir!"

I liked classic cars, particularly the 1950 and early 60 Corvettes. I also liked the 1956 and 1957 Thunderbird, the ones with the porthole hardtop, like the colonial white 1956 Suzanne Sommers drove in

American Graffiti. Unfortunately, on a cop's salary, owning a classic was a dream, however, after tonight, I might not even have a job. I drove the 1964 Impala Super Sport, probably the closest I'd ever come to getting behind the wheel of one of these beauties again, as carefully as I'd hold a new born infant.

The damn car was worth seventy to a hundred grand depending on the market and who was hot to trot for it. Under the hood was a chromed-out 350 big block, even the hoses were chromed and braided. On the underside of the hood was a mural of a half-naked, gorgeous Mexican girl tossing back a shot of tequila laughing at three Mexican cowboys who obviously wanted her. Her breasts were bigger than the engine. The mural was masterfully painted and clear-coated.

The interior of the black beauty was black leather. The seats were soft and luxurious. The dash had an inboard television, Bluetooth, a backup camera, and a horn button separate from the driver's horn that, when pushed, played "Bad Boys" in Spanish. Halfway down the driver's seat, which would be between the legs of whoever was driving the black Super Sport, was a concealed button that looked very much like it was part of the upholstery, which it actually was. In this case, if you pushed that button, a compartment opened, and within reach of the driver's outstretched hand was a pearl-handled 357.

"Where the f**k did you get this car?" Rocky asked, looking at me in amazement.

I drove south on the 5 freeway and said, "We have our ways. We have our ways."

"If you so much as scratch this baby, you'll be paying for it until you make captain," Rocky said.

"I doubt either one of us will see that day."

"What's the plan, Stan?" Rocky asked.

I thought before I replied then bit my lower lip. "For now, all we need to do is make contact with the Hernandez brothers. Once we get to them, we'll find out where Roberto is, I frickin' guarantee it."

Rocky didn't respond, my look was resolute. I loved my career and had high hopes of climbing the APD ladder. But that was history. The whole Hernandez family was f*****d up beyond repair and needed to be taught a lesson.

You f**k with the bull, and he sticks his horns up your ass until they come out your mouth. These assholes had f****d with the APD bulls. Now it was our turn to stampede. I signaled and was very careful to check my mirrors, all three of them, to look over my shoulder, to recheck my mirrors, and to slide over one lane at a time until I reached the exit lane.

"Bro, it's almost Showtime," I said.

Rocky reached into his shirt pocket for a pack of smokes.

"Not in this car partner. Didn't you see the no-smoking sign?"

Rocky laughed. "I get really irritated when I can't smoke. I guess I'll have to take it out on a couple of Mexicans."

I had never seen so many cars and motorcycles in my life. The show was a fundraiser to benefit the legalize marijuana camp in the sunny State of California. Being law enforcement, I had mixed emotions about making the herb legal. If I had to vote tomorrow, I'd vote against legalizing it. Cars were parked not only in the massive Dodger Stadium parking lot but also on the side streets that led to the Los Angeles Police Department Academy and the street that led to Elysian Park. Every place I looked were classic automobiles.

The entry fee was by vehicle. The charge was twenty bucks. I pulled a bill out of my pocket, asked for a receipt, then was instructed to go to isle 27A where the Chevys were parked. The "parking lot" or display area was amply lighted, making the black Super Sport look like a tiger tooth in the night. I drove slowly, taking in the millions of dollars of metal, chrome, and paint. I thought it must be nice…..

Rocky said, "If you don't hurry up and find a damned parking space I'm going to have a nicotine attack."

"F**k the cigarette, give the surveillance team a call. See where these wetbacks are."

Cheech and Chong were where they should have been, in the section with the low riders. In all fairness, they accompanied two absolutely gorgeous cars. The 1957 **Chebby** Impala was red with red and white interior. Under the hood was a custom 350 Chevy small block. The paint glowed. The interior of the **Chebby** was impeccable. The engine was chromed out. The rear boasted a custom continental kit with a nude lady on the back who had tits the size of a f*****g freight train.

What the hell was with these Hispanics and their huge breasted bitches?

Of course, Cheech or Chong converted the American made Chevy to a low, low rider. The other vehicle was a black Chevy four-door gangster car with suicide doors. It was a 1930 something. It had a visor over the front windshield, running boards, and machine guns mounted inside the car in the back. Of course, a big busted bitch was painted on the front door. I was afraid to look at the passenger side of the Chevy. Rocky and I rolled up in our Impala SuperSport not only to annoy the brothers, but we also wanted to get their attention.

When I leaned on the horn, everyone within earshot gave us a look. Contrary to what you see on television and on the big screen, cops are fraternal. Sure we may jerk each other around when something out of the ordinary occurs, we may get hammered and "fight" with one another when we're boozed up, but if someone outside of the fraternity f**k's with us, the entire brotherhood will come down on you like rain clouds pissing bricks and mortar.

Such was the case here. ACOP Rolando let those who needed to know, those who might be able to help with personnel and or equipment, that an outsider had f****d big time with one of our own.

Like a domino effect, the word got out. We had every piece of equipment, intelligence, staff power available to us. We literally had a green light to do what we must to accomplish our mission. Any mess would be swept up after the fact. It was like finding and taking out Osama Bin Laden.

"Wiggly Hernandez," the slightly shorter of the Hernandez punks, was probably so nicknamed because he couldn't sit still or standstill. Probably from all the coke, the asshole had to bounce around in his f****d up body. His brother went by the moniker "Stiff" probably because he couldn't get it up.

Rocky and I found a parking space a couple of spots down from the punks we were after. We parked, left the car windows down, threw open the doors, and strolled slowly around the vehicles in our proximity, making our way to Stiff and Wiggly.

Rocky and I were admiring the beautiful Chevy. "Pretty baby homie, ain't she?"

"Gorgeous," I agreed, "Bro gorgeous."

Within thirty seconds, Stiff and Wiggly were giving us the life story of their vehicles. Then Wiggly said, "I see the SuperSport around before, bro."

It was more of a statement than a question. "I just bought it. Guy got himself in a bind, a big bind bro. He needed cash in a hurry, and the pawnshop wouldn't give him what he needed. I had the cash. He saw the green put the ink to the pink and bro, the car is low."

"You interested in turning her over to make some quick green?" Wiggly asked.

I responded, "Anything's doable, bro. What did you have in mind?"

Wiggly introduced us all around. "I have to check her out all over. It might take a while. If she looks as good up close as she did coming in bro, we might be able to cut us some deal."

I nodded and said, "When you're ready to look her over, give me a holler. I'll move her away from traffic, so we can talk in private. We're going to check this shit out while you're getting ready."

I drove the car to a fenced area away from traffic, cars, and people. We needed to be fairly isolated to pull off part two of my scenario. We waited. The longer we waited, the more pissed off I grew playing and replaying the tape Assistant Chief Rolando had played for us in his office. There was no way this scum, and all with whom he associated, deserved anything but pure hell.

And they were about to get it. In my short police career, I had observed a lot of shit. I had witnessed badly beaten kids, sexually abused kids, husbands beating wives, wives beating husbands, families tortured during home invasion robberies, people mangled in drunken-driving accidents, but this took the trophy, uncontested.

Threatening a youngster in this manner was unconscionable, unforgivable. In this case, I was going to be the jury, the judge, and the executioner if necessary. I programmed myself to do whatever had to be done to get Roberto back. Rocky had called LAPD. They had arrived in style. Two plain-clothes officers drove up in a dark-colored bakery truck with blacked-out windows. They parked behind the Impala. The second truck was a television broadcast truck that read **Fusion United Cable Kingdom Unlimited**, across its body. It took me all of thirty seconds to figure the acronym. The truck's side windows were totally blacked out. The Ford truck parked next to the "target."

Two plain-clothes, Hispanic officers exited the vehicle. The field was set. Now we were just waiting for the players to arrive. It didn't take long. When I was in the academy, I swore to myself that you would never catch me doing anything illegal or fundamentally inappropriate on the street.

REMINISCING ABOUT THE PAST

I broke that ethic on my first day on the street. My first Field Training Officer and I were assigned a call of a male and female engaged in a loud argument. They were in a white pickup truck that was parked across the street from a park. It was spring, it was sunny and clear. I was the brand new booty on the block. My FTO's instructions were, "You're my shadow. Where I go, you go. If I don't tell you to speak, shut the f**k up."

Those were his exact words! We arrived on the scene, found the truck, and contacted the husband and wife, who were inside the truck screaming at each other…in Spanish. Neither my FTO nor I speak much Spanish. I had three years of Spanish in school, but that's as worthless as a castrated horse. We called for a Spanish speaking officer. On scene arrived a young, attractive, Hispanic officer, Officer Pena. My FTO cut me slack.

He told me to take the male half of the 415 disturbance call to the west curb and do the best I could to find out what the hell was going on. He and Officer firm tits and tight ass escorted the female to the east

98

curb to investigate. I asked asshole very politely what was going on. He did speak English, not a hell of a lot, but enough to get by.

"Dinero," he said.

That's a universal word. I knew dinero meant money. "What about **MONEY?**" I asked.

"She wants money, I don't have. She gets pissed and starts arguing."

"I'm going to pat you down for officer safety." I made a gesture with my hands. He held up his hands, so I assumed he understood. The guy was clean. "Do you have licensia?"

"Si," he replied.

How the f**k you could get a license in this damn state without speaking the language was beyond me. "Let me see it, please." He showed it to me. I looked it over.

I was trying to decide whether or not my FTO would want me to run the guy for warrants when I observed Pena and my FTO walking across the street. The female had returned to the truck. Pena said something to the guy that I couldn't understand. She spoke faster than a ten round magazine being emptied at a target in three-point five seconds.

My FTO asked, "Did you get a license?"

I handed him what I thought was the guy's license.

"Did you graduate from the academy or acting school?" "This is a f*****g Cal ID card."

I could feel the heat in my face. I knew I was red. Pena tried to hide her laugh. She failed miserably. My FTO ran the asshole for warrants. He was as clean as new underwear. He handed the ID card to Pena, who said something to the guy in Spanish then handed him his ID card. She motioned for him to hit the road. He tucked the ID card in his right pants pocket. As he walked south, he intentionally shouldered me. This guy had to be taught a lesson, but Pena was present. I was certain my FTO wouldn't object if I used a bit of muscle, but I didn't know how this female cop would react.

My left hand made the decision for me. Up it came in one sweet, sweeping, rapid arc. I grabbed his belt then turned him toward me none too gently. Behind him was a metal fence. I slammed him against it jamming my forearm under his neck.

The guy was gagging. "You mother f*****g Mexican cocksucker. If you ever do that to any police officer again……" I felt my FTO's arm on my right shoulder. He leaned over and whispered in my ear.

 "Do what you need to do, but there are people across the street in the park watching you. Keep yelling, *sir, please cooperate.*"

I leaned forward, putting more pressure on his neck. "Sir, please cooperate, sir. Please cooperate."

"Me, sorry, sorry, sorry, sorry."

 "You pathetic prick." I let go of his neck. I thought he was going to fall to the curb. "Get the f**k out of here," I said.

He walked by me quickly, not fast enough. My right foot had a mind of its own. It came up swiftly, kicking asshole square in the ass. Pena looked at my FTO, at me and at *pathetic* walking down the sidewalk.

Pena walked to her unit, got in, and drove off.

I turned to my FTO. "Who do I give my badge to?"

"What the f**k are you talking about?"

"I put my hands on him…"

"And he had it coming. If you didn't do what you did, *I'd* be ripping that badge off you.

"Some of these punks out here need special handling. He's one of them. That's the first decent thing I've observed you do out here. Get in the car, we'll do some more police work. And by the way, if I let you have lunch today, you're buying."

SO MUCH FOR REMINISCING

The brothers Hernandez came walking around the corner. Both carried huge smiles as if they knew something we didn't. I had a flash for these clowns. They didn't know shit. The smaller of the Hernandez Brothers approached me. The other dipshit approached Rocky. Slowly I guided Hernandez toward the back of the SS. Rocky told the other brother he wanted to show him the engine and engine compartment. We had found a small area that was secluded, dark enough, we hoped, to conceal what we were about to enact.

The trunk's entrance was keyless. I pushed a button, and the trunk opened. Every piece of hydraulics was chromed to the max. The glare was blinding. This car had to be worth twice my annual salary and then some. I probably couldn't afford the insurance. Hernandez nodded, he was grinning broadly.

"You like?"

"Si senor, I like mucho."

Yeah, you little prick, I thought. In a few minutes, I'm going to give you something you're not going to like.

"Let's check out under the hood."

Hernandez and I walked around the passenger side of the Chevy, and on cue, Rocky and the other brother walked around the driver's side of the car. Under the hood of the car, Hernandez was so engrossed in the restoration that he never heard or saw LAPD's finest in action. The van's rear doors opened quickly, smoothly, quietly. Three officers from LAPD's Special Tactics Units earned their pay.

They were on the wetbacks like the Houston Astros were on trash cans in their dugout. No doubt, they were going to accomplish their mission. I have no idea what was on the towel, they threw over Hernandez' face. I do know he went down like the sack of shit that he is.

And just like a magician making the rabbit disappear, the Mexican was out of sight. At the back of the car, the same operation was in full swing. Three LAPD undercover coppers swung open the van door as the asshole was savoring the hydraulics in the trunk. They "toweled" him and dragged him into the van.

CHAPTER 9

BREAKING THE KIDNAPPERS

P hase Uno was accomplished without incident! Every once in a while, I would screw around with the horses and wager on a long shot. I never won on any of those long shots. Every once in a while, I would even put a couple of bucks on a penny stock. One of those stocks tripled in value overnight. I made a few grand but unfortunately didn't get out in time to reap the profits. The company went under, and so did my money. This was the longest shot of my life. I hoped like hell it was going to pay big dividends! Hernandez woke up. He was seated on the wooden bench seat against the truck's wall.

"Stand up, punk," I said, looking into his glazed eyes.

He looked at me, and in perfect English, he asked, "Who the f**k are you?"

"I'm your worst nightmare, puke pot!" I punched him so hard in the gut my right hand stung.

 He doubled over. His hands were cuffed behind his back. I watched him grimace in pain. I loved it so much I hit him again. It was about three minutes before he could speak.

"You're making a big mistake, my friend. You're f*****g with the wrong man," he managed to say gagging and coughing.

"Let's understand something. You're not a man. You're a piece of shit, a piece of Mexican shit. Let's understand something else.

"I want to know where Roberto is. I'm not going to stop pounding your wetback body until you tell me. Very slowly and very deliberately, I asked, "Where………is………. Roberto?"

Hernandez sat down. He looked up and laughed at me. I pulled him up by his shirt. "You forgot to ask, '*may I*' sit down." I kneed him in the balls. "Do wetbacks have balls, puke bucket?" I looked at Hernandez. I smiled. "Again, punk, where is L'il Roberto?"

I could see the tears in his eyes as he fell to the floor. He spit blood, he coughed, choked, he finally passed out. The van had a bathroom. I found a small plastic bucket. I walked to the bathroom, filled it with cold water, walked back to where Hernandez lay semiconscious.

I threw cold water in Hernandez's face. He looked up. He was dazed, confused. "Where's Roberto?"

"Eat shit, pig," he managed to say.

"I don't like your mama's cooking asshole. Where's Roberto?"

Hernandez blacked out.

I felt the van move. I didn't know where we were headed. I didn't care. LAPD knew what they were doing. They understood what the operation was all about. They were informed a child's life was at stake. It was one of their own. I had no concern with LAPD. I had a concern with breaking Hernandez. I had taken a couple of classes in interrogation technique. These classes dealt with things psychological, like chair placement in the interrogation room, voice control, eye contact, fear factor, etc. Probably great if you had time on your side; we didn't.

We had half-a-day plus to break this asshole, he was a tough customer, the toughest. The asshole was a professional criminal, but I too was a professional. Under normal circumstances, we wouldn't stand a chance. In the first place, before we started the questioning, he would demand an attorney.

That would short circuit the game before the first pitch was thrown. When we did get to questioning him, his attorney would object to the world. Assholes like Hernandez didn't have a public defender; they had the money to hire the real deal. We'd had two strikes on us before we came to bat. Unfortunately for the wetback, he had no such luxury. All the rules were out the window.

This game was going to end one of two ways and only one of two ways. Either numb nuts was going to tell us where Roberto was being held, or numb nuts was going to die. This game was not going into extra innings. While Hernandez was taking a "nap," I phoned Rocky on my cell. I wanted to know how things were going with him and the other Hernandez brother. I also wanted to run an idea past him.

I told Rocky, "His vocabulary is limited to 'asshole.' His favorite phrase is 'f**k you pig.' I've about had it with him."

"We could trade suspects," Rocky offered.

I shook my head and said, "I'm having too much fun with this asshole."

Then I ran my plan by him. "You're crazy," Rocky replied.

"Do you have any better ideas?"

"How are we going to get all this stuff together with the time we have left?"

I said, "I'm on it like the Broncos on Washington."

Rocky bet a couple of guys at the Station that the Broncos would handle Washington even without the spread. The bounty in each case was a carton of cigarettes. Maybe God was trying to tell Rocky to quit smoking.

I said, "I'm calling the office, and we're going to set this thing in motion. It beats the shit out of standing here with my thumb up my butt, especially if we can't break the brothers Hernandez."

My plan was reckless, hastily put together. It probably wouldn't work. Since we were going to get fired, possibly go to jail for what we had done, it didn't matter. I really was prepared to kill for Rolando and Roberto. It fascinated me how an individual can be law-abiding his entire life, and then a situation presents itself, and everything changes. This was the case! I reminded myself, *I keep the peace.*

Nothing mattered anymore. I was trying to justify what I was doing and what I was about to do. I didn't need justification. I knew better than to play God. Here I was judge, jury, maybe even the executioner. I looked at my watch then quickly got on my cell. I made several calls in succession. It's amazing what the right people will do for you on the spur of the moment if you've treated them right in the past.

Everyone I called offered me not only what I needed, but each also offered me one hundred ten percent support. Maybe this wasn't such a damn long shot after all!

In less than forty five minutes, Little Roberto's rescue crew was in position. Flying overhead was our air support, SAS 1, sheriff's Air Support. The chopper was deliberately flying low, as requested. The noise was annoying and distracting, as requested. The spotter sheriff in the chopper was on his loudspeaker.

It was difficult to understand what he was saying. It didn't matter. That, too, was designed to be a distraction. City Road Department had a crew on the ground. Their job was to block the street for us. They were on point. City lighting was asked to dim the street lights to the point of near blackout. They had done their job. The trailer truck was compliments of Victory Trucking out of Vernon. The truck and trailer was a training rig.

It took Rocky only a few minutes to find and not grind the gears. Everything else needed was in place, supplied by our city friends. It appeared we had a lot of friends, more than we realized. Then again, the brothers Hernandez had been a pain in the ass to the majority of good citizens of Amity and surrounding cities.

Most of the population of Amity wouldn't piss on the Hernandez boys if they were on fire. So, they were only too glad to help. We had thirteen hours left to break the older Hernandez brother, who was convinced he was bulletproof. Maybe he was, but was his brother?

CHAPTER 10

FLASHBACK

My mind flashed back to a blind date Paula arranged for me. It all started when I was driving us back to the barn to go EOW a week ago. Rocky's cell phone rang, playing the beginning of "Bad Boys." From his conversation, it was Paula. From further conversation, she had made a dinner reservation at the Olive Garden. I liked the Olive Garden, and I loved "wop" food, but it would be a cold day in hell before I'd go on another blind date. Even when the blind date was cute, it blew up in the end.

"I love you, babe. See you in a couple of hours or so, depending on traffic. Sure, he'll join us. He'll like Mac." Rocky hung up.

"Who the hell is Mac?" I asked.

"Calm down dude, why do you have to think the worst of every situation?"

"Because I'm a cop, and I'm trained to think of the negative, so I can deal with any situation," I responded.

"Relax, Mac is the Chippie who pulled Paula over on the 14 two weeks ago," Rocky said.

"What for, don't her plates come back to APD?"

"Yeah, but I guess Mac stopped her before the plates came back."

"What was she doing?"

"87 in a 65."

I smiled. "You gotta' be kidding me. Paula doesn't usually drive like that."

Rocky nodded. "I know, she wasn't paying attention since she was talking on her cell phone."

"To you?"

"Who else?"

"Did he write her?"

"No. When Mac found out her hubby's a cop, Mac cut her slack. She was lucky," Rocky said.

"So this is payback. Paula's buying Mac dinner?" I asked.

Rocky nodded. He insisted I join them.

I said, "Why not, I'll just run home, change and shower and meet you guys at the Olive Garden." I checked my watch. "Seven, seven-fifteen work?"

The Rock nodded. "Affirmative."

I shaved, showered, threw on a navy blue suit over a white pullover shirt, a pair of black loafers, grabbed my Glock, and was on my way.

The only thing I forgot to do was pee. By the time I reached the Olive Garden parking lot, I had thought I was going to piss myself. The lot wasn't quite full, lucky for me. I parked, rushed into the lobby, and started straight for the men's room.

And then…..I saw her; actually, I saw her tight brown slacks and the revealing panty lines. I stared, I couldn't help it. I had a panty fetish. When all else fails, I'd wrap a pair of nylon panties around Peter and have sex with my right hand. Sometimes, for novelty, I'd use my left hand. A few of my girlfriends knew about my fetish and donated to my cause. The agreement was as long as I used *her* panties, I could go to town.

I kept staring, then I noticed the blonde hair. She was about five-nine with low heels. She had on a white blouse, but I could only see her from the rear. I had no idea what her headlights looked like. Her ass was tighter then the handcuffs I'd slap on a suspect who pissed me off. I envied her husband or the guy she was with.

I was hard. Whether it was from having to piss or it was that tight ass and those panty lines, or maybe it was a combination of both. Unfortunately, it didn't matter; I made a beeline for the bathroom. I walked out of the bathroom, feeling relief. I scanned the dining area, sighting Rocky, and walked to the table.

As I got closer, I observed blonde hair, then brown slacks and panty lines. What the hell was she doing at the table?

Rocky jumped up when he saw me, "Tony meet Mackenzee. Mackenzee meet Tony."

I'm rarely at a loss for words, but momentarily I was speechless. I sat down next to Mackenzee. I said smiling, "A pleasure to meet you, Mackenzee."

I took her hand, it was warm. She smiled a provoking smile. Her blue eyes said she knew something I didn't. She probably knew a lot that I didn't.

She said, "My friends call me Mac, please call me Mac."

I picked up the water glass looked across the table at Rocky, and Paula then raised the glass. "To friends," I said. I gave Paula a warm smile. We tapped glasses.

"To good friends," Mac offered. I thought there was a challenge in that toast.

"I hear you're a Highway Patrol Officer," I said.

"Triple-A with a gun," Mac offered.

I looked at Rocky, I was poker-faced. I caught Mac's blue eyes as I smiled. "What's Triple-A with a gun?" I asked.

"Yeah, right," Mac countered. "And what's a Miranda warning?"

She was attractive, she was gorgeous, stunning. Her medium length blonde hair accentuated her blue eyes. Those eyes were warm. Her white blouse was tight against her breasts, very tight. I couldn't help looking, a long look.

Mac noticed that I noticed then said, "You can get a ticket for moving too slow."

I was embarrassed, but at the same time I wanted Mac to know I was interested.

I looked over at Paula. "Paula, I hear Mac cut you some slack, or is that part of the charade also?"

Paula smiled, "Mac gave me professional courtesy."

Mac reached below the table with her right hand and patted the top of my knee. "Only special people get professional courtesy."

She was looking at Paula when she said that, but I was certain it was meant for me.

The waitress interrupted, "Good evening, folks." I'm Monica, "I'll be your server tonight. Can I get you something from the bar?"

Paula and Rocky both ordered a beer.

"Mac, professional courtesy says I'll buy you a drink," I said. "What would you like?"

"I don't drink, I'll have coffee, black," she said to Monica.

"Give me a shot of Seagram's, please," I said.

When Monica walked away from the table, I said to Mac, "You're off duty. You're allowed to drink, that is unless you're not twenty-one yet."

"Cute, I'm keeping score. A couple more like that and you might get a get *into* jail free card."

113

"As long as you handcuffed me first." I said. "How long have you been Triple-A with a gun (highway patrol)?"

"It's going on five years," Mac replied.

"Why join the CHP?" I asked.

"I like the fit of the uniform." Those blue eyes sparkled, her lips parted, she ran her tongue across her lips, and she smiled then said, "I had a tough time growing up and got into some trouble. I tried LAPD and the Sheriff's, but they wouldn't overlook some issues I had. The CHP cut me a break. We'll talk…I hope."

"I'm sure we will." I corrected myself. "I hope we will." "How long have you been with APD?" Mac asked.

"Just for a few years, I was told I'd either love it or hate it. I can't get enough of it, it's like an addiction. Does your not drinking have anything to do with not being able to go with LAPD or Sheriff's?"

"My drinking got me into enough trouble that my background became an issue." Mac took a breath just as our drinks arrived. "I couldn't control my drinking. I'm a sober member of Alcoholics Anonymous."

"Wow," I said, not meaning for the words to come out. "Does our drinking bother you?"

"Not in the least. So, relax and do your thing."

I raised my shot glass. Paula and Rocky hoisted their beer. Mac held up her coffee cup.

"To the now," she toasted, "To the here and the now with new friends." And as she lifted her coffee cup, Mac added, "Yesterday's a canceled check, tomorrow's a promissory note and today is a gift, that's why they call it the present."

Nearly two hours later, I walked Mac to her car. "Nice ride."

"He's a 1996 Corvette Grand Sport." She said proudly.

The Grand Sport was a blue convertible with black rims and red hash marks on the front fender. *He* didn't come cheap. Then again, CHP made more money than your average city police department.

"He's handsome. I said, "Now I know why you're Triple-A with a gun. A car like that is a radar magnet."

"I've only been pulled over twice since I was sworn in. I try to play by the rules. The CHP gave me a gift, they hired me. What I give to the team and the community is my gift to them."

"Like Karma."

"Like Karma," Mac said as she smiled broadly. She followed that with, "Follow me home."

"Do you need protection?"

She didn't bat an eyebrow. "No, but if you're lucky, you might."

I nodded and started to walk toward my car, which was a few spaces away. I turned to check the license plate on the Vette. It was a personalized plate, *DCZDMND.*

I followed Mac while trying to decode her personalized plate. I was usually good at that. In this case, I couldn't crack the code. We sat in Mac's tastefully decorated living room, on the light tan "L shaped" couch. She pushed a button. The fireplace lit up adding atmosphere to the evening and to the mood. I was comfortable in her company on Mac's turf, which was unusual for me, probably unusual for any cop.

"What does the plate on your Corvette say?" I asked.

"DISEASED MIND."

I laughed, "That's funny. Is it accurate?"

"Stick around, judge for yourself." Mac looked very serious for a second as she said, "There were two of me. The me who wants to do well, and love, and be happy and free, then there's the me who wants more and more and more, me with the hole in the gut that no amount of *more* can fill up. That's what AA is really about. It's not about drinking, we know how to drink. Hell, real alcoholics have PhDs in drinking. We don't know how to live.

"AA is about living. It's about being happy, joyous, and free. It's about balance." She stopped suddenly. "Sorry about that, sometimes I talk too much." Mac smiled. "I like you."

"I like you too. Without being too nosey, what did you do to keep you out of LAPD and the Sheriff?"

"Which time?"

"You gotta' be kidding?" I said. "With all that baggage, it's amazing the CHP hired you. Hell, a couple of speeding tickets or a low FICO score is enough to get you DQ'd from most departments."

Mac nodded. "I had some leverage, I had some contacts. I had God on my side."

"So, what did you do to keep you out of other PDs?"

"I'll give you one example, and then I want my lawyer," Mac said.

"Go for it."

"I slapped a cop."

"You what?" I said, astonished.

"I had a few drinks, my boyfriend and I got into it. I got pulled over. One word led to another. I slapped the cop."

"Obviously, you were arrested?" It was a question.

Mac nodded. I could see the seriousness in those blue eyes and on her face. It was obvious Mac was replaying the incident.

"I was arrested, taken in handcuffs in a unit to the station. A phone call was made."

"A phone call?"

"I knew the right people."

"So, you used your contacts to extricate you from a situation of your own making?" I teased.

"I want my attorney, smart guy." Mac leaned closer. I kissed her softly, and then I pulled back and looked into those beautiful, soft blue eyes. I kissed her again, longer, more passionately. She didn't resist, at least not for several seconds.

"Too much heat here," she said. Her left arm was on my shoulder, "Tony, I like…..I like what I'm feeling a lot, but let's pull back a bit."

I understood, "I like it too. I like it a lot. When would you like to go out again? I have tickets Thursday night for the Big Top Circus at the Performing Arts Theater in the Valley. How about it?"

Without hesitation, she replied, "I'd love it. Let me see if I can get someone to change shifts with me. I'll let you know."

"Why are you a cop, and why APD?" Mac asked.

"I did two tours in Afghanistan. I guess I didn't see enough shit. I needed to see more. I love being a cop. It's the system that's screwed up. I've literally seen bad guys 'bond out' before we finish the paperwork. There are more guns on the street than ever. Get caught with a gun, and if you don't have a prior, it's a misdemeanor.

"Get caught with a nightstick in your car, if you don't have a badge, it's a felony. More drugs come across the border daily than illegal fruit. We have a death penalty, but we don't use it even though the people want it. I find all this challenging."

"Did you kill anyone in Afghanistan?" Mac asked.

"Five kills, two hand to hand." I took a breath, "The first one was the hardest, and it got easier after that."

Mac nodded.

She leaned into me, pushed me down on the couch, and kissed me hard with half her body on top of me.

When she broke the kiss, she said, "That's so you don't forget me."

I looked directly into those captivating blues, "Trust me, Mac, I won't forget you, I can't, you're almost as exciting as a pursuit."

She looked down at my crotch. I didn't have to piss. She smiled and then said, **"ALMOST!"** The accent was on almost. She continued to look at my crotch. "We'll let the evidence speak for itself." She looked me in the eye and said, "Get out of here before I rape you."

Rocky was merciless with me in the unit about my feelings for Mac. I spent almost as much time talking on my cell with Mac as Rocky did with Paula. The only thing I was missing was Mac's panties. I was absolutely positive there would be little need for them.

"How many times have you and Mac been out now?"

I didn't have to count, "Four, not counting our initial dinner date with you and Paula. As a matter of fact, Mac is an Angel's fan, and as you well know, I am a devote Dodger fan. I happen to have four tickets, box seats, to the freeway series next weekend. Interested?"

"Are you serious?" Rocky yelled! "Which night is it, Friday, Saturday, or Sunday?"

"It's Friday night at Dodger Stadium."

"Love to go, partner, thank you. I'll even drive."

We were sitting at a table in a dark corner of Applebee's. Mac was eating a chicken salad and sipping hot black coffee. I was eating Caesar Salad and drinking coffee. I wanted a shot of Seagram's, but since Mac didn't drink, I felt uncomfortable drinking in front of her. However, I did feel comfortable sharing my panty fetish with her. Figure that one out.

 "So how many runs do you think the Dodgers will beat the Angels by?" I asked.

I thought Mac was going to choke on her coffee. She replied, "The Angels will take the first and third games. They'll feel sorry for the Dodgers. They'll *allow* them to win the middle game."

"Okay, name the wager," I said to Mac.

Mac was wearing a snug-fitting pair of blue jeans and a tank top. She looked beyond good. We did a lot of verbal sparring but had yet to reach the physical part of the relationship only, or so I thought, because of circumstances. Our shifts, for the present time, were not conducive to building this relationship. We talked almost every chance we got, but Mac worked when I was sleeping, I was sleeping when Mac was at work. As far as I knew, Mac wasn't dating anyone else. I sure the hell wasn't interested in dating anyone else.

Mac rubbed her chin, "Here's my suggestion, wise guy, for a wager.

If the Angels win game one of the freeway series, I handcuff you, blindfold you, and game on. If, on the other hand, the Dodgers win game one, I'll take my panties off in the car on the way home, and they're yours since you were man enough to let me in on that particular fetish; although I thought you would prefer to get in them rather than play with them." Mac paused, "Whatever gets your baton rock hard, I guess."

My face must have been red. My dick was hard. I tried to hide both. I was zero for two. "I can't lose," I said.

"Neither can I. It's a win, win for both of us."

So much for the flashback, Roberto is still in trouble!

CHAPTER 11

THE PLAN TO FREE ROBERTO

Icame back to reality with a smile. Everything was a go. The streets were blocked. The lights were dimmed. Air support was overhead. Among other objectives, air support was asked to shine its light on the windshield of the van Hernandez was riding in to obscure his vision. In the first van was the older Hernandez brother, who I hoped against hope would crack. He was cuffed, bruised, battered, and bleeding, but I didn't feel one bit sorry for the bastard. I did feel sorry for Roberto.

The second van was gone, and these animals couldn't care less about human life. Their only concern was the all mighty f*****g American dollar. Most of that illegally earned money went across the f*****g border. The rest went up to their collective noses. It was past time to fight them at their own game. F**k them and the wetback f*****g horse they crossed the border on.

I keyed the mic. "Baker to Charlie, are we in position?"

Rocky responded immediately. "Charlie to Baker, we're ready to roll, sir."

"Go for it, Charlie. Go for it!"

I heard the truck's engine, then a backfire, then the grinding of gears. It had been a while since Rocky climbed into the cab of a truck. Pushing a black and white around the streets was a lot easier than hauling a tractor and trailer. The truck bucked as it slowly moved forward. I observed a hand come out the window then thumbs up. We were engaged.

The van had a glassless window partition separating the rear of the van from the driver's area. The partition had a wooden slide. I slid it to the right giving Hernandez a somewhat obstructed view of the truck. This was intentional.

I pushed Hernandez's head against the opened partition window. "See anything you recognize, asshole?"

It was dark. The city workers had dimmed the street lights. Hernandez blinked, trying to focus.

"Look up, asshole at the top of the truck." Hernandez finally got the picture.

"That's my brother, my little brother!"

"Good for you, asshole, your wetback eyes are 20/20."

I forced a smile and was doing what I was doing because, in this case, the ends justified the means. That didn't mean I had to like it. In his case, I was enjoying my work immensely.

"Where's Roberto?" I asked as Hernandez' face turned bread white. I had scared him Caucasian.

"What the f**k are you doing?" he asked.

I was surprised at his clear English, and his missing accent.

"Here's the game, numb nut. That's your brother tied to the top of the truck, vertically. We are headed toward the Soto Street overpass. I figure two minutes should do it, three if we hit a red light or two. The clearance of that overpass is just over fourteen feet.

"That cross, with your brother tied to it, is damn near twenty feet. Do your math, asshole, do it in English wetback, but do it. Tell me where the f**k Roberto is or your hermanos, or however the f**k you say it, dies a hard, horrible death."

"You're a cop, you wouldn't do it. You're bluffing," he said.

Hernandez's eyes were locked on the top of the truck, to the cross, to his little brother, who was securely strapped to that cross.

"I'm a police officer, wetback asshole. I will do it. I don't give a shit. Got it, moron! I'm not going to be able to live with myself if Roberto is harmed or killed. So, your brother's life, whether he lives or dies, is in your Mexican hands."

I heard the low flying chopper overhead. That added to Hernandez's utter confusion.

"Baker to Charlie, give me an ETA," I asked Rocky.

The truck stopped at a red light. Hernandez could see his brother's shirt flopping around lazily in the light wind. He could see the large wooden cross secured to the base of the top of the truck. Attached to that cross was.....his brother!

"We're rolling now. If we don't hit any more lights, ETA is about a minute thirty," Rocky said.

"Hear that ass wipe? Your brother has ninety Mexican seconds of breath unless you give up that address."

As the truck picked up speed, the jeans, the shirt, the arms, the legs, flailed in the breeze. Hernandez kept staring upward at the truck at his brother.

I said, "Fifty seconds wetback. Give it up."

The overpass was in view, the chopper was hovering between the overpass and our van. Hernandez knew he didn't have much time.

"Tell him to stop! Tell him to stop!!! He yelled!

"Baker to Charlie, slow it down a bit, just a bit." I heard the gears grind as Rocky downshifted.

"Give it up. You're brother's almost a dead man."

"Okay, okay, it's 3344½ Kingston, Bell. It's the rear house."

"Again," I said.

"It's 3344½ Kingston in Bell, the rear house. "Stop him! Stop him!"

I keyed the mic. "Baker to Charlie, full throttle."

I heard the gears grind again. Rocky shifted into a higher gear. There was no stopping him now, the cross and its companion slammed into the bridge. Body parts were scattered all over the street. Red stains were visible against the bridge abutment and on the street.

125

Hernandez looked at me. "You pig, you killed my brother."

I hit him as hard as I could in the ribs for Rolando, then for Roberto I kneed him in the balls. He went down hard. I got on my cell and called to the waiting special tactics team. I gave them the address. We waited.

BACK AT THE STATION

The older Hernandez brother sat in the interrogation room. Asshole sat on one side, his attorney sat across from him. Next to Hernandez' attorney, sat the Lieutenant, the assistant district attorney, Rocky, and me.

"They killed my little brother. I gave them what they wanted, and they killed him anyway. I want them arrested. You bastards, you sick bastards."

Hernandez' attorney put his hand on Hernandez' shoulder. "We're going to take care of all of this, trust me."

I laughed out loud. Rocky looked at me and started laughing.

The attorney shook his head and waved his hand. "I don't see a damn thing funny. You're being accused of a serious crime, premeditated murder."

"First of all, counselor, let's look at your upstanding client here. He's been dealing drugs for years. Because the old man is to go to trial, your upstanding client is a party to the kidnapping of a little boy. He turns some faggot loose on that child and threatens to let the faggot

126

do his thing if we testify against the old man. And you want me to feel sorry for your client?"

The attorney looked me directly in the eye, "You're alleging all this."

"I'm not alleging shit, counselor. I have all the evidence I need to put your asshole client away for life."

"Where and what is your proof?" The attorney asked.

"Yeah, right. You'll have your shot at that when it's time for discovery. In the meantime, ask your coke choked client what proof he has that we *allegedly* did his little brother."

Fox looked at Hernandez then nodded. Hernandez said, "I saw the whole thing. They made me watch. They tied him to the top of a truck and ran the truck under an overpass that wasn't high enough for my brother to get under."

Rocky looked the attorney in the eyes and said, "Your client's brain is fried counselor. He's been watching too many TJ Hooker reruns."

Hernandez jumped up. He moved toward me. I was out of my chair in less than a second and shoved him back down in his chair.

"See what I mean, counselor. He has no control. His brain is fried. If I were you, I would cop a plea."

Before Fox replied, the interrogation room door opened, and accompanied by two uniformed officers was a handcuffed younger Hernandez.

CHAPTER 12

DRUGS & MAN VERSUS TRAIN

Rocky was, as usual, tied up on the phone talking with Paula. I handled the driving and the radio. "13 Adam, we're going to be 1038, Glaze west of Acacia on 8 Adam William Adam 221. We'll advise on a back."

Rocky ended his call. "The plate is expired registration," I said to Rocky, "One male, Hispanic in the vehicle, worth a check."

Dispatch came back. "13 Adam, your vehicle has no wants or warrants. Expired 2/13."

"Copy that." A vehicle can be impounded if the tags are more than six months in arrears. In this case, the tags were a year old. "Is there a RIP?" "RIP" stood for registration in progress.

"That's a negative, 13 Adam."

If a registered owner couldn't afford to pay the full registration fee and he worked out a payment schedule with DMV, it would show when dispatch ran the plate. Normally we wouldn't bother someone who made a good faith effort to pay the fees. Times were tough; many good people were experiencing tough times.

"Copy that. We'll advise on a back."

Rocky and I exited the car. The lone occupant of the vehicle had his hands on the steering wheel. Rocky approached the passenger side of the red Chevy Nova. I approached the driver. He looked straight ahead.

"Can I see your license, registration, and proof of insurance, please?" That was strike one. People with nothing to hide usually look at you when they respond.

"Sure, he said, it's in my suit jacket pocket, the inner one."

He was wearing a well-pressed navy blue suit with a white shirt and a solid blue tie. He was dressed well enough to be the D.A.

"Go ahead, get me the license," I said.

I was watching his hands as he reached for his left breast pocket. My Glock was not out of its holster, but my hand was on the butt, when suddenly, Rocky yelled, "Gun partner!"

I pulled my Glock out of the holster so fast Wyatt Earp would have made me his deputy. "One move asshole, I'll blow a hole in your head wider than Grand Canyon. Get your mother f*****g hands on the steering wheel and don't even breathe."

Rocky had already called for a backup. I added, "Roll me one additional. Roll it code. We have one 417 suspect in the stopped vehicle."

When three backs arrived, everybody wanted in on the party. We pulled asshole out of the car, cuffed then searched him. The gun was

129

a 9 with one in the chamber. In other words, he was ready to go to war. This meant he either had a warrant or something in the car that didn't belong in the car or both. Rocky took control of the suspect. I searched the car; there wasn't a damn thing in the car that didn't belong. I walked to the trunk. I didn't need his permission to pop the trunk because I was impounding his car.

I had to inventory it to make sure he got everything back that was in the car when it was impounded. In the trunk, under a blanket, was enough cocaine to satisfy the entire state of New Hampshire. One of the backing units ran the guy for wants and warrants. He had a warrant out of Las Vegas for possession for sales.

The "clean up" work at the scene, including taking pictures of the stash, writing the CHP 180, the impound form for the car, photographing the gun, waiting for APD tow truck to arrive on the scene, and other incidentals, took us just over an hour. This did not include the time it was going to take to book the idiot, tag and book the evidence, run the gun to see if it was stolen, question the perp, and write the report.

We'd see overtime tonight. We had just finished booking the evidence in at the annex and were walking across the parking lot to the Station when ACOP Rolando called us on the portable. Rocky and I walked directly upstairs to Rolando's office. Rolando was smiling. He extended his hand first to Rocky then to me.

"Congratulations on a helluva' bust, guys. You got a weapon off the street, you took a warrant suspect off the street, and you seized a sizeable amount of nose candy. Not a bad day's work."

130

Rocky looked at his watch, "I would say half a day's work, sir."

"I know, and you're correct, Rocky," Rolando said, still smiling. "But the way your partner writes, the report will probably take you guys until midnight to get it approved."

"Not funny," I said.

Rolando walked over to me and slapped my back. "Seriously, I wish all my team worked as hard as you two. Speaking of hard-working." Rolando walked to his desk.

"Here, these are paid for. They're for four, you and Paula, and Cannoli and Triple-A with a dart gun."

I shook my head, "How the hell do you know about Mac?"

Rolando shrugged his shoulders, "I'm a cop; it's my job to know EVERYTHING!" Then he continued, "This is from our family and me for what you guys did for Roberto. You put your careers on the line. For that matter, you put your lives on the line. And speaking of careers on the line, Adolfo Gonzalez wants to know what you did with the mannequin and the clothing. I answered for you.

"I told him you were practicing a new sexual position. Also, a city yard employee said to tell you, you could have done a better job cleaning up the street and the overpass. They said they found half an arm from a mannequin in the bushes, torn clothing stuck to the overpass abutment, catsup stains on the concrete, and pieces of rope in the street. It sounds to me like someone had an early Halloween party."

"Great deduction, sir, sounds to me like you solved the puzzle." I got serious for a second and asked, "How's Roberto doing?"

Rolando shook his head then said somewhat solemnly, "He'll probably live with that for the rest of his life. They didn't do anything physical to him, but they threatened to. He said the more they drank, the mouthier they got. They told him they were going to do things to him that I haven't even heard of…and I'm Hispanic.

"Remember when we were in school the talk about the donkey and the lady? They told Roberto they were going to turn a donkey lose on him. They said the donkey's name was Gay Turd.

"A bunch of slime ball pigs. These sick pricks are real losers. Too bad they didn't give our boys a reason to take them out of their misery."

Rolando turned away from us but not soon enough. I observed the tears welling up in his eyes. When Rolando recovered, he said, "Both of you guys, get back to work, again, thanks."

We waited until we were back in the unit and on the street before we each opened our envelope. Inside were reservations at the Meadowlark Motel in Solvang, a very high class bed and breakfast accommodation that included a room with a fireplace, hot tub and a Jacuzzi outside the room. You had your own private Jacuzzi and fenced backyard. I know because I had taken a date there for a weekend a long time ago. The price tag on that puppy was big bucks.

It cost me an arm and a leg then. I could just imagine what it cost Rolando and his family. Hopefully, Meadowlark showed love. Rocky and I were closer than most married couples. Rocky knew Mac and I were close, but he didn't know to what extent. The fact that Mac's schedule and my schedule preempted our seeing each other as often as we would have liked, however, didn't keep us from talking to one another frequently, very frequently.

As a matter of fact, when I was riding shotgun in the unit, I was beginning to resemble Rocky with the damn cell phone glued to my ear. This is how Rocky knew Mac and I were building a solid relationship. According to Mac, and there was no reason not to believe Triple-A with a gun, she was not seeing anyone else.

I had reciprocated her announcement by telling her I was not seeing anyone else either. Then I raised the ante by telling Mac that I had no desire to see anyone else. Rocky, Paula, Mac and I made reservations for the Meadowlark. I couldn't wait. We were going to have a blast.

We decided to go up during the week. First of all, the traffic would be lighter, it would be less crowded, and we'd have better access to the restaurants and the shops. The girls were as excited as were Rocky and I.

"13 Adam, a possible 273.5 now at 6829 Rita Apt 221C. The R/P is Lucy, who stated Gloria's husband, who is still in the apartment, slapped her three times because she poured his beer down the sink. I have her on the phone, and I can hear loud arguing."

"13 Adam, we're around the corner. ETA is less than two."

"Copy 13 Adam, 25, and 26 will back."

25 and 26 radioed their ETA. We took the elevator to the 2nd floor of the apartment complex. As the elevator door slid open, we could hear

yelling from an apartment down the hall. Rocky and I approached apartment 221C cautiously. I knocked and then stepped to the side of the door. Rocky stood across from me. He had his hand on his gun. Rocky stood to the other side of the door. The shouting inside the apartment subsided.

I heard footsteps. I heard the lock turning. The door opened first a crack, then a bit wider, then completely. A short, heavyset woman in her fifties held out her hand, inviting us in. Cautiously, Rocky and I stepped across the threshold, our eyes scanning the room. The male half of the reported 273.5 was seated on the couch. He had on black slacks and a short-sleeve sport shirt that did nothing to hide his beer gut. He had a day old growth of beard.

I looked at Rocky. He looked back at me. I said, "Houston, we have a problem."

I spoke briefly with the female R/P, reporting party. Rocky spoke with the male half of the 273.5. The couple was Gloria and Daniel Gomez, who were long time owners of a clothing store on Pan Am Boulevard. They were police positive. It was Gloria and Daniel who gave us the mannequin and the clothing to make the older Hernandez brother think we had little Hernandez strapped to the damn truck.

Gloria had a few marks on her cheek where Danny had admittedly slapped her because she poured his beer down the sink. The law states that if either subject has visible marks, we MUST make an arrest. It doesn't matter that the victim may not want the spouse arrested. We *must* make the arrest.

Rocky and I went into a huddle. How the f**k do you bust someone instrumental in thwarting a crime and probably saving a life. There is an easy answer to that, you don't! I spoke to Danny, who then literally got down on his knees to apologize to his wife. He swore to Gloria, in front of Rocky and me, that he would only drink three beers a day, no more.

To emphasize this, I borrowed a piece of yellow lined paper from Gloria and hurriedly scrawled, "Under penalty of law, I Daniel Gomez, do solemnly swear that I will not drink any more than three beers a day during the next 365 days." The four of us signed and dated the bullshit agreement. Gloria was happy with that. I canceled the backing units.

Daniel was happy with that. Rocky and I didn't have to make an arrest, and f**k the state of California! We walked out of the apartment, smiling. We climbed into the unit. Before I started driving the black and white, I called Mac. I didn't so much want to make love to her, although I had a raging hard-on thinking about her, I just wanted to be with her.

I wanted to talk with her, have a bite to eat, look at her, hold her hand, touch her hair, and drink a cup of coffee with her. There was a lot of like there; an awful lot of like. I started the car, smiling.

We were back on patrol waiting for the next call. I couldn't have been in a better place. I had life by the tail. I was swinging with it. Rocky was in a great place too, it was finally quiet. We had a good bust under our belts. I had a beautiful lady in my life, even if she did work for Triple-A, and the Meadowlark vacation was coming up. We couldn't ask for more. Maybe a winning lottery ticket, but first you have to buy them, I don't.

I was westbound Glaze, a four-lane road, two lanes in either direction with parking on both sides of the street. I was doing about thirty in a thirty-five in the number two-lane. I heard the warning horn of an approaching train that runs parallel to the street. As I glanced to my right, I observed a figure on the tracks, walking toward that train.

"Holy shit, Rocky!" I pointed. "Look at that!"

Rocky turned in time to see the figure nailed by the train. I looked in horror as pieces of body flew hundreds of feet in every direction. Rocky got on the radio. I jumped the curb. I drove as close to the scene as I could without disturbing the scene. We exited the unit, still in shock. As cops, we see a lot of shit. I had never observed anything like this. I had watched people die. I had seen my share of dead bodies.

I had been on the scene when a guy was shot, who survived. I was on the scene when another suspect was shot. He succumbed at the hospital. I was at horrible accident scenes. I had helped badly injured victims. Up close and personal, I had never watched an individual get struck by a train. Contrary to what some people believe, police are human.

I put my underwear on the same way the public does, one leg goes through at a time. I'm no different than the accountant, the teacher, the stockbroker, the salesperson. I bleed when I cut myself. I feel sorry when a child is injured or killed. I love my country. Sometimes I don't sleep well at night because I worry about bills, taxes, or romance.

We're no different than the average Joe Doe. We're not immune to pain, physical or mental stress. Sometimes we're right, sometimes we're wrong, just like any other person. However, this was different. I knew this image was going to stay with me. I actually observed it! Saw it; it was inked into my brain. Rocky and I walked closer toward the scene. The train was stopped about a quarter-mile from the POI, Point of Impact. No one on the train was injured, even though it came to an abrupt stop.

The victim's body parts were scattered, some in front of the train, and some under the train. I actually felt sick to my stomach. I watched Rocky light a cigarette and momentarily turn away from the scene. I heard sirens in the distance. We were certain the paramedics weren't needed. We could be on the scene for hours waiting for the coroner.

A death scene investigation is not difficult. We'd interview any witnesses, take standard POI information, and make certain the train's staff weren't under the influence then, if possible, establish the victim's identity. We'd pass all the information we gathered to detectives. We would most likely not be making notification to next of kin. From all appearances, it looked like the subject walked into the train intentionally.

137

What caused the incident, at the moment, is up for grabs. Was he or she intoxicated, high, or was it a suicide. Was he deaf, blind, or just stupid? At this point, my best guess would be suicide. What a way to die. More units arrived on the scene. I understood why a person would commit suicide: you lose all hope.

When I die, I wanted to die with my head between Mac's spread legs. I especially didn't understand how the hell you could walk in front of a train if you weren't on drugs. A clear-headed person has to be in unbelievable pain to step on the tracks, knowing the train was only seconds away, and so was the end of your life.

Rocky interrupted me. "Let's get statements from the people on the train."

The on-scene investigation revealed the deceased, or what was left of the deceased, according to his California Identification Card, was Pedro Gomez Calderon of neighboring Trenton. He was thirty-three years old. The train's conductor was too shook up to speak with us. We asked paramedics to tend to him. Rocky and I placed a short red cone next to each of Calderon's body parts. We found eight different body parts. We searched for more. There were only two witnesses who weren't on the train, Rocky and me. There were no witnesses other than the conductor who didn't observe anything useful to the investigation.

Unless you've been there, you cannot imagine what it's like to see a hand severed from a body lying yards from where it belonged; or finding the right leg twenty feet from the left leg. It's horrific. It would be a hot day in a Russian winter before I forget this day. I could only guess what big brother Hernandez thought when he observed what he thought was his little brother about to collide with the overpass. I'd feel for him if he wasn't such a vicious, violent POS.

CHAPTER 13

NEVER REALLY BORING!

It was Monday, Rocky, and I had switched shifts so we could take the ladies to Solvang and the Meadowlark for three days of R and R. It was another one of those beautiful sunny southern California days that bring the best and the worst to our fine state. Life was good. The work of a policeman is normally boredom, coffee, donuts and women who like the uniform.

The life of a cop is often paperwork, court, long days, and short nights off or long nights and short days off. Sometimes, the sewer backs up. That's when the dregs of the city surface. That's when police work goes into high gear. You have to be ready for anything because you never know when the sewer will clog, and the cities shittiest will hit the streets. Today was boredom. We were driving around the city, hoping it remained that way until we were EOW.

I had Mac on the cell. Rocky had the wheel of the Crown Vic. We were more than halfway through our shift. We hadn't so much as handled an arrest. That was unusual. We had our "stats" for the month. Although no officer is officially supposed to carry a quota, it's common knowledge within the Department that if you don't write so many cites, if you don't make so many felony busts, the brasses' smile turns to a frown.

Rocky and I had always hit that magic number. We did our job. If you did your job in APD, you hit your numbers. If you hid in the alley, your team resented you. You had more to worry about from your shift crew than you had from the brass. The Union could usually protect you from serious discipline by the bosses.

No one could protect you from the crew. If you weren't pulling your weight, the "boys" would take you on the side. Nobody wanted that. That was the main reason APD was doing well, and crime was down noticeably. It was all about teamwork.

"All units standby, 3 SAM is in pursuit."

A "SAM" unit is a sergeant, and in this case, 3 SAM was Sgt. Patterson. Patterson was **humored** to be bipolar. I say "humored" not "rumored" because everyone knows he wasn't bipolar. He ran hot and cold like the water that comes out of your faucet. He could be the warmest, happiest, calmest cop in the world one second, the next; he would be his ugly, unnecessary acting twin.

Several of us, one night in the not too distant past, had chased three felons in a vehicle that had robbed a Pan Am Boulevard jewelry store. We cornered them in the parking lot three miles west of the robbery. We immediately took two into custody as they exited the car. The third suspect fled into the rear of a building complex. We set up a perimeter and had him virtually boxed in. He had no way out but to come back the way he went in.

141

By this time, we had all available units at the scene and a K9 unit. Chewy was a ferocious-looking German Sheppard who had more legitimate bites in his file then I had written traffic citations. In short, the perp was f*****d. We had him! Whether or not he was armed, we didn't know. Although none of the suspects presented a weapon in the jewelry store, they all claimed to be armed. The two perps who had been taken into custody were unarmed. We had cover and were awaiting an airship to illuminate the area where the asshole was hiding. We were in no particular hurry.

All of a sudden, Sergeant Patterson yells, "Enough of this shit. I've had it!"

Patterson goes charging into the darkness like some f*****g cartoon character driving aimlessly over a cliff. We were in shock. Three-point two minutes later, Patterson came out with the perp in handcuffs. The crazy sergeant could have gotten killed. He could have gotten us hurt. He took unnecessary risks, to say the least, but he's the sergeant. We wrote the report accordingly. The guy wasn't liked. Aside from his personality that changed like New England weather, he was a range master and was always on everyone about improving their shooting skills.

The sergeant, a former Navy veteran, was tall, in his forties, and out of shape. We kept telling him he needed more exercise because, in the field, you use your fitness and dexterity more than your f*****g gun. He laughed and patted his holster. To say the least, Sergeant Patterson was a bit off-center.

"3 Sam, I'm westbound Western from Pepper Lake Park. The vehicle plate is personalized, ADAM CHARLES LINCOLN UNION HENRY 8 ROBERT. It's occupied one time and is wanted for speed only at this time. The vehicle is a blue Dodge Viper hardtop."

Dispatch reiterated this information feeding it to the troops who were now driving to the location west of the pursuit. Within minutes they would be in a position to assist Patterson or to set up a perimeter if the suspect stopped, foot bailed, went rabbit.

"3 SAM, what's your 20?"

3 SAM responded, "Westbound Western approaching Elm. Speed is 55, traffic is moderate."

"21 ADAM, we're with the SAM unit, and we'll call out the pursuit for the SAM unit."

"I'll call my own pursuit," Patterson yelled into the radio. "I've got this clown."

Rocky and I were rolling to the far west end of the city for coverage. I looked at Rocky and laughed.

"Dr. Jekyll and Mr. Fried. I would hate to be the perp if Patterson catches up with him."

Rocky said, "The best thing that guy could do would be to pull over, and run like hell. 3 SAM would never catch him on foot."

"No, but he might shoot the guy in the back."

I said, "True."

"3 SAM we're still westbound Western west of….." The radio went dead.

"21 ADAM, we blew a front tire. We're out of the pursuit."

3 SAM sounded beyond excited; his out of breath voice clouded the airwaves. He yelled, "Subject is out of the car, running across Western. He's on the east side of Western…." You could hear Patterson gasping for air. "He's running southbound into…."

Units arrived within seconds. They didn't find the suspect, but they found Patterson lying on the curb, spitting snot and puke all over the curb. He was so out of breath, I thought he was going to have a heart attack.

I couldn't help myself, and as the lieutenant was sending out directions to set-up a parameter to box and lock in the suspect, I leaned close to Patterson.

I turned to Rocky and said in a voice disguised, so Patterson, if he lived, wouldn't know it was me. "Let's go to the range after EOW and get in some extra shooting practice."

We broke the perimeter after roughly an hour and a half. The GTA suspect got away. Patterson had every excuse in the book. Everyone on the crew knew the truth. We went home laughing, all of us except Patterson. We were one shift away from Solvang and fun, fun, fun. Don't get me wrong. I don't like my job, I love it. But every so often it's good to get away. The game-changer was Mac. I wanted to spend time with her, and the miracle was that Mac wanted to spend that amount of time with me.

144

The fact that Mac and Paula had become great friends, the fact that Rocky and I were as close as sprinkles on ice cream, made for an awesome foursome. We could have just as much of a blast playing miniature golf as we could, sitting around the fireplace in Rocky's house watching an old movie or playing pinball machines in the game room at my place. I don't think I was ever happier. I know I was never happier than I was today. I was willing to bet I'd be happier tomorrow. This was the blue line of life and death for a cop.

Mac tried to get me to carry a pair of her panties in my police pants pocket when I went to work. She said it was for luck. I think she wanted me to think about her all day and remember her kinky side. I could see it happen. A fight with a suspect goes down. I'm transported to the hospital. My clothing is taken from me at the hospital, and somehow Mac's panties are discovered in my pocket. I would be the laughing stock of APD. Some wise guy would probably post a picture of the panties on Twitter.

I begged off. Mac offered to let me have any color panties I wanted to carry around. Then she offered me a different color every day. I laughed, and politely declined. But Mac was as sharp as a bull's horn. She put the thought in my mind. More often than not, her damn panties would come to life in my mind, and I'd smile. I'm sure Rocky thought I was as crazy as a 5150 subject; that I should be sent to the Looney bin for observation. I looked at Rocky and smiled. We cruised over to Alameda Street to check on the casino. Everything appeared quiet and peaceful.

"How about getting a cup of coffee?" Rocky asked.

"Sounds good to me, let's drive over to the 7-11."

"We can have coffee, and I can cop a smoke out of the unit for a change." Rocky nodded.

At one time, I'd been a heavy smoker. When I decided I wanted to become a cop, I hired a friend who owned a local gym to get my ass in shape. What a mistake that was. The friend's name was Candy. He wasn't so named because he was "sweet." Candy worked me hard, very hard. He built muscles on me that I never knew were hiding within my body. He got me in awesome shape. Most of my female friends were impressed with my muscles. You have to do a lot of running in the academy. Candy had done his homework.

One day Candy said to me, "Today we run."

"It sounds good to me."

The gym was about a tenth of a mile from the corner. "Run down to that parking meter and come back," he said.

"Why don't I just run around the block?" I asked.

"Because I don't have an ambulance here, and I'm not about to give you mouth to mouth. Now get your ass down to that parking meter." Candy fished in his pocket. "Here's a dime. When you get to the meter, put that dime in. That'll give you a chance to catch your breath."

I took six running steps and thought I was going to puke, that my heart was going to stop. I walked back to where Candy stood in front of the gym.

146

"Why don't I just run around the block?" Candy, who was built like a sculptured rock, laughed.

I walked into the gym, into the locker room, got my Marlboro cigarettes out of my shirt, and threw them across the gym. Everyone in that f*****g gym laughed. I said, "I quit!" They laughed harder.

One of the gym rats yelled, "Better men than you have tried quitting cold turkey."

 I never had another cigarette. I didn't have the desire. What was strange was that I went to Vegas quite a bit and played "recreational" poker at the tables. Most of the players smoked. It never bothered me. The year I got out of the academy, I ran the L.A. Marathon in three hours forty minutes. Not too bad for an ex-smoker!

 I pulled into the 7-11, scanned the parking lot, found a place where I could park the car, and could see it from inside the 7-11. I backed the car into a vacant space. Rocky had just lit his second cigarette. I hadn't quite finished my coffee when the call came out. It was possible shots fired call up in the Richmond Strip, which is the northeast corner of APD and a heavy gang area. According to dispatch, she received only one call, which meant it, could have been a firecracker, a backfire, or a round.

I dumped my coffee in the trash and slid behind the wheel of the unit. Rocky took his cigarette with him into the car. I headed east to the Richmond Strip.

"21 Adam, we're 97, and we're code 4. A couple of neighborhood kids are playing with firecrackers left over from the 4th. We'll talk to the kids and mom and dad." That took care of that adrenalin boost.

It was dead quiet. It was getting dark. We were almost EOW and soon to be on our way to Solvang. I headed west on Saturn toward Pan Am Boulevard., where there had been several grab and run or strong-arm robberies. One of apparently two players and possibly three would observe a victim wearing a gold chain. One of the pair would jostle the victim while the other suspect grabbed and ran.

At times, these assholes were daring enough to just grab the jewelry and take off. There might have been the third subject with a vehicle parked in the vicinity because these clowns always managed to make a clean getaway before we got to the area.

We had a vague description but nothing more. I asked the Watch Commander if we could use a couple of Reserves for a stakeout. He said he'd kick it upstairs. APD had a dozen Police Reserves. Reserves came in three levels. A Level 3 Reserve was restricted mainly to inside the station and could not be anywhere an arrest might occur. A Level 2 Reserve could be teamed with Level 1 Reserve or full-timer. A Level 1 Reserve has the same police powers as a full-timer. A Level 1 Reserve could be in the field on his/her own.

The level rating depended on how long you were in the academy. A Level 1 Reserve went through the same academy as a full-timer. A number of Level 1 Reserves "tested the waters" before becoming full-timers.

APD used the Reserve contingency as a major league baseball team might use a farm team. Rocky started out as a Reserve when he was driving big rigs. He loved police work to the point that he went full time. He took a major pay hit.

I stopped for the light at Saturn and Pan Am. I could see evening shoppers to my right peering into store windows. The sidewalks were crowded with shoppers on the main street's business district. This was a good thing, especially since the American economy had long gone south. The light changed. I began my right turn. As I completed the turn, I thought about Mac and her damn panties, the pink ones.

Immediately, I observed what looked like a Hollywood movie set or a war-torn Afghanistan where I had spent two tours. I saw fire and people running in all directions. I heard people screaming. I heard what could have been gunshots. I got closer and stopped. We're taught to "survey" the scene before we take action. We're no good to anyone dead. Rocky grabbed the mic. I opened the door of the unit. A car was on fire. No, it was a van or an SUV.

I thought I saw a couple of guys with a weapon, a rifle, maybe a shotgun, maybe an assault rifle. I started to back up toward the unit for cover. I observed Rocky's door open, out of the corner of my eye. I watched Rocky moving forward slowly. I smelled tear gas. My world went black.

End of Part One

CHAPTER 14

THE WORST POSSIBLE SCENARIO

Everything was white. The room was white, the sheets on my bed were white, and the curtains were white. Tubes were coming out of every conceivable part of my body. I looked like a f*****g road map. As if on cue, the door opened, and more white stepped into the room. I tried to clear the cobwebs from my brain. My thinking was hazy, my memory worse. The doctor wore a white gown. Two steps behind him was a crisp, well-pressed blue suit, APD blue. It was Assistant Chief Rolando.

The doctor put his stethoscope to my chest. He cocked his head and listened for a moment then, in a somber tone, said, "How do you feel, Tony?"

That had to be the second stupidest question I ever heard. The guy may have been a doctor, but he was Dr. Asshole. *How the hell do you think I feel?*

"I feel like playing poker," I said. "As a matter of fact, let's go to Vegas. Look at me, man, how do you think I feel?"

I knew it was me talking, but it felt like the voice was coming from a different world. I just stared at him. The doctor was standing on the left side of my hospital bed. He looked serious, way too serious for my liking.

"You've been through hell," he said. "You're working your way back."

"We've had you in a medically induced coma for damn near two weeks. We almost lost you three times during four different operations. You just mentioned Vegas; the odd makers were betting you wouldn't make it. They lost, you beat long odds, son."

The guy had a sense of humor. "What the hell happened?"

I was trying to clear my head to remember. It was cloudy like the New England sky before a summer rain. Nothing came clear. The last thing I remembered was driving the unit into some f*****g Hollywood movie set. I remembered...I remembered stopping the unit. I recalled getting out of the unit. I remembered Rocky getting out of the unit. I remembered the smell of tear gas or something like it. I remembered nothing after that.

"Normally, I wouldn't do this, but the assistant chief asked that I leave the two of you alone. Assistant Chief Rolando will talk with you in a minute," the doctor said.

The good doctor changed the subject, "I want you to know that this hospital is here to help you in any way we can. I'm here to help you. You have a long, long road ahead of you. At times that road is going to be bumpy, it may feel insurmountable. When that happens, we have staff to assist you. When you're released, we won't drop the ball. We'll still be available for you."

The doctor paused to rub at day-old stubble on his face then ended with, "Good luck. Show Vegas you want to take more of their money."

I had no idea whatsoever what the good doctor was trying to tell me. Obviously, Rocky and I had driven into the middle of some sort of "situation." After that, I was blank, totally blank.

I looked up at the doctor, who was probably in his fifties. His long black hair looked like he had just gotten out of bed.

"Thank you, sir." I was more confused than before.

The doctor left the room, leaving the assistant chief and me alone. There was an upholstered chair in the corner. Rolando slid the chair within inches of my bed. ACOP sat down, never taking his eyes off me. He held my hand for fifteen seconds, looking down at me as if he wanted to apologize for something he did. I could swear I saw a tear in his eye.

"I asked the doctor if I could be the one to tell you."

I hadn't seen Rolando look this way since Roberto was kidnapped and threatened. I exhaled. My mind was clearing. It was coming back to me. We were in the unit, Rocky and me. We were on patrol.....

"Tony, I've got bad news, and I have worse news. I'm sorry, my friend. I am so, so very sorry."

"You're going to make me cry. What the f**k is going on?"

152

"You drove into the middle of an armored car robbery. It was one of those things… that just happens. You guys did nothing wrong. You had no way of knowing. Rocky is dead!"

I looked at Rolando in total and complete shock, "What the f**k did you just say?"

"I'm sorry, Tony. I'm so very sorry. Rocky is dead. They killed him at the scene."

"Holy shit!" My world stopped. My head couldn't make sense of those words. "Did you get them…the shooter?"

"We have three in custody, actually, three dead. We believe Rocky's killer got away. He also got away with the money, we think."

The tears rolled down my face. I didn't give a shit. The sobs came. I let my partner down. The man who was always there for me, I let him down. I wiped away some of the tears.

"How's Paula?"

"Not good. She went back to be with her folks…at least temporarily."

I managed to ask, "When's the funeral?"

Rolando took a breath. "Rocky's already been laid to rest. You've been in a coma for almost two weeks, Tony. We didn't know if you were going to make it."

"You said bad news and worse news. Nothing can be worse than what you just hit me with. What else?"

I watched the little chief inhale very slowly. He didn't exhale. "You lost your left leg at the knee."

Instinctively I reached down where my left leg should have been. I pushed down on the white sheet. The sheet didn't stop moving. There was no left leg below the knee. I wailed. The tears wouldn't stop. I didn't know whether I was crying for Rocky for me or for both of us. I fell asleep.

The first thing I did when I awoke was remembered what Rocky told me a long time ago when I pulled a tatted down gang banger over for expired tags, which I misread. I apologized to the guy for my mistake. When I got back in the unit, Rocky, being the senior officer, said to me, "There are two things a police officer never does. First, he doesn't ever say he's sorry. Second, he never cries."

I looked up at the ceiling, "You're wrong, Rocky," I said aloud. "A police officer does say he's sorry. I'm sorry as hell that you're gone. I'm so, so sorry, Rocky, I f*****d up!"

I wanted my Glock, I was thinking I was a dead man walking. That was funny. I wasn't walking, probably never walk again at least not unassisted. Police work was over, my life was over. I wanted to end it all. F**k the world! I was twenty-eight with a leg and a f*****g half. The door opened, and in walked Mac in that tight-fitting f*****g triple-A with a gun uniform clinging to that beautiful body. That relationship was dead. I couldn't look at her. She kept walking closer to the bed. I wanted to get up and run, but I had too many tubes in me and no left leg.

"Hey." I said.

Mac was leaning against the bed and started to reach for my hand. I moved it. I didn't give her a chance to lean over the bed to kiss me. I didn't give her a chance to hold my hand.

"I need a favor." I looked down at where my left leg once was. "Leave. I need time. Leave." I never looked up.

She was silent for several seconds, "I'll leave after I get a kiss."

"That ain't gonna' happen, so just leave, please."

"That ain't going to happen either until I get a kiss."

"Get the f**k out of my room. You're supposed to be working, which means you're on taxpayer time, so get the f**k out." The tears rolled down my cheek.

"I'm off duty. I've been here every day since you were brought in. Each and every goddamned day, so don't do this to me. "I've even slept here, showered here, and then go back to work. Don't do this to me, Tony." Tears rolled down her cheek. "You know….." Mac was raising her voice higher than I had ever heard it. "Do you know why your favorite word is asshole? Do you, damn it? It's because you are an asshole, that's why! A f*****g wuss asshole. That's you. You don't know real love when it goddamn bites you, you asshole.

"I'll leave, but bet on this one, Tony. I'm not done with you *yet*. You and I have unfinished business. You've got one f*****g hour to quit this bullshit. You can feel sorry for yourself all you want, but I don't give a shit how busted up your mind and body are. You'll heal asshole, we'll heal together. Whether or not you realize it, we're a team. Do you think Rocky would want you playing this tune? Do you, asshole? Do you?"

I was getting hard listening to Mac's cursing, ranting. At least I knew that worked. Maybe I had another fetish I wasn't aware of until Mac starting screaming at me.

I swallowed hard. "Please leave."

"I'm going downstairs to grab something, some coffee, maybe a sandwich. I'll be back in an hour."

Mac turned to leave then said, "You can save the kiss for when I get back. I'll bring you back a set of balls!"

I dozed, which wasn't difficult. I was higher than a kite. I don't know how long I slept. I woke up in a cold sweat.

I had a damn dream, a real frightening nightmare. Too damn real. It was so real it scared the crap out of me. I was in court. I was facing the judge who was seated behind his bench. His nameplate read, Judge Karma. The Judge said to me, "You know why you're here, and you know what you did. You've paid the price. Now get out of here and live with it. As I was trying to shake off the terror of the nightmare, the doctor came and had little to say except that in the next couple of days, the staff shrink would be in to see me. After that f*****g nightmare, maybe I did need a shrink. I also needed a f*****g left leg. I needed Rocky!

At 1530 hours, in walked Mac. She was smiling as if nothing happened. She walked from the door toward the bed and didn't stop. She looked like a cop on a mission. She was both. I had to give her

156

credit. She knew what she wanted. Mac was determined. So was I. The relationship was over. My career was over. Rocky was dead. I wanted to die. When she got to the bed, without saying a word, she reached under the blanket and the sheet. I felt something between my legs and knew what it was immediately. Mac was rubbing her panties against my dick.

"I've been wearing them all day. They have my scent on them. They're probably a bit juicy. I was laughing so hard earlier today I may have even peed in them. Wanna' sniff?"

She kept rubbing. It felt good. Real good! The door opened, it was a nurse. She was older, heavyset, and stern-looking. Mac didn't stop rubbing.

Over her shoulder, she said deadpan to the nurse, "This is official police business. I'm conducting an investigation. I'm also doing a search. I need you to leave, please, NOW!"

Without hesitation, Florence Nightingale left my room.

Mac pulled one of two chairs over to the side of the bed. She sat.

"Are you through feeling sorry for yourself?"

"Do you always go where you're not wanted?" I gave Mac an ice-cold stare. At least I tried to.

"That goes with the badge." She smiled. "I'm wanted. You just don't know it yet. I know you've been through a lot, a helluva' lot. But you've got a lot of fight left in you. This bed doesn't become you.

Neither does that ugly hospital gown, although I'm tempted to tear it off you and see if I can make a cop cum in five minutes."

I shook my head from side to side. "It's over, Mac."

"It's over when *I* say it's over. You don't listen well. I told you before I'm not finished with you."

"Mac, let it go. You're a helluva' lady. I *was* falling in love with you. But I'm not good to anyone this way. I have no left leg."

"Quit the happy horseshit. The mind is in….well I guess that's up for grabs, shit happens. We've both seen enough of that. You gotta' get back up on the horse and ride. If all else fails, I will get you a job at IHOP." Mac rubbed her hands together. "Before I leave, is there anything I can get you when I come back?"

"You don't need to come back," I said slowly, deliberately, meaning it.

"I want to come back. I will come back. Despite you, we're going to get through this.

"The first word in the Big Book of Alcoholics Anonymous is *WE.* We can do what *you* can't. We'll get through this together." She got up to leave.

"Has Rocky been laid to rest?" I asked, forgetting or trying to deny what I had been told earlier.

Mac nodded. "When you're able, we'll go see him at the cemetery."

"You're a stubborn bitch!" I finally managed a smile.

158

"I love it when you talk dirty. It gets me wet." She walked over to the bed. She put her recently worn panties under the pillow.

Another doctor came in, a different doctor. He examined me. "How do you feel?"

"Scared!"

The doctor was tall, thin in his late forties. "I'm sure you're frightened, you have every right to be." He put his stethoscope around his neck, "You're out of the woods; however, it was touch and go for several days, more than several days. You were in a medically induced coma for quite a while. The worst injury you suffered was the loss of your left leg at the knee."

I looked at the doctor. My head was starting to clear just a bit. My body hurt all over, my head hurt more.

"Why did I lose my leg?"

"There was an explosion. You took shrapnel. There was heavy gunfire. You took eight rounds in your leg. We did everything we could to save it. I'm sorry."

"What killed Rocky?"

"It was the same thing that almost killed you."

"Did he die fast?"

"I don't want to lie to you. He was alive when he arrived here. He died in surgery. For what it's worth, I don't think he was in much pain. The explosion knocked your partner unconscious. The gunfire did the most damage to him. The rounds penetrated his vest. What else can I tell you?"

I shook my head.

"We're here to help you. You'll be here a while longer. I can't pin it down right now. That's going to depend on how fast you heal, both physically and mentally. When you leave here, you'll go to rehab. Let's take it a day at a time."

CHAPTER 15

THE INCIDENT

About three o'clock that afternoon, APD detectives visited me. It was a welcome break from the Dr. Phil show, which always seemed to be on the hospital television. I was questioned about "THAT NIGHT." Detective Gall, a high school teacher, turned police officer, then detective, led the team in questioning me. Gall was short and squatty, in his forties, easy going with a sense of humor. He was dressed in what looked like a blue Sear's suit with a white shirt and blue tie. He stood with his partner Mike Samuels at the foot of the bed.

"What is the first thing you recall about that night?" Samuels asked.

I grabbed the remote off the nightstand table and silenced Dr. Phil. "We were.....I was driving west on Saturn. I stopped for the light at Pan Am Boulevard, in preparation for a northbound turn on Pan Am. Everything was quiet. It was our last shift before a few days off... Rocky..." I swallowed hard and then coughed, trying to cover up the lump in my throat, "Sorry about that."

Samuels looked down. "Tony, it's okay, we understand. We feel the pain too."

Gall said, "You're stopped for the red at Saturn. You're about to make the northbound turn onto Pan Am….."

"Yeah, the light changed green, I proceeded. I remember seeing flames, people scattering, and what looked like a dark-colored SUV covered in flames.

"I remember my first instinct was to run to the SUV to pull out anyone who might be in the vehicle. Then training kicked in. I looked at Rocky, who was on the radio. I surveyed the scene. I got out of the vehicle and used the driver's door for cover. I thought I saw a man in dark-colored clothing with a ski mask and a semi-automatic rifle in his hand, but by the time that fully registered, it was game over.

"Everything went black. Oh yeah, one other thing. As I exited the unit, I observed Rocky exit the unit. That was the last time I saw Rocky before the lights went out."

Samuels asked me if I could identify the guy.

"It's hazy, sir, really hazy. I'm going to say five-ten to six-foot. He wasn't thin and wasn't fat. I didn't see his feet or shoes. Like I said, he was wearing what appeared to be a black ski mask. Do I get a question or two?"

Gall nodded.

"What was this all about?"

Samuels, who was the senior of the two, was a few inches taller than Gall, which made Mike about five-ten. Samuels did double duty. He also served as a range master for APD. Mike Samuels had been with

APD forever. Like Rocky, Mike started as a Reserve. He was quiet and serious; off duty Mike had a sense of humor that could have put him on stage as a comic. He often headlined at our annual Christmas party.

"Here's what we know, Tony." Mike pointed to Gall indicating he should lock the door. "This was a robbery."

Mike continued. "The van was a money van. There were two couriers in the truck.

"It was the SafeGuard armored truck that would normally pick up the casino receipts on Alameda, then make the rounds of the shops and banks on Alameda and then head east to Pan Am and Western working its way north on Pan Am making indicated stops.

"Preliminary estimates say approximately three and a half million dollars was seized. That's not a hard figure. Here's where it gets interesting. We have scant witnesses; however, from what we have to date, four pros pulled this off. It was well planned. Somehow, and this too is still in investigative stages, a bomb was planted under the truck.

"It was set off remotely, and then the truck was torched. Tear gas was fired at and around the truck to dispel the crowd and take out the driver and partner, who were shot and killed, execution-style. These were and are 'real nice guys.' But I'll get to that. We think they may have had inside help. It sure looks like that. We're trying to get a plant on the inside, but that's going to take time. We need to be really careful. If it was an inside job, we don't want to spook anyone.

"The only hitch was they didn't expect your unit, you and Rocky, to be on top of the situation. When you showed up, they opened up. You and Rocky had no chance. None, zilch, nada, zero!"

Mike took a deep breath. He ran his tongue across his lips.

This gave me a chance to ask, "You said four guys pulled off this heist. Three of them are dead. Obviously, we know who they are…..were. I'm lost, did Rocky take them out?"

Mike answered in a solemn tone. "Rocky never had a chance. We believe Rocky was hit before you were hit.

"Your guy, the guy with the auto, killed them all. Most likely so he could keep the money. We identified the three dead perps. They had jackets longer than Pete Rose's hitting streak. They were bad dudes. The one that got away, we think, is Austin Martin, an import from New York who did some mob hits several years back. NYPD was unable to build a case. They also tried to build a RICO case against him, but that failed too.

"We pulled prints off the stolen they were driving. Since the prints don't belong to any of the three dead perps, nor do they belong to the husband, wife or teenage son who is attached to the stolen, we think they belong to our man. We have BOLOs out all over the world for the scum bag. It's just a matter of time. You can't deposit three million-plus dollars into banks domestically. Even ten grand at a time gets questioned. Either he's got it hidden, or it's deposited in offshore accounts.

"Since the robbery and killings, we've had sightings of Martin in Italy, France, Hoboken, New Jersey, Brazil, and Thailand. We're not certain which are legitimate sightings. We do know two things, the money's gone, and we have six dead."

"Six and a half," I piped in. "Three robbers, two guards, half my leg and Rocky."

Mike said, "We'll get this prick sooner or later. Hopefully, it'll be sooner. When we get him, we intend, and I didn't say this. When we get him, we're going to balance the books the best we can."

START OF A NEW LIFE

I slept for under an hour. I heard the theme from CHIPs. When I finally figured out that I wasn't dreaming, I realized it was my cell. I reached over, grabbed it.

I said, "Hello."

"Are my panties still damp?"

I exhaled my annoyance. "Mac, please listen to me. I really was an asshole yesterday, the day before yesterday, or whenever the hell it was. I apologize for that. And yes, I did play with your panties the best I could with all this hospital shit in me. But, it's over, we're history. I really do love you, which amazes even me. But I have enough problems right now, so please let it be."

"Tony, I love you. We'll work through this together," Mac said.

"There's nothing to work through. It's over."

"No, it's not," Mac insisted.

"Are you at work?"

"I'm off."

"Where are you?"

The door opened, "I'm right here!"

Mac walked to the bed. She kissed me on the cheek, slid her hand under the pillow, pulled out her panties, then scrutinized them.

"Got it, you did enjoy them, I'm glad." She pulled a pair of blue nylon panties out of her pocket. "These are for tonight, or tomorrow or later. I don't know how much temporary damage the meds are doing. But whenever you feel up to it, no pun intended, you can reach out and touch yourself with these." Mac put the panties under my pillow.

I don't know whether it was Mac, the panties, or both, but I was getting hard. Mac noticed me through the sheet.

"You do miss me."

"What the f**k am I going to do with you?"

"Keep me."

There was a knock on the door. This place had more foot traffic than a Compton crack house. Two very well attired gentlemen entered without waiting for an invitation. They both wore blue pinstripe suits, white shirts, and solid red ties. They both had short black hair and were about five foot eleven. Both were in their early forties, wore the

166

same black shoes, and were out of the same cookie cutter. They wore government shoes.

"Edgar and Hoover," I quipped, "Come on in."

The robbery, which involved banks, Federal banks, made this also an FBI case. Contrary to what you see on television, we welcomed the help of the FBI. They had access to manpower, equipment and investigation expertise that we could only dream of.

"Tony, I'm Hoover, and he is Edgar. Seriously, I'm agent Busher. John Busher. This is agent Mark Clark. You know why we're here."

"The lady," I said, deliberately not giving up her name or occupation, "was just leaving."

"The lady," Mac said, "Is going to grab a bite to eat. I'll be back in an hour or so."

Before I realized it, out of my mouth came, "Thanks, angel, this is police business. Something you wouldn't know about."

Agent Busher asked, "If you don't mind my asking......"

"Sally," Mac lied convincingly. "My name is Sally." Mac was walking toward the door.

"Police?" the agent asked.

Mac looked at me then at Busher. "I work for Triple-A."

Agent Busher put a small black Sony recorder on the white food table next to the bed.

"Do you mind my recording this session? It makes it easy when I reduce this to a computer file."

"As long as you don't read me my rights, I'm comfortable."

Busher laughed. He spoke today's date, my name, and the purpose of the interview into the recorder. Then the gentle questioning began. I was able to tell the agents the same thing I told Gall and Samuels.

"That's all I can recall. The doctor's said more might come back after a while, then again, none of it might ever come back."

"Occasionally, in cases like yours," Agent Clark offered, "hypnosis can be of assistance in jostling thoughts free. Would you be willing to give that a shot?"

"Gentlemen, if you think it'll help, I'm willing to give it a shot." I was surprised at how my attitude was improving.

"Good, we appreciate that."

"There's nothing to appreciate. We're all in the same game here. We're all after the same end. The sooner we get our asshole, the happier we'll all be."

I was finally allowed, visitors. It was as if someone cleared the sewer drain, and the water started pouring in. I didn't know I was so popular. The room now had flowers, balloons, a stack of magazines, a few novels, and a smuggled in fifth of Seagram's. I was suddenly feeling a bit better. The doctor said no more than two visitors at a time, which is like telling Yasiel Puig not to steal second base. My room was filled with well-wishers who were trying to cheer me up. It was working. My favorite visitor was Mac.

I had a serious problem with our relationship. I loved Mac. I hadn't known her long, but she was everything I wanted in a partner, in a relationship. But now I was limited since losing the better part of a limb. I wasn't feeling sorry for myself, but I was no longer a whole man. With the loss of that limb went my career. That meant I'd have to be trained to do something else.

I couldn't see myself doing anything but police work. Life could be a bitch! I had my associate of arts degree. I had gone to college to study journalism. I wanted to be a newspaperman.

In my final months at community college, I secured an internship with a local newspaper, a small newspaper with a solid readership. I was allowed to accompany a full-fledged reporter on his assignments. Before the internship was up, I was assigned to write two stories of my own. I had space on the inside page of the newspaper. I had a byline. I enjoyed it but realized it was too restricting for me.

I needed more excitement at my job. On one of my assignments, I interviewed a police officer who rescued an elderly woman from a blazing apartment building. I knew right then that I wanted to be a cop. After the academy, after getting hired by Amity PD, following my FTO training and after getting off probation, I enrolled in a police science class, thinking I might want to advance into management. I got an "A" in the class but decided, at least for now, I belonged on the street. Life really can be a bitch, a great big f*****g ugly bitch!

169

The door opened and in walked Dr. Seuss "Everyone out," he said with a smile. "We need to do some tests, and I need our guest to roll over, so I can stick a needle in his butt. Tomorrow is another day."

Everyone exited the room, but Mac. "I'll be back after the doctor plays with your ass."

"We're going to let you out of here next week. We've done everything we can for you." He sat on the edge of the bed, "You'll heal, the only permanent physical injury you'll have is your left leg. My concern is your mental condition. I've been watching you closely as have other members of our staff. We're concerned. It's normal to go through a stage when you've been through what you've been through. It's not unlike what you'd experience if you've lost a loved one, in fact, you lost Rocky. The loss of the leg compounds the situation.

"I'm not a shrink, but I've seen similar cases to yours in my many years on the staff. Here's my prescription. When you're comfortable with it, go visit Rocky at the cemetery. Make peace with that loss. After that, let's see what we can do about the leg. Medicine and science have come a long way.

"If the DA and the police don't work together, law and order suffer. If medicine and science don't couple, we're not fair to the patient. Finally, and this is none of my business, don't shut Mac out of your life. Let her help you through this. She wants to help and, whether you realize it or not, you need her help."

I had mixed emotions about Dr. Seuss sticking his nose so far into my business. I knew he meant well.....but..... "I'm not a whole person anymore."

Dr. Seuss, in no uncertain terms, said, "Tony, that is so much bullshit that I really don't want to hear it. I have a present for you. Do you remember Roy Campanella?"

"Sure. Campy was a Brooklyn Dodger catcher who was in a terrible automobile accident back in the 50s, in the middle of his great baseball career. He skidded on a patch of ice and rolled his car. He damned near died."

Dr. Seuss continued, "He would have died, not because of his physical injuries but because he damn near gave up. Don't quit on yourself. Somebody once told me, and I'm not a religious man, I am spiritual. Someone told me God doesn't close one door without opening another."

"I'm not religious, either. But if there is a God, why does he want to f**k with me?" I asked.

"That's God's business, Tony. Sometimes the seemingly bad turns out to be not so bad. Campy lost a career but how many people did he inspire to push for greatness, to push for survival. You don't know what tomorrow will bring. You don't need to drive yourself crazy projecting the future on one and a half legs."

Dr. Glaze handed me a hardbound copy of Campy's book. "Read the book before you leave here, that's an order. And in the meantime, turn over and pull up the ugly looking hospital gown so I can plant this needle in your butt."

Mac spent a few minutes with me. Before she left, she put a couple of stapled sheets of paper on my nightstand.

As Mac was getting ready to leave the room, she said, "When you get bored, read this. You…we have an entire life ahead of us. Nobody knows what tomorrow is going to bring. Remember, yesterday is a canceled check, tomorrow is a promissory note, today is a gift, which is why we call it the present. Don't forget that!"

A few minutes later, Mac left to go to work. I was getting antsy. The drugs were starting to wear off. I was feeling a bit of pain. I was restless and took that as a good sign. I plucked Campy's book off the night stand and started to read, *It's Good to Be Alive.* "Campy," was a helluva' catcher. I knew before I opened the book, from previous readings about Campanella, that he was often called "half breed." Campy was half-Black and half- Italian. What a combination, a Black wop! Being Italian was handicap enough; being a Black Italian was a real bitch.

The man endured all sorts of bullshit as one of the first blacks, or partial blacks, to break into baseball. He was feisty, he was small, he was smart, but most of all he didn't know the meaning of the word QUIT! The man was a fighter. He was also the MVP three times, pretty awesome for a catcher. I knew Campy was paralyzed as the result of an auto accident.

What I didn't know until I started reading the book that on a January night in 1958, Campy was on his way home from the store he owned in New York. He hit a patch of winter ice rolling the station wagon he was driving. His neck was broken. Here was a major league catcher, tougher than that junkyard mutt, now he lay in a hospital bed, not even able to feed himself.

He wanted to die. He felt as sorry for himself as I felt for me. Somehow, he found oneness with God. He realized there was a reason for his survival; that there was a purpose for still being on this earth. With the help of friends, Campy again became the fighter that we Dodger fans knew and loved. As a matter of fact, the Dodgers moved to Los Angeles in 1958. Several years later, Campy came west. Eventually, Campy became a Los Angeles Dodger coach.

Wow and a half! I put Campy's book on the nightstand. I put my head on the pillow, face down. I reached under that pillow and pulled out Mac's panties of the day. They were perfumed, and they were pink. I had a new pillow for my face. I guess it was *good to be alive*. Forty-five minutes later, the door opened, and I couldn't believe what I saw. This wasn't real, it really wasn't. Wheelchair Willie motored into my room. *Goddamn medication*. Now I was hallucinating.

"What the f**k are you doing here, asshole, get the f**k out!"

CHAPTER 16

SHOCKING REVELATION

Willie was well dressed in jacket and slacks. He held up his hand and said, "Hang with me a minute."

"Get the f**k out. If I could get the hell out of this bed, I'd get up and throw you out. Get out!"

Willie held up both hands, "I'm sorry about Rocky, I'm truly sorry, Tony. I know how close the two of you were. Rocky was also my brother. I'm sorry about your leg."

This guy was out of his f*****g mind. "What the hell is the matter with you? I'll have you arrested. Get the f**k out."

"I'm sorry for everything," Willie said sincerely.

Wheelchair Willie suddenly pushed himself out of his wheelchair and stood up. The son of a bitch had grown legs.

"I'm an FBI agent. I was…..am working a sting in cooperation with APD. I had to offer my condolences. I am sorry."

"You got to be kidding me. You're not a f*****g cripple. You're one of us."

Willie nodded. "The only one who is in on our game is your Chief. It had to be that way."

I nodded, then said, "Rocky didn't know?"

He shook his head, "Rocky didn't know, just your Chief. It has to stay that way. They'll bring me in from the cold in a couple of months, then we can talk." Willie wheeled his scooter around and disappeared out the door.

I laughed myself to sleep. I was watching the six o'clock news when they "broke" for breaking news. There was a pursuit on northbound 405 freeway, just north of the 118. I propped up my pillow, police pursuits fascinated me. A pursuit was like a good poker player trying to win a large pot on a bluff. In the case of the asshole being chased, usually you didn't know why he wouldn't pull over. In a pursuit, the primary unit always has the option of nixing the chase or, of course, the WC could call it off.

Because cops were getting blamed when the pursued took out an innocent victim, or when the shit hit the wall at the pursuit's end, more and more pursuits were being questioned. The guy who came up with a sure-fire way to end the pursuit would be a rich man. The other reason I loved watching pursuits was that they rarely broke for commercials. The car being chased was a 2014 pale blue custom Toyota. The rims and spokes were polished and chromed. They must have been worth almost as much as the freakin' car.

There was a mural on the trunk, but the chopper couldn't get close enough to hone in on the mural. The Toyota was stolen out of San Diego. The CHP was in pursuit. There were two choppers overhead.

175

Traffic was light. Had this been a weekday instead of a Sunday, the freeway would have been jammed packed with commuters. I wasn't sure if Mac was on duty. If she was, odds were she wasn't in the vicinity of the pursuit because she didn't work out of the northern area CHP Station. The news chopper reported speeds of 75 to 85 miles an hour. He also reported there appeared to be one male behind the wheel.

At this point, the chopper spotter said, "The driver is wanted for GTA and various traffic violations." There had not been an identification of the driver. He weaved from the number three lane across several traffic lanes and into the diamond lane. He signaled before changing lanes. "That was nice of him," the spotter quipped. "The best thing this guy can do is pull over and take what's coming to him. These chases have a habit of ending badly, badly for the fleeing suspect or badly for an innocent victim."

Five CHP units were trailing the Toyota at various distances. With the helicopters above, it was wise to not get too close to the stolen. The suspect could be armed. He could suddenly slam on the brakes and come out shooting. The guy could be high on PCP or coke. Then again, he may have taken the car for a "joy ride." He may have no criminal record at all, not likely, but possible.

I'd never had the chance to be in another pursuit. I'd never write another ticket. I'd never arrest another felon. All I could do was watch it on television. F**k me! I watched as the suspect again crossed over the diamond lane then back across several traffic lanes damn near side swiping a white pickup truck. He decided he wanted to enter the 14 freeway. I was familiar with the 14 freeway, it went north and up into

176

the desert and eventually out of Los Angeles County and into Kern County.

While the freeway offered plenty of opportunity for speed, if he exited the freeway and attempted to lose the CHP on the many dark and lightly lit surface streets, he'd be in trouble. The choppers overhead would follow him. There was a little cover of trees on these streets; this was a desert, barren desert. The Toyota was now north of Agua Dulce. According to the news chopper pilot, speed was now as high as one hundred. The CHP was following. The choppers had him in sight. He was a dead man driving, but apparently didn't want to admit it.

The news chopper flew low and got a close angle shot. Just as the tight shot of the Toyota flashed on the screen, the driver's side tire blew out. A piece of the tire slammed against the rear quarter panel of the car, cracking the fender. The car veered right, left, back to the right and rolled over and over and over. It was still rolling when it burst into flame. Somehow, it didn't hit another vehicle. The CHP units behind the flaming Toyota stopped freeway traffic.

This pursuit was over. It ended the way it should have ended. Only the suspect was dead. I was not a bleeding heart liberal. If you steal a car and got killed in the process, you made a choice. You live with it, or you die with it. In this world, we have options. You play by the rules, or you break those rules. Eventually, if you break the rules, it'll come back to bite you. Karma with a capital *K!* I was going to miss the hell out of police work.

I was waiting for the nurse to come in to give me my pain shot. I was also waiting for Mac, who was causing me more problems, at the moment, than my injuries. I looked over at the nightstand next to my bed. There were the stapled sheets Mac had given me to read. I slid them off the night table. It was a copy of a newspaper article that read: "Injured CHP officer returns to work on 'bionic' legs." The article was an Associated Press story written by Don Thompson. It was dated September 19, 2007.

Okay, I thought, some cop was injured in an on-duty situation and returned to work running code three sitting behind a f*****g desk. That didn't have anything to do with me. Besides, I didn't want to rack up miles behind a desk. I wanted back in the field. That was in-f*****g possible! I was curious enough that I kept on reading. The CHP officer was out of West Sacramento, California.

I read the story: A California Highway Patrol officer who lost both his legs in a traffic accident last year is returning to work on "bionic legs" after proving his fitness with tests such as running the 100-yard dash in 20 seconds. "I probably still could outrun four or five guys in my office, even on these legs," Officer Mike Remmel joked on the Wednesday after demonstrating his new prostheses at the CHP training academy in West Sacramento.

"Remmel, 47, is the first double amputee ever to be cleared for field duty after passing the CHPS's 14 difficult 'critical task' tests using what officers call his *bionic legs*," said CHP spokesman Tom Marshall

Besides having to sprint the length of a football field, new cadets and veterans returning from injuries must run 550 meters in two minutes, climb a steep hill, drag weight and complete several agility tests. Remmel, spent more than a year in rehabilitation and training before passing the last test and getting his medical clearance August 10, exactly 19 months after he lost his legs. He quietly returned to work four days later. CHP brass recruited him to give a motivational talk to cadets and invited the media.

Cause of the injury: Remmel was completing a traffic accident investigation just after dusk January 10, 2006, alongside Highway 49 in the Sierra Nevada foothills near his hometown of Sonora. A confused 80-year old driver struck him at 45 mph, sending him flying 23 feet over a tow truck. He lost his left leg above the knee, his right leg below the knee. Tow truck drivers used tourniquets to keep him alive until he could be flown by helicopter to a hospital.

Three days later, Remmel came out of sedation after a near-constant series of surgeries. He almost immediately began telling the CHP officers crowding around his bed that he would one day rejoin them on patrol. "'I'm setting my goal to return to the field, to field duty'" Remmel recalls saying, 'no one believed me.'

He learned to use a $40,000 computerized leg that can gauge his stride and react accordingly – technology recently developed largely for wounded soldiers returning from Iraq. A $10,000 carbon fiber leg fills the spit-and-polish black uniform shoe on his right leg. To pass the CHP running tests, Remmel used a $30,000 pair of lighter, springier, metal legs. He ran the 100 yards in 17.2 seconds – 18.6 seconds when he's wearing his bulletproof vest and gun belt.

"'When I first starting doing this, I was falling every 10 yards or so,'" Remmel said in an interview. Now he is so fast that he is considering competing in sports events for athletes with disabilities. Remmel is two inches shorter now than his original six feet. Though he asked his prosthesis-maker to make him an extra inch taller, they opted instead for a lower center of gravity.

Using his computerized legs, Remmel played golf again for the first time since the accident and shot a better score than before the accident. In June, he kayaked five miles up a lake and then hiked the last mile to one of the prime Sierra fishing lakes where he and his buddies used to backpack before he lost his legs.

"I needed my old life to come back as much as possible," Remmel said of his internal motivation, "'I needed to know that nothing 'ended'– and so far, it hasn't.'

With 20 years in the CHP, Remmel could have retired on disability. But he said his experience as an officer helped drive his determination to put on the uniform again. "I've watched people's lives change in a moment through no fault of their own," Remmel said. "'It was just my turn." Remmel never sued the driver who hit him, although she was cited and lost her license.

"Money's fine, but I needed to feel like I was doing something with what I had after the accident," Remmel said. "To sue, you'd have to ask, what's a leg worth? And I couldn't come up with an answer."

I held the pages in my hand. My mouth was wide open in awe. My mind was also wide open. It was made up. I had a leg up, so to speak. I had only lost part of one leg. If Remmel could do it, I sure as hell could do it. The old fight was back. F**k anyone who got in my way! I checked out of the hospital Wednesday morning. Mac took the day off so she could wheel me out of the hospital.

I was scheduled for a rehab appointment Thursday morning. Mac also took Thursday off so she could be with me for my first rehab appointment. As Mac was wheeling me out of the hospital, several nurses, a few doctors, and a couple of patients I had met during my stay shook my hand and wished me well. Eight fellow officers were lined up outside the hospital entrance to see me exit the facility. One of them tied a balloon to the back of the wheelchair.

I hated that hospital. Not because of doctors or nurses or even the food. It meant a change of life and lifestyle for me. I didn't like change. Most of all, I was scared to leave the hospital. I didn't know what the future held. Mac accompanied me to the rehabilitation facility in Downey. We had a 9:45 AM appointment with Doctors Remington and Sterling. At ten o'clock, we were ushered into the office.

Mac pushed me into the office in the wheelchair, a going-away present from the hospital. The slightly deflated balloon was still attached. Dr. Remington was young, blond, tall, and adventurous looking. His thin build gave him the look of a distance runner. He was wearing a grey pinstripe suit that was complemented by French cuffs and a tie that had a picture of the three stooges on it. His cuff links were his initials.

Dr. Sterling was only about five foot nine. He had a potbelly *almost* well hidden under a solid blue three-piece suit. His hair, the little that

181

was left, was grey. His face showed his age, which I guessed to be about sixty. He looked annoyed. Dr. Remington made the introductions. Dr. Sterling stepped into the batter's box.

"We read your file." He smiled, "Then Dr. Remington and I consulted. The bad news," the doctor said slowly, "Is it's all behind you. You could live a perfectly normal life from here on out depending on your attitude and your ability to overcome what some might call a handicap. You have months of hard work ahead of you."

I thought, *You gotta' be kidding,* **what some might call a handicap?** *What do you call it, a leg up?* I probably would have made a smart ass comment, but respecting Mac, I kept my mouth shut. I really didn't want to piss her off. I wanted to get laid later. Pissing Mac off would not help my cause.

I asked, "What are my limitations giving that I'm missing a limb?"

"Actually," Dr. Remington began, "You're not missing a limb. You're missing half a limb. We can take care of that with a well-fitted prosthesis that will allow you to do everything you used to do except maybe play professional soccer. And that maybe only a few short years away. We've made terrific progress with replacement limbs in the last ten years. We'll do our job. The rest is up to you."

He sounded like one of my goddamn academy instructors. I hated her ugly ass.

Dr. Sterling looked at Mac. "Is your husband a fighter?"

Mac didn't correct him. "He can be when he wants to be. Right now, and I think it's understandable, he's still coming to grips with the totality of the situation. He's better than he was."

Mac looked at me. "I've got two good legs, and if need be, I'll put the right one-halfway up his ass."

I looked at Mac and smiled. "I think you'd have better balance if you stood on your right leg and put the left one up my butt."

Mac raised her eyebrows, "You might like that. Then I'd have something else to worry about."

Dr. Remington was amused. He said, "I see you have a sense of humor. Humor is the best medicine in our prescription pad. Keep taking heavy doses of it."

"Make no mistake, he will," Mac assured both doctors.

I had some burn sores and a couple of bullet wounds that would leave scars but nothing too telltale. I had been fortunate that I didn't have the shit burned out of me. I was also fortunate in that I didn't lose an eye or my arms. Luckiest of all was that I still had my life. The good doctors told me there was no need for me to be an in-house patient. Dr. Sterling quipped that they needed the beds for the really seriously injured patients. I liked the sound of that.

"Prosthesis comes in many shapes and sizes. Obviously, we want to find the easiest one for you to put on and take off, the one that is least restrictive, the one that is most comfortable for you. Does that make sense?" Dr. Sterling asked.

"Yeah, it does," I answered.

Mac stepped closer and took my hand. She opened her purse. Inside were pastel panties. She deliberately held the purse close so I couldn't help but notice the panties. She took out a tissue and dabbed her eyes.

"Once we select the prosthesis, we need to train you to wear it. So, once we accomplish the former, we're going to ask that you come in five days a week for a month." Dr. Seuss then said, "We'll have you working with a therapist who will see to it that you learn to use the leg properly. When you're ready, he'll take you out walking in it, then running and even driving with it. Of course, he'll teach you how to put it on and take it off and how to take care of it."

Mac said, "Look at the bright side, you won't have to trim the toenails on your left foot."

I wanted jokingly to tell her to go f**k herself. But because the doctors were sitting across from us, I didn't. I did say, "I love you too."

I felt like Campy must of felt. Here I was a cop who had physical capabilities far above that of the average individual, now I was going to learn to walk again.

"Tony, do you or your wife have any questions?" Dr. Seuss asked.

"When do we get started?"

"We can pick out the prosthesis tomorrow. We'll take measurements, make a model, then go from there. We'll need two to three weeks to accomplish the design of the prosthesis."

I joked, "Can I get a designer prosthesis?"

Dr. Sterling said, "We were thinking about one shaped like a police car."

I ignored his attempt at humor. "Can I use crutches instead of this damn wheelchair?"

"I'd prefer you to use crutches," Dr. Sterling said. "It'll keep the circulation going. It'll also get you used to standing. So, by all means do, the sooner, the better."

We said goodbye and left the same way we came in, with Mac pushing me in the wheelchair.

"If you have time, let's stop at a hospital supply house so I can get me a pair of crutches."

"Good idea. If you get ornery, I won't have to shove my foot up your rear and get it dirty. I can kick a crutch out from under you."

The best medicine for what ailed me was Mac. Her sense of humor was dry, dirty, and loveable. Her ability to "get inside me" was uncanny. Mac's devotion to my rehab process, and I realized it was going to be a process, was incredible. For the first time since the incident, I felt like I was going to survive. However, I might not survive the way I wanted to survive.

I might not return to that which I really loved, but I was going to make it. With Mac by my side, most things were possible. The biggest problem I would have would be accepting the fact that police work was behind me. Mac found a store on the way home that sold crutches. That was our next stop.

CHAPTER 17

MAC'S FREEDOM FROM ALCOHOL

Mac said, "How about we get you crutches so if you start aggravating me, I can kick them out from under you and then, depending on time, you go to an AA meeting with me?"

I was puzzled at the comment. "I don't have a drinking problem."

"I understand that. But since this relationship has gone beyond the point of pleasuring yourself in my panties, I thought you might like to see what a big part of my life is about."

Mac had a valid point. Support goes both ways. "Is anyone allowed to go to an AA meeting?"

"To open meetings yes, however, closed meetings are only for those who identify as alcoholics. The reason being, suppose I am a police officer, not just Triple A with a gun, and I attend an open AA meeting, a meeting anyone can attend. Someone who isn't in AA might see me then let everyone and their Aunt Betsy know that I am an alcoholic. Anonymity is a big thing in AA. On the other hand, everyone at a closed AA meeting *is* supposed to be an alcoholic. Make sense?"

That was as clear as stained glass. "Somewhat?"

"More the reason for you to attend a meeting with me, AA is not about drinking. We know how to drink.

"We got perfect scores in drinking 101 and in graduate drinking. We didn't know how to live. AA gives us rules for living. They're called 12 Steps and 12 Traditions. We read them at every meeting. Someone told me I was put on this earth without operating instructions. AA gives me those operating instructions, the 12 Steps."

We pulled up to the "Crutches R U" store. Before we got out of the car, I slid my hand under and up Mac's skirt. I kissed her slowly, passionately, lovingly. Mac returned the favor and played with my medium size Ben through my blue cop pants.

"That's almost as long as you're left leg."

I didn't believe she said that. "Get the f**k out of the car before I arrest you for assaulting a police officer."

Mac said, "It could be a lot worse. It could be ADW, assault with a *dead weapon*."

Mac rolled me in the hospital supply store. Hopefully, this would be the last ride in a wheelchair for me. I wondered if they'd take a trade-in, the wheelchair, which I didn't own, for a pair of crutches. Picking out a pair of crutches was easier and quicker than buying a pair of shoes. I found lightweight, adjustable, aluminum crutches that seemed to work just fine. I practiced walking with them as I would a pair of new shoes. I checked myself out in the mirror. For a warrior who had been through hell, I returned almost whole, almost.

"Let me drive home," I said to Mac as if I was a teenager asking mom for permission to drive her car.

"Are you out of your mind? Drive my car? How many meds are you on? How many legs do you have? It would take more phone books than the county has for you to reach the clutch. Weren't you listening at rehab? You'll be taught how to drive."

"I f****'n know how to drive."

"You couldn't even pass a field sobriety test. Did you take a funny pill this morning? You bring out the best in me, but with a leg and a half you ain't driving my Vette. If you shut up and stop whining like a little bitch in heat, I'll even open the door for you."

"I can open my own door, thank you." I held up one crutch to show off. I lost my balance and damn near feel to the curb.

"I'll open your door for you."

"Never mind."

"Right now, you couldn't even steal second base on a balk. Get in the car." Mac looked at her watch. "I want to make it to the AA meeting, and then you can take me to lunch. I'm starting to get hungry."

The last place I expected to end up was an Alcoholics Anonymous meeting. Yet, here I am. The room was large, with folding chairs set up against oblong tables that ran the length of the room in a large U-shape. Against the wall were additional folding chairs. There was a book at the table at most every place a person could sit.

189

There was a kitchen, which had a very large, silver coffee urn. Next to the urn were coffee cups, the large size cups, creamer and sugar, both diet sugar packets and regular sugar. People were quickly filling up the room. The attendees were clean, casually dressed, and friendly.

Most said hello to me, some even introduced themselves. This was not what I expected to see. There were a lot of young people in the room. There was even a girl...a lady who couldn't have been more than 23 with a baby in a stroller. Mac stopped to talk with several people. They asked her how she was doing.

I had no experience with alcoholics other than those I dealt with on the street. Those may not have been alcoholics at all. Just because you got popped for DUI or for drunk in public or for drunk and disorderly doesn't make you an alcoholic. I had no idea what an alcoholic was, but I suspected those worn-out men and women who slept in doorways downtown, covered with newspaper to keep them warm in the winter, were probably alcoholics. No one in my family drank heavily. Everyone in my family drank. No one in my family was an alcoholic.

Mac asked me if I wanted a cup of coffee.

"Sure."

"I'll get it. Get us a seat."

"Where do you want to sit?"

"At any one of the tables?"

I was doing well with my crutches. I felt like I was born with them. If my prosthesis worked this well, I'd be in good shape. My mind, which sometimes works in strange and mysterious ways I've been told, flashed back to an acting class I took years earlier. I was on vacation, I was bored. I read an ad on "craigslist" for an acting class run by a former star of one of those television sitcoms. I always wanted to take an acting class. I had even done some extra work while waiting to get into the academy. I signed up for the class.

Halfway through the class one night, I was talking to, flirting with, a cute, tall, lady in her twenties who said she wanted to become a cop. We were seated next to each other on the floor.

"What's stopping you?" I asked.

"I was in a motorcycle accident. I lost a leg, my right leg, from the knee down."

I laughed, "Seriously, why don't you put in applications? LAPD is looking for officers, especially female police officers."

"I told you I only have a leg and a half." She was wearing tight blue jeans and crossed and uncrossed her legs.

I watched her, both her acting and her ass. She was attractive. I was single. She walked as well as I did…as well as I used to walk. Before class ended, we continued our earlier conversation.

"In other words, you're afraid to try for the cops."

She slides the jeans up her leg. She had a prosthesis.

"I'm sorry. I thought you were screwing with me."

"Don't worry about it. You're not the first person to think I was playing."

 "You walk…..it's not noticeable."

She smiled, "I've gotten used to it."

"How long has it been?"

 "I lost the leg five years ago. I was on the back of my boyfriend's Harley. We were T-boned by a jerk that had been drinking. He ran a stop sign. My boyfriend was killed."

"I'm sorry."

"Me too, I was lucky."

Mac came with the coffee. We sat at the table.

The meeting started at 1:30. A lady probably in her fifties banged her hand on the table and announced, "My name is Anne. I'm an alcoholic."

There was a chorus of "Hi Anne," from the people in the meeting.

"I want to welcome everyone to the open afternoon meeting at the 'In Group.' If you have a problem with alcohol and/or if you have a desire to quit drinking, you're in the right place. Let's go around the room and introduce ourselves."

The introductions worked themselves around the room with everyone introducing themselves by first name and the fact that he or she was an alcoholic.

When it was Mac's turn, she stated, "I'm Mackenzee, and I'm an alcoholic."

I then said, "I'm Tony. I'm here with Mackenzee."

When the intros were done, the leader said, "At this meeting, we read a portion of Chapter 5 from the Alcoholics Anonymous Big Book. Today I have asked Bill to read a portion of chapter 5."

A gentleman in the back of the room, near the kitchen, said, "I'm Bill, and I'm an alcoholic." Bill read a portion of Chapter 5 from what they called the Big Book. "Rarely have we seen a person fail who has thoroughly followed our path.

"Those who do not recover are people who cannot or will not completely give themselves to this simple program, usually men and women who are constitutionally incapable of being honest with themselves. There are such unfortunates. They are not at fault; they seem to have been born that way. They are naturally incapable of grasping and developing a manner of living, which demands rigorous honesty.

"Their chances are less than average. There are those too who suffer from grave emotional and mental disorders, but many of them do recover if they have the capacity, to be honest. Our stories disclose in a general way, what we were like, what happened, and what we are like now.

"If you have decided you want what we have and are willing to go to any length to get it---then you are ready to take certain steps. At some of these, we balked. We thought we could find an easier, softer way. But we could not. With all the earnestness at our command, we beg of you to be fearless and thorough from the very start. Some of us have tried to hold on to our old ideas, and the result was nil until we let go absolutely.

"Remember that we deal with alcohol---cunning, baffling, powerful! Without help, it is too much for us. But there is one who has all power---that one is God. May you find Him now! Half measures availed us nothing; we stood at the turning point.

"We asked His protection and care with complete abandon. Here are the steps we took, which are suggested as a program of recovery. (1) We admitted we were powerless over alcohol-

194

--that our lives had become unmanageable. (2) Came to believe that a power greater than ourselves could restore us to sanity. (3) Decided to turn our will and our lives over to God as we understood Him. (4) Made a searching and fearless moral inventory of ourselves. (5) Admitted to God, ourselves and to another human being the exact nature of our wrongs.

(6) "Were entirely ready to have God remove all these defects of character. (7) Humbly asked Him to remove our shortcomings. (8) Made a list of all persons we had harmed and became willing to make amends to them all. (9) Made direct amends to such people wherever possible, except when to do so would injure them or others. (10) Continued to take personal inventory and when we were wrong promptly admitted it.

(11) "Sought through prayer and meditation to improve our conscious contact with God as we understood Him, praying only for knowledge of His will for us and the power to carry that out. (12) Having had a spiritual awakening as the result of these steps, we tried to carry this message to alcoholics and to practice these principles in all our affairs. Many of us exclaimed, 'What an order! I can't go through with it.' Do not be discouraged. No one among us has been able to maintain anything like perfect adherence to these principles.

 "We are not saints. The point is that we are willing to grow along spiritual lines.

"The principles we have set down are guides to progress. We claim spiritual progress rather than spiritual perfection. Our description of the alcoholic, the chapter to the agnostic, and our personal adventures before and after makes clear three pertinent ideas: (a) That we were alcoholic and could not manage our own lives. (b) That probably no human power could have relieved our alcoholism. (c) That God could and would if He were sought."

"Thanks, Bill," Anne said.

"My name is Anne, and I'm an alcoholic." "It says here, (Anne was reading from a typed sheet of paper) that I should briefly qualify, so here goes.

"I started drinking when I was thirteen. Most of my friends drank. Before I started drinking, I was getting A's and B's in school. I was a cheerleader; I was editor of the school newspaper. Life was good. Then I took a drink one night with a group of my friends, and life was even better. I wasn't overweight, and I was attracted to boys.

Better yet, boys were attracted to me. By fourteen, I was no longer a virgin. I was becoming more and more popular with the boys.

"I was popular because I *put out.* I thought it was because of my looks. My body and I came from great parents who drank occasionally. They had rules. They were loving, caring parents. We were comfortable financially. My dad had a good job. My drinking drove them crazy. By twenty, I had two DUI's and one arrest for drunk in public. It didn't stop me. What did stop me was a drunken-driving accident that injured a young, pregnant mother.

"Fortunately, no permanent injuries resulted from the accident. Of course, I was arrested for my third DUI. The judge sentenced me to 24 AA meetings and took my license for one year. The bottom line was I came to AA, got a sponsor, and worked the steps. I have been sober for almost five years. I am a teacher's aide at a local elementary school. I have my license back. I have a relationship with a great guy who is a 'normie.' And I've lost thirty-seven pounds.

"Most of all, I've found a new way to live, and I sleep very well at night. Life has its ups and downs, but drinking isn't going to make anything better. If you're new to this program, give it a shot. Come to meetings, get the Big Book and the 12 and 12, read them, and get a sponsor. Most importantly, find a God of your own understanding and let Him or Her into your life."

"Thank you. The meeting is now open for sharing," Anne said.

A heavyset gentleman sitting across from us spoke. "My name's Jack, I'm an alcoholic."

"Hello, Jack."

Jack said, "Let me share quickly what it is like for me, what happened and what it's like now. I was a doctor, actually a surgeon. I had one honor after another bestowed upon me and was living the American dream. I had a gorgeous home, a beautiful wife, great kids, three cars, a boat, a vacation home, money in the bank. I had it all, but I just couldn't stop drinking. One drink and I was off to the races.

"I got pulled over numerous times for drinking and driving. I knew the majority of our local police. I even operated on some. I was **protected,** you might say. And it almost killed me.

"I drank until my right to practice medicine was suspended. That got me to AA. Did I quit drinking? No. I believed I could handle it; that my life was not unmanageable. I was in denial. I hit a parked car driving drunk. I busted myself up. I was arrested. The judge sentenced me to six months of confinement and thirty AA meetings. My wife left me while I was in jail. It was a long, hard road back to normalcy.

"But God, AA, and these rooms brought me a peace I never thought I would find. I believed I would die drunk. I'd like to tell you my wife came back. She didn't. She's happily married and living in New York. My kids, who wouldn't talk to me for years, now visit me regularly. I have my license back and have a small family practice a few miles from here.

"I live in a small townhouse. I have one car and money in the bank. I have more today than I ever had when I was drinking. I have peace of mind. If you're one of us, if you're one of those people who can't stop drinking, if you're one of those people whose behavior is self-destructive, if you hurt like hell inside, we might have the answer for you. Here's my suggestion. Try this program for six months. If it doesn't work for you, I'll buy you your next drink. You can't catch alcoholism from us. Thanks for allowing me to share."

The sharing went on for about forty-five minutes. One of the speakers said something that made sense to me.

"If you're familiar with the Doctor's Opinion in the Big Book, our Alcoholics Anonymous Book," he explained, then you know that we have a physical allergy to alcohol; that our bodies are different from a "normy's" body.

"The doctor tells us that once we take just one drink, a phenomenon of craving sets up in our bodies, and we can't stop drinking." That made sense to me. He said, "Numerous times I had sworn off booze. But once I took one damn drink, I couldn't stop drinking. Think about that, the only remedy for us, according to the doctor, is complete abstinence."

"We have time for one short share," the leader said. "Are there any takers?" Anne asked.

"My name's David, I'm an alcoholic. "I'm five-five, is that short enough?" There was laughter.

"Let me share quickly what it was like, what happened, and what it's like now. I was just shy of my 28th birthday. I had a Master's Degree from Michigan State, along with a teaching credential. I was teaching school in Calabasas. I was about to be promoted to administration. With a partner, I had a lucrative business in Canoga Park, which we built from the ground up. Next to our business was a bar. After school, I'd drive to the business. I rarely made it past the bar (and I'm not an attorney). If you didn't get that, see me after the meeting.

"I was warned by my principal that students were complaining (and so were the parents) that they could smell alcohol coming out of my body pores. I said it was Listerine. Fast forward, I was in a coffee shop in Woodland Hills. It was after the bars closed. I was sitting at the counter. Someone tapped me on the shoulder. When I turned, I saw four LAPD officers standing behind me.

"One of them told me to stand up, which I did. He handcuffed me and searched me. There was a student of mine in that diner.

"He walked over to where I stood surrounded by cops, handcuffed and about to be stuffed into the back of a black and white for drunk and disorderly and drunk in public. I had little recollection of the event when I got out of jail later that morning. By mid-week, I had no teaching job. I lost the business to my partner. I was evicted from my apartment. My car had a "For Sale" sign on it.

"Somebody from a different AA club gave me a job digging house foundations for five dollars an hour under the table. I came to AA for me. I thought AA was a bunch of losers when actually, I was the loser. Today, I'm a winner. I attend meetings regularly. I work with others. I read the Big Book, and I let God into my life. This is not a religious program, it's a spiritual program.

"A priest once said religion is manmade, spirituality is God given. In the back of that black and white that morning, on the way to lockup, God gave me a gift of spirituality. What I give back is my gift to God. Today I write detective novels. As a matter of fact, I just published my second novel. If you'd like an autographed copy, see me after the meeting. I'm kidding. Thanks for letting me share."

The meeting closed with everyone holding hands and reciting the Lord's Prayer.

CHAPTER 18

MEMORIES REVISITED

I started to daydream. I was getting bored. I give major credit to people like Mac, who realized they had a problem and were willing to do something about it. But I didn't have a problem. AA wasn't for me.

My thoughts went to Rocky. I felt guilty as hell that I was alive, broken but alive. Rocky was dead. I'd never let go of that. I wanted, no, needed to visit Rocky. I had to go to the cemetery. Mac wanted to do lunch. After lunch, I'd ask her to drive me to see Rocky. We dined at Applebee's. Good food and affordable for a cop and Triple-A with a weapon. Triple-A, who made more each month than this cop.

"Do you have any comments about AA?" Mac asked.

"No, but I give you major kudos for turning your life around. I'd like to hear more about how the hell you did it. How you managed to get into the PD with an arrest record."

"You will. Every so often, I go to a meeting. I'm what they call the main speaker. I speak for about 45 minutes. If you'd like to hear my story, if it won't bore you like the second half of the AA meeting did, I'll invite you."

Mac was perceptive as hell. She was trained to be. She also knew me like a book. That was more than fine with me.

"I want to go to the cemetery after we eat. Is that okay with you?"

There was a lump in my throat and tears burning in my eyes. I could feel the tears. I knew Mac could see them. I wasn't embarrassed. I knew she understood.

"You gotta' get the puss out before the wound can heal," Mac said.

"This wound will never heal," I answered.

Mac added quickly, "I was taught always put *YET* at the end of a sentence. This wound hasn't healed *YET*."

That, I thought, was great when you cut yourself, you fail to get a promotion, or you don't get laid. This was life and death, in this case, death. I'd live with this for the rest of my life since I was driving that f*****g unit. I drove us right into that mess. I should have surveyed the scene before I drove into it. I relived that scenario twenty f*****g times a day. I couldn't get the scene out of my mind. It was like watching a bad f*****g movie over and over again.

I once went to a dentist. He gave me "laughing gas" before he started drilling. The gas put me under. I dreamed I did something illegal and was sentenced to two consecutive years of constant drilling of my teeth by various dentists. Finally, I awoke. This wasn't a dream. I wasn't going to wake from it.

"Do you mind if I have a drink?" I asked Mac.

"Not at all, Tony."

"Are you sure?"

"Positive."

I called over the waitress. "Hon, bring me two shots of Seagram's, please."

Mac stayed in the car. I stood over Rocky's grave. Rocky's headstone wasn't in place yet. I fell to my knees. I'm so, so sorry, Rocky. I'm so, so sorry. We were a hell of a team. I learned more from you than you'll ever know. More than that, we were friends. You were always there for me. If I could only go back, I'd change things, you know I would. It would be me instead of you; I mean that it would be. I know you're up there puffing on a damn cigarette, cruising the streets in a unit, if they even require them up there.

I know you're looking down watching over me and every other cop at APD. Do me a favor buddy, watch out for Mac too. The tears poured down my face. I waited until they subsided. I wiped away some of the tears. I stood up. I'll see you one day buddy, don't take on a permanent partner. One day I want back in that unit with you. May God rest your soul, Rocky, you sure earned it. I patted the ground under which Rocky rested in peace. See you later, friend.

THE HYPNOTIST

Mac had to work, and I had an appointment with the hypnotist to see if there was anything he could do to bring back memories of "that evening." The appointment was in a small office building less than eleven miles from my house. They sent a car to pick me up. I wasn't quite certain what they were after. Three men were dead, who APD identified as the perpetrators. The loot was gone. One suspect was at large who had been tentatively identified. I wasn't sure how I could be of help.

I was ushered into a plush but comfortable office. The colors on the wall were solid and soft. No doubt to relax the "patient." I was relaxed. The furniture was mostly couches, with deep pillows and soft cushions.

"I'm Dr. Tarnower." He offered his outstretched hand. "We met in the hospital." He fumbled for words. "It was during the early stages of your stay, you probably don't remember."

The doctor was dressed in a sports jacket, slacks, sans tie.

"I don't remember, sir. Sorry about that."

"Nothing to be sorry about." He smiled, "After what you've been through, I wouldn't be surprised if you couldn't remember your name. Please have a seat. Pick a couch, any couch," he kidded.

I looked, decided, and sat. The couch was as comfortable as it looked. I dropped my crutches in front of the couch. I was eager to get this over with.

"Let me tell you what we're going to do. What you see on television and in the movies is sometimes totally unreal and, at other times, pretty close to what's going to happen here. I'm going to try to bring you to the point of relaxation where you and I can bring to the front of your mind the facts of that evening. Often, when we go through a traumatic incident, for reasons of pain, it could be mental, physical, or both, we force the incident to the recesses of our mind, so we don't have to deal with that pain."

I was uncomfortable. I didn't want to go back to that day.

"Now that you've had time to adjust to what occurred, now that it might be a bit less traumatic, we're going to see if we can come up with any details that might not have been clear when you were interviewed in the hospital."

I nodded. "I've got it."

"There's a tape recorder, which you can't see, nor will you be able to hear. That recorder is used for multiple reasons. First, we don't want you to think we're hiding anything from you. We can replay it after we've finished the session. You can even have a copy if you like. Next, there may be some facts that the department wants to analyze. We'll supply a copy of the tape to APD, and to the FBI. Is that a 10-4 with you?"

I nodded my approval. "Wanna' sell me the couch?"

"You're not the first person to ask that question."

I looked at the walls. They were decorated with diplomas, certificates and several soft, pastel-colored paintings and prints, nothing too ornate.

"How do you feel?" he asked.

"I'm comfortable and relaxed. I'm nervous as hell." I sat back.

"We're going to get started. I want you to close your eyes and think of the one thing you really enjoy watching on television more than anything else. Think of anything but police shows. If you're a sports fan, think about your favorite team enjoying a comfortable lead, and you're sitting back with a friend or two, on a soft couch, enjoying the game. You're so relaxed, you're starting to fall asleep….."

I thought about the Dodgers, about Mac and me watching the game together. I had a bet with her. I was ahead to the point where I knew I was going to win. The bet was…..

"Think back to *that night.* You were on patrol with Rocky. Do you remember that?"

"Yes."

"Where were you?"

"We had just left the station. Rocky left something in his locker he wanted, a pack of cigarettes. We drove to the station to get it. Rocky was driving. When we walked back to the parking lot to get the unit, Rocky asked me if I'd drive for a while. He wanted to grab a smoke. He wanted to call Paula. That was fine with me since I liked to drive. This was our last shift before going to Solvang. My mind was on Mac, on her….. I made a southbound turn out of the police lot and then a westbound turn on Saturn.

"I was stopped for the light at westbound Saturn at Pan Am Boulevard. I was trying to decide which way to go. It was a calm, quiet, early evening. The usual shoppers were walking Pan Am Boulevard. Since we had several grab and run thefts on Pan Am, I decided to go north on Pan Am, go up to Almador and come back southbound. I made the turn on Pan Am. I immediately observed a vehicle engulfed in flames.

"I sped up. I remember taking deep breaths to calm myself. I stopped the car close enough to the vehicle that was burning but not too close. I wanted to get out, but my training kicked in. I surveyed the scene and noted a lot of haze. I attributed that to the burning vehicle. I smelled an odor that I thought might be pepper spray, but I pushed that thought aside.

"I decided it was okay to get out of the unit. Out of the corner of my eye, I observed Rocky on the radio. I could hear his voice but didn't actually know what he was saying. I opened the door of the unit. I stepped out of the car. I stayed behind the door for cover.

"I observed Rocky step out of the unit. I observed a man in black clothing, about five-eight or nine, holding something in his hand. He had something black over his face, probably to shield himself from the smoke and fire. Fire extinguisher registered in my mind. No, I thought, you can't fight that fire with a car fire extinguisher. Getaway before it blows up.

"I stepped out from behind the door. I noticed Rocky, who was still on the passenger side of the unit, was a few feet forward of me. I heard what I thought were firecrackers or rounds being fired. I heard an explosion. Everything went black. I awoke in the hospital."

I heard the doctor's voice. It sounded like it was off in the distance.

"I want you to recall that pleasant time you were thinking about. The fun you were having with a friend or friends. Do you have that thought with you?"

I said, "I do. The game was at the top of the ninth. The Dodgers lead was insurmountable. My bet was a sure winner."

"Good, now I want you to continue to think about that for a minute. Okay?"

"Sure." A minute later, I opened my eyes. "Well, how did I do?"

The doctor was reviewing papers inside a file folder. "Well, what?"

"How'd we do?"

"You did fine. How do you feel?"

"Relaxed."

"Good, I'm looking over notes from your hospital interview. Nothing new surfaced. In your initial interview in the hospital, you stated the outstanding suspect was taller by a few inches than you said under hypnosis. That's not all that unusual. In real life, under stress, things look bigger than they really may be. When someone points a gun at a victim and threatens to kill the person, that person and that gun look a helluva' lot larger than they really are.

"You know that from the classes you've taken. You know that from your real-life experiences on the street. I'll review the recording. APD detectives will review the recording. The FBI will go over the recording. If we have any questions, we'll call you."

Shopping for a prosthesis is not that different from shopping for a pair of shoes. In this case, I needed a leg that was durable, comfortable, and looked good. The hospital had a special department for arms, legs, hands, fingers, and toes. I was escorted through more double doors than in a maximum-security psychiatric ward. After I thought we might stop for a break, we reached our destination. Nurse Gale turned me over to Dr. Bouche and his protégé Dr. Wentworth.

We shook hands, then he said, "Let me take your crutches and go ahead and have a seat."

I handed over my crutches then sat in a straight back black chair.

Dr. Wentworth said, "We're going to find you a leg that is perfect for you. If we do our job, which we will, you'll be almost as good as new. In some aspects, you may be even be better than new. But the only way we can get the job done is to work together as a team. At times, the process may become frustrating.

"If, when that happens, ask us for a break. We'll all get a cup of coffee or in your case, maybe a soft drink, or Dr. Bouche' mentioned, maybe something a bit stronger. I have a bottle of Seagram's in my desk."

How the hell did Dr. Bouche' know I preferred Seagram's? I could only guess. That wasn't important. What was important was that I was making progress. Whatever the hell my future held, I needed a complete set of limbs to do that job. This was step one.

"Will I walk out of here…? I caught myself. "Will I leave here today with a leg that you will design for me?"

"No, most likely, we're not going to find something that fits. Occasionally that happens, but don't expect it. More likely, I will find something close that works, shape it and then send it out. There's an entire process. It could take two to six weeks. Once that is accomplished, we will have you do some exercises or rehab to get you and your prosthesis compatible with one another. We'll even get you out in Dr. Wentworth's Ferrari for practice driving."

"Funny, Dr. Bouche.' You're a much better doctor than you are a comedian, much better"

The doctors had me try on five different legs. Each leg was too long or too short, too thick or too thin, too uncomfortable, cumbersome, or all of the above. After each try, they questioned me about fit and took copious notes.

"How about a short break, Tony?"

"That's fine with me."

"Would you like a drink?" Dr. Bouche' asked.

"A cup of vanilla nut coffee would be great."

He handed me my crutches, "Let's take a walk to our Café de Style."

MY NEW LIMB

I couldn't believe how comfortable my new leg was. I could do just about everything I could do with my real leg. I took doctors on, one at a time, in a game of one on one basketball in the back of the building. I won both games. Whether they threw the game or whether

210

the fact that I was nineteen years their junior had something to do with it, didn't matter, I won. My attitude was 180 degrees from where it had been only a few short months ago.

Two things remained front and center in my mind. Rocky was a source of guilt. I imagined Rocky would always be a problem area. I couldn't ever imagine not blaming myself for his death. The second source of severe irritation was not being able to go back to my job. Some people see work as a grind, but I loved my career. It was the major slice of my life. I had to find something to replace that slice of life.

I drove Mac's Vette for my driving lessons, which wasn't a problem since I didn't use my left foot for driving. That damn Vette was one hell of a car. The second night with my new leg, which Mac named "Luigi," the three of us went dancing.

We danced to slow music, to fast music, to rock to country. No one gave me a second glance, which is surprising because I have two left legs on the dance floor. I was amazed as was Mac. I actually was a better dancer with a prosthesis.

She held me close, then said, "I commend you, you've been through the wringer. You've come out the other end." She looked down at my crotch. "As long as you keep coming, we'll both be fine."

"It is amazing, and so are you. Without you, I wouldn't have made it."

"Sure you would have, but thanks for saying that. That means a lot to me."

I pulled Mac's head back from my shoulder. I kissed her on the lips, then pulled away, saying, "I love you."

There was no hesitation, Mac kissed me back. "I love you too."

We danced until the nightclub closed.

Mac was working. I was on paid medical leave. My attitude and emotional temperature vacillated. One minute I was fine. The next minute I was suicidal. Sometimes, most of the time, I'd fight off the temptation to punch a wall or kick the bottom of a door. I had only two holes in one wall. I had the bruises on my right fist for my effort. The doctors said it would be this way for a while. They gave me a prescription to "soften" my mood when it grew seriously maudlin.

I rarely popped one of those pills. I was no more a pill taker than Mac was a drinker. *"This too shall pass,"* Mac constantly reminded me. *"This, too, shall pass."* Often when I was with Mac, I was myself, thrilled to be alive, enjoying life. I went to the cemetery three times the first week I was out of the hospital. I was a fighter, physically, and emotionally. I realized that if I learned to use the leg as if it were my own God given leg, I would be less depressed. I tried to do everything as if I had two of my own legs.

Surprisingly, most of the time, although sometimes clumsily, I succeeded. When I allowed frustration to get the better of me, Mac reminded me that, "You don't fail until you quit trying." If it weren't for Mac, my walls would have looked like the holes in Swiss cheese.

A mile and a half from my house is a gorgeous city park that boasts a football field, a beautiful fenced baseball diamond, a soccer field, a swimming pool, a meeting hall, and dirt track that ran one mile inside the park. I took my ass and my prosthesis to the park. I walked that track three days out of five. I was at the park, walking that track, at 0730 hours. It felt good physically and mentally. I had daily meditation meetings with myself as I walked the track.

Before I realized it, I was mixing walking with running. I felt like I had two legs, and in a very real sense, I did. I'd finish up walking and running at the track. I'd go home, shave and shower and call Mac. Mac was concerned about me emotionally. I could hear it in her voice and could read it in her words. Our love was growing, but I was still fighting it.

Mac gave me a copy of the book Alcoholics Anonymous which AA's fondly referred to as the Big Book. I started to read it. It discusses a spiritual way of life for alcoholics but will probably work for anyone who wants to try it. The first half of the book talks about how it works and what doctors think about the "illness" of alcoholism. I knew the second half of the book was devoted to stories, and experiences of alcoholics, how they drank, what happened to them, and how they recovered. Mac told me that most alcoholics were self-destructive before they became involved with the program.

I hadn't yet gotten to the second half of the book. Mac also gave me a copy of another book they use in AA called the "Twelve Steps and Twelve Traditions." I hadn't gotten to that book yet.

CHAPTER 19

THE CHALLENGE

Monday morning, I awoke in a piss poor mood. I put on my sweats and headed for Ronald Reagan Park. I hit the track with a vengeance and didn't bother to warm up. I started jogging at a slow pace. I talked to myself as I ran the track. "Asshole, this isn't what Rocky wants for you, and this isn't what Mac wants for you. This isn't what all your buddies at the station want for you. You have an entire life ahead of you. Quit f*****g feeling sorry for yourself. Remmel did it. You can do it. You will do it."

Then the other side of my screwed up brain argued, "But you lost your livelihood, what you loved doing. That makes you a loser." I didn't like the word loser. I was in control of my destiny. I could do whatever the hell I wanted to do, *almost*. Again, I argued with myself. Remmel did it, you can do it, and you will do it! I recalled the license plate on Mac's Vette: DCZDMND.

I ran two miles on that track. I was sweating like a f*****g addict who tried to outrun a cop. I walked two more miles to cool down. I felt like I had just shot a perfect score on the combat range when I climbed into my car. "F**k me," I said out loud, "f**k me." I'll do whatever the hell I want to do and f**k any asshole who gets in my way." I was already formulating a plan in my mind. I told myself I'll talk it over with Mac at dinner, although I already knew what Mac would tell me.

Mac would say, "If that's what you want, go for it, Adam Henry. You can do anything you want if you're willing to put forth the effort."

Mac had taken to calling me Adam Henry, police parlance for "asshole." There was a story that circulated around the station. How true it was I didn't know, but it was kinda' funny and goes like this: A police officer pulls a guy over on a traffic violation. The guy is obnoxious, calling the cop everything but a police officer. The cop issued the citation, and after the offender drives off, the officer makes the usual notes on the back of his copy of the ticket.

On the back of the citation, the cop writes, "Acting: Adam Henry." In other words, the cop wrote that the guy was acting like an asshole. In court, the guy's attorney, who was doing his job, and was good at it, asked to see the officer's copy of the ticket. The barrister knew that cops almost always made a notation on their copy of the ticket because it could be months before the case was called to court; you're bound to forget the happenings at the traffic stop. The smart ass attorney got the officer on the stand.

"Officer," the not so young attorney began. "Isn't it true that most officers make comments on the back of their copy of the traffic ticket so the officer who wrote the cite can later refer back to it?"

"That's correct, sir."

"After you cited my client for allegedly running the stop sign, did you make comments on your copy of the ticket?"

"I did counselor."

"I have that ticket in front of me, officer. Do you recall writing, 'Acting Adam Henry' on the back of the citation?"

The attorney was attempting to show the court that the officer had an attitude problem.

"I did, sir."

"Would you tell the court, in police terms, what Adam Henry actually means?"

The attorney was sure he had the cop against the ropes. The officer was about to go down for the count. Ali called this ***rope a dope***. Buying time the officer on the stand coughed, then coughed again.

"Counselor, your client was aggressive, rude, and profane when I contacted him. He continued that stance during the entire contact. I asked him to sign the ticket. I explained to him that signing the citation was not an admission of guilt; it was merely a promise to take care of the ticket. I further explained to your client that I had written his court date on the citation, that he had every right to meet me in court. That he could plead not guilty.

"Your client, counselor, told me I could go f**k a New Jersey cow. Sir, after your client pulled away from the scene, I did make a notation on the back of the copy of my ticket. I wrote, 'Acting Adam Henry,' the officer on the stand smiled. That means counselor that your client was acting **very *ANGRY and* very, very *HOSTILE*.**"

The counselor looked at the cop on the stand. He starred at him for several seconds. The attorney realized he had been swallowed, digested, and shit out. He tossed a wry smile at the wise officer.

"No further questions, Your Honor."

The asshole was found guilty of running the stop sign. Three weeks later, the same officer pulled over the attorney for speeding.

They had a pleasant conversation, and a good laugh. The officer let the barrister off with a warning. A week later, the cop received a card in the department mail. The note simply read, 'attorney is Adam Henry, *apologetic* and *happy,' Thank* you, officer.

ON A MISSION!

During the next eight months, some things changed, and some things remained the same. I gave Mac a key to my place; she gave me a key to hers. I completed all the physical therapy that my doctors' thought was necessary. I finished the psychiatric therapy required by the department. I was still on paid medical leave. I was jogging and running six miles, five days a week at the park. I was playing with the few weights I had at home regularly. I was probably in better physical shape now than I had been when I was in the police academy.

I went to the cemetery regularly, not because I felt guilty but because I wanted to *see* Rocky, I wanted to talk with him. The department shrink said that it was good therapy. Mac said she understood. Beyond that, I didn't give two shits what anyone else thought. I went to Alcoholics Anonymous meetings occasionally with Mac. I heard alcoholics say if you're restless, irritable, and discontented, you're not working the program. I sure the hell wasn't an alky, but I was sure as hell restless, irritable, and discontented. I wasn't sure why.

The AA program tells the alky if you're unsure, talk with your sponsor, the person who you select to work with you, and write about it. I opted for the latter. I sat down with a pen and paper. (1) I missed Rocky. (2) I missed police work. (3) I wanted to move forward with our relationship. (4) I was bored. The Serenity Prayer, said in many AA meetings, taught me to accept what I couldn't change, and to ask God for the courage to change the things I can. I wasn't religious by any means. I was somewhat spiritual.

I believed in a higher being or a *higher power* as some in AA referred to Him. I couldn't change the fact that Rocky was dead no more than I can change whether or not there was life on Mars. I could sit down and have a heart to heart with Mac, who I knew wanted to move the relationship to the next level, whatever that turned out to be. Going back to police work, to patrol which I loved, was out of the question; or was it? I heard in the meetings that I went to with Mac that *faith without works is dead,* meaning that I could trust in God all I wanted to trust in God, but if I didn't get off my dead ass and do something, nothing would change.

AA's says, "Do the footwork, leave the results to God." In other words, put one foot in front of the other, then step aside and get the hell out of your own way! That meant, go see the Chief. The Chief might laugh, but nothing ventured, nothing gained. And it wasn't the

Chief I suddenly decided I would make an appointment to see. It was ACOP Rolando. If anyone would bend over every which way to help me, it would be Rolando. If anyone at APD was honest with me, it would be the assistant chief. I'd run it by Mac later, but I already knew what the next indicated step was for me.

The search for the fourth man in the robbery and killing of Rocky yielded nothing more than what APD and the FBI already had. The guy had been seen, supposedly, all over our country and outside of it. In other words, he was nowhere to be found. Airlines were on the lookout for him. Interpol was on the lookout.

Newspapers and television had promoted his picture, the television show Cold Files did a sixty minutes airing of the robbery and murders. The TV drama depicted his likes, his haunts, even the fact that he was a heavy gambler. He might be in some of the posh resorts enjoying his gambling obsession. So far, all that added up to zero.

I promised Rocky, at his gravesite, that we'd get this Adam Henry and put him where he belonged, on a gurney with a needle in his arm. Austin Martin, to date, was one very lucky, very rich killer. But his luck would run out. I'd see to that.

Mac and I just finished a romp on my thickly padded white living room rug. We were soaping each other off in the shower. My back was to her as Mac rubbed soap all over my front, all over.

"Do you think I should give the assistant chief a call?"

"What have you got to lose? If you do nothing, you've gained nothing. The worst that happens is that he says no. You can always go above him to the chief and appeal his decision."

"I wouldn't do that," I said.

Mac was getting me hard from rubbing the soap in the right places.

"I have something I want you to read…later…much later. First…"

Mac rubbed the soap between my legs, then slowly under my testicles and in the crack of my butt. With one hand, she played with my butt, with the other, she stroked my cock. Life was beautiful.

"Damn, I love you, even when you're not horny," Mac said.

ACOP Rolando was only too happy to meet with me. As a matter of fact, he suggested we meet for lunch at his favorite, fattening Mexican restaurant. He had continued to visit me in the hospital. Several times a week he'd call me. We'd chat for fifteen or twenty minutes. The phone calls continued even after my discharge. The Little Chief was a good guy. He was sincere. He cared. I knew Rolando was charting my progress.

I loved Mexican food, but I was also weight-conscious. I ordered a Mexican salad, somewhat of a compromise. I ordered two-shots of Seagram's with the meal.

Rolando ordered Carne Asada. He went right to work on the chips and salsa when it arrived. I was nervous, anxious, but as Mac said, nothing ventured, nothing gained. All I could do was the footwork. The rest is completely out of my hands. The first shot of Seagram's fortified my courage. The second shot brought it to the surface. Rolando was reaching for another chip to dip into the salsa.

"Sir, I have a request."

He stopped before the chip and salsa could get to his mouth. A bit of the hot, red sauce hit the table.

"What's up?"

"I'm ready to come back to work."

He put the chip in his mouth. He looked at me, swallowed, smiled, and nodded, then said, "I thought you'd never ask."

"You mean….."

"You're going to have to pass a complete physical, a medical, and an agility test. You're going to face a psych eval. Are you up to that?"

"Shit, sir, I'll fight a f*****g bear with my arms tied behind my back if that would do the trick."

"You're also going to have a partner. I already ran it up the chain expecting you'd want to come back in. Because of the leg, and other circumstances, the Chief wants you to have a partner."

"And that would be…?" I asked.

"I'm still trying to work out those details. I'll keep you posted. Okay, here's the calendar for you. Get yourself ready for the agility test. My suggestion is that you contact LAPD and get their permission to train

221

on their turf. They have the entire academy package on-site to get raw recruits ready for the real game. You can take Mac with you and let her run just in front of you for motivation."

He laughed so hard I thought he was going to choke on his chips and salsa. "I have a game plan, but I won't give that out till you clear all the hurdles. I will start the paperwork rolling. I'll contact you when you're ready for your first test."

He took another chip from the bowl as the waitress set his carne asada in front of him.

"Are you driving?"

I nodded affirmatively.

"Hon, when you get a chance, bring my son another shot of Seagram's please, and bring me a diet coke."

All that f*****g fattening Mexican shit and diet coke, I thought.

GETTING IN SHAPE

Mac and I had a helluva' time at the LAPD Academy.

"You know what, if you run in front of me with that tight black 'thing' you're wearing, I bet I could run the marathon in under three hours."

Mac stopped running the track. She stepped off to the side. I followed her. She put her arm on my shoulder.

"You're probably in better shape than you have been in years."

We had been running three days or three nights a week, schedule permitting, for weeks.

"That goes both ways." We laughed. "Let's go play with that wall they'll make me jump over."

LAPD had the obstacle course that all candidates have to pass or they're history for the Department. The wall was cinderblock, and it was six feet tall. Women had a tough time of it because most lacked upper body strength. The name of the game was practice. Like anything else, if you wanted it badly enough and you worked at it, odds were that you would make it. Mac could go over that wall like a champion. Obviously, she had worked at it. Mac had developed the upper body strength to accomplish it.

She actually taught CHP recruits the art of getting over that wall, men and women. Brains, beauty, and a tight ass like Mac had, I was one helluva lucky guy. Contrary to what many will say who can't pass the arduous physical agility test, the departments do not want you to fail. Most departments, if you make it as far as the agility test, send you a written copy of the tests you will take. LAPD will train you to pass those tests, no matter what department you're shooting for. So, as Mac's AA would say, ***"faith without works is dead."***

I ran toward the wall. I had all but forgotten that my left leg, below the knee, was bought and paid for. When I reached the wall, I pulled up my right leg so that my toes hit the cinderblock about forty percent of the way up the wall. That momentum carried me forward until my hands hit the top of the wall.

Momentum and my upper body strength carried me to the top of the wall. My legs reached the top of the wall. I pulled myself over the wall. I hit the ground harder on my right side than on my left because I was favoring the prosthesis. I couldn't get used to landing hard on my left side. It didn't matter. To pass the damn test, all I had to do was get over the wall. I could do that with ease. I didn't want to break any bones.

We took five, ran the obstacle course, and cooled down. We called it a night. We drove back to my place. I was satisfied that any physical agility bullshit they threw at me, I could handle; that is Mac, my strength, Luigi, my new leg from the left knee down, and I could handle it.

The biggest challenge would probably be a psychological test. I still had bouts of depression. They were fewer and farther between, but I still had some major depression. Occasionally, I'd wake up in a cold, damp sweat from a nightmare of being shot and badly burned. Or I'd wake up wanting to scream to Rocky to get behind the car. I didn't know how the department shrink was going to deal with that, but I was going to take one step at a time.

"Do the footwork," Mac reminded me, "The rest is none of your business."

CHAPTER 20

A POSITIVE ATTITUDE = SUCCESS

March 13th, I drove to the LAPD Academy for the first of my tests. Mac had to work. I had no cheering section. I put my prosthesis on at the house. Physically I was all set to go. Mentally, my mind was conjuring creative ways of failing the test. As Mac had taught me, when I'm thinking too much, I'm in a bad neighborhood. Today I was not only physically in a bad neighborhood, I was stuck in heavy traffic.

As a cop working a tough, busy city, I dealt with confrontation and threats all day long. I almost always held my own. This was a lousy physical agility test that I could pass with my eyes closed. I was frightened. Could I pass it with my phony leg? I had to force myself to recite out loud what Mac had reminded me of dozens of times during my rehab; "*Do the footwork and let God do the rest*."

Normally, when LAPD is running the test, several officers will break up the group into teams of five or six depending on the number of wannabees. In this case, it was just me. I was a couple of minutes early, so I walked the track then I ran some short sprints to warm up. I was doing a few stomach crunches when a middle-aged, well built, African American man approached.

"Officer Kano?"

"Tony, sir."

"I need to see some identification, please."

His smile was warm. He was as least five foot ten and as solid as a brick fireplace. He was wearing blue gym shorts and a white tee-shirt that said, **_LAPD Academy Trainer._** I showed him my police ID and my driver's license. Kahlil White matched the ID to the license then handed both back to me.

"Let me run them back to the car."

I had parked close as we had the academy to ourselves. I ran both ways. I was as nervous as a bank robber who came out of the bank to find his getaway car gone.

"We're testing your fitness for duty today, Tony. I am here to give you all the help you need. You'll be running, climbing the wall, going over barriers, dragging the dummy, running the obstacle course, and hanging from the bar. Normally, this is a timed event. In your case, we just measure fitness for duty, so don't worry about the time. We'll deviate a bit with some of the tests. It's pass or fail. I have no doubt you'll pass. How do you feel?"

I laughed. "I'm nervous. I've been working out hard, but I'm nervous."

Trainer White nodded. "Understandable."

He put his right hand on my shoulder, reassuringly, "You'll do fine. We're both on your team. Let's do it. I want you to run and/or jog for fifteen minutes without stopping."

White nodded. I started jogging. There was no sense of burning myself out at the start of the test. My running was smooth and consistent. I barely broke a sweat.

The more I ran, the looser I felt. I inhaled, held it a few seconds then let it out. I repeated that three times. Then I said aloud, ***"God, I did the footwork, the outcome is not my business."*** I looked up at the blue sky. ***"The rest is up to you."*** I spread the palms of both hands upward and tossed it to God. ***"I'll accept your results."***

While I ran, I focused on getting back into uniform. I wanted that badly. That would cure much of my depression. I looked at my watch. I had run and jogged for about twelve minutes. I lost track of the laps I ran. I thought about Mac and our romp in my shower. I had a hard-on as I ran, probably the second-best medicine for my on and off depression.

"Well done, Tony. You're already doing better than many of our recruits. Want to hit the wall next?"

"I'd rather go over it than 'hit it;' your call, sir."

"I like your sense of humor. We need more blue suits with your guts. Ever thought of lateraling over to LAPD?"

"I'm flattered, sir. But Amity is my home. I want back in APD. I seriously want to get back to work with my family."

White nodded, "Let's get the wall behind us."

We walked over to the wall. As we walked, we talked. "How's your therapy coming?" White asked.

"I'm ready to get back to work. That's what this is all about."

"Didn't you lose part of a leg?" White asked.

"I lost the left leg from the knee down."

"You'd never know it. Not even a limp. It's amazing what science and medicine can do." Then White added, "And you're set of guts."

Officer White pointed to a thick, white chalk line. "I want you to stand behind that line. Get a running start and get over the wall. It doesn't matter how you get over the wall, just get over it."

"Got it, sir!"

I took a couple of deep breaths, focused on the top of the wall, and jogged the first few feet then ran hard. My right foot hit the wall. The rest of my body continued forward; a body in motion tends to remain in motion. I went over that wall like a champ.

"Nice job, Tony, you have no problems."

"There in my head."

"It'll clear in time. Trust me. Let me tell you a quick story. I was in my third year in the Department. I was out on patrol with an officer who had less than five years in the department. We get a call of an armed 211 at a liquor store. My partner and I are right around the

228

corner. It's raining, and it's dark. A guy wearing a ski mask comes out of that liquor store. He is casually walking east.

"My partner pulls to the curb behind him. He keeps walking. I open my door, and I'm standing behind the door for cover. Now I yell at him. Suddenly he turns and reaches for his waist. I double-tap. He goes down. He's dead before he hit the sidewalk. He was unarmed.

"I still run that around in my head. The call was an armed 211. The guy told the liquor store owner he was armed. He had his hand in his jacket as if he had the hand wrapped around a weapon.

"He had no gun. He was unarmed. The memory never goes away completely, but it fades; you learn to live with it. It goes with the badge. What people tend to forget is that we're as human as they are. We bleed red just like they do. We have a wife and kids just like they do. We laugh we cry just like they do."

White looked like he was back on patrol. I was sure his mind was replaying the shooting.

"Let's see if you can hang from the bar for three minutes." He said.

I probably could have hung from the bar all day long and part of tomorrow. I had great upper body strength, not good, great. I talked with White while I was hanging. The body drag consisted of pulling a one hundred seventy-five-pound dummy out of a car then dragging that dummy across a sandpit. The only thing I had to worry about was keeping my balance. I bent low for the drag.

I figured if I put more pressure on my right side, this would compensate for the prosthesis. This was the one test I hadn't practiced. I hadn't a damn thing to worry about. It was as easy as writing a jaywalking ticket.

We did the rest of the tests, then White said, "You passed with ease. You're better than a rookie. Nice job. I'll notify Rolando, who will handle the paperwork. Congratulations, Tony, the best to you. When you're ready for retirement, you might think about coming to LAPD. We can sure use you as a training officer."

I passed my physical agility, that was step one. I took my medical the following month and aced it. The psych test was next up in April. That bothered me. I still had scars. The physical was easier for me than the mental or psychological.

It had always been that way even when I was a kid. Now it was just magnified. The doctor was a middle-aged man who had been a cop before deciding he didn't like the streets or the lack of money. He went to school nights and worked the day shift. I had to give the man credit. Going from cop to doc must be shell shock at its finest. I guess, either way, you see a lot of blood. We sat in his office. The interview was made to appear informal. It really wasn't. He sat behind his mahogany desk in a blue suit and red tie. I sat in front of the desk. I was nervous.

"I'm Dr. Lopo. I'm here to assess your ability to go back to work and to handle yourself as you did before the shooting. Before we begin, do you have any questions about me, about the process, about anything?"

"No, sir." I shook my head.

"This session is being taped, beginning now." The good doctor said.

I guess any question about the process remained to be seen. The doctor pushed a button on a small Sony tape recorder that was on the mahogany table.

"We tape the session, so if any problem arises later, we can go back and review the session. Is that acceptable?"

As if I had a choice. If you read me my Miranda warning, at least, I could decide if I wanted an attorney before speaking with you.

"That's fine," I said dryly.

He sat up straight in his black upholstered chair. He turned off the recorder.

"Now that the formalities are off the table, let's talk a moment before we do the assessment. You and I come from the same side of the street, the dirty side. We observed the worst over and over again. Being a cop is almost a disease; it's in your blood, or it isn't. If it isn't, and you don't pull the pin early on, you'll end up going crazy, running your family into the ground, committing suicide, or you'll become an alcoholic. If it's in your blood, you're hooked, like an addict. You have to have your daily fix, or you go crazy.

"It's almost like withdrawal, I know, I've been there. It's in your blood Tony. You have to have it. To get through this, I just want you to be honest. Like I said a couple of minutes ago, there are no right or wrong answers. I'll write an evaluation of the session within several days of this test. I'll send it to the powers that be in the department.

One hundred percent of the time, my recommendation is gold. Copy that?"

"10-4, sir." I was starting to like this guy a little more.

"I want you to relax. I will not let you know my appraisal after the session. Within one week, I will send my recommendation to your Department. You will receive a pass or fail letter from me. You will not receive a copy of that report from me."

I nodded my head, indicating that I understood. I didn't like having to wait for the results, but I was told to accept that which I couldn't change. I couldn't change the department policy. He switched the recorder to on.

He got right to the point, "How do you feel about Rocky's death?"

"It's still very painful. I'm guessing in time it'll be easier to live with, but I also believe that it'll never leave me. And it shouldn't.

"Rocky and I were the closest of friends. In many ways, he was a mentor to me. What can I tell you? It hurts."

"It should, that's okay. It's part of the process." He leaned back in his chair and then asked, "Do you blame yourself for Rocky's death?"

I hesitated. I wanted to give a truthful answer. "To a degree, however, it's better than it was immediately after I woke up in the hospital and found out he was killed." I drew a deep breath, "I was driving. I drove us into that hell hole."

The doctor smiled, "I was a police officer for six years."

I nodded, "I know, I did my homework."

He grinned. "Checking up on me, huh?"

"I was just being prepared, sir."

"How are you coping with your injuries, specifically the loss of your leg?"

"I only lost half a leg, doctor policeman. It happened, I can't change it. I was feeling sorry as hell for myself in the beginning. One of my doctors gave me a book to read about Roy Campanella, the Dodger catcher paralyzed in an auto accident. Then my lady gave me an article to read about a California Highway Patrol Officer who lost both his legs in an on-duty accident. He's back on patrol, **actually back ON patrol.** That renewed my fighting spirit. If he can do it, I can do it!"

"Wow, he lost both legs, and back on patrol?"

"He lost his left leg above the knee, his right leg below the knee. He has what his colleagues call bionic legs. Incredible, huh? I'll send you a copy of the article."

"Pretty much. That's quite an accomplishment."

"It's amazing what the human spirit can do when we put our mind to it. The feeling sorry shit is behind me. I understand they'll be setbacks. But as long as most of the movement is forward, I'm in good shape."

"Supposing, the department says no to your plan."

"Honestly, I haven't thought that far ahead. One day at a time. Someone once told me life is hard by the yard but a cinch by the inch. I'll take baby steps for now. Right now, all I want to do is get past this part of my process and move on to the next step."

"I see you're not married."

"Correct."

"You've never been married?"

"Not yet. A lot of women out there like the uniform but only want to get laid. They don't want to put up with a cop full time. But I met a lady a while back, through Rocky and his wife Paula, she's the one, I know that." I turned my head to look out the picture window over the doctor's desk.

"How is she handling your ordeal?"

"She's a brick; she kicks my ass whenever it needs kicking."

"How often does it need to be kicked?"

"It gets less and less every day."

Dr. Lopo laughed, "That's good. I'm curious, what does she do for a living?"

"Mac is a California Highway Patrol Officer."

The doctor paused. He looked at me, quizzically, "Mac?"

It was my turn to laugh. "Don't sweat it. Mac is short for Mackenzee. She's all woman, trust me."

"How do you sleep at night?"

"Better and better, however, I always wake up in the middle of the night. Sometimes it's the result of a dream related to the incident, and sometimes it's because I have to pee. Every so often, it's because Mac or I want to make love."

Again Dr. Lopo laughed. "You're a refreshing interview. I appreciate your candidness. Where would you like to be three years from today?"

"I'd like to be back on patrol in Amity, married to Mac, maybe kids."

The questioning went on for half an hour. I tried to read the doctor's expression. I drew a blank. Following the last question, the good doctor nodded, and he was a good doctor. He was probably a damn good cop. "Anything you'd like to add?"

I shook my head. "I'm good."

"You are good and you're getting better every day."

"We're done here; you'll have my letter within a week."

The doctor stood up. He walked out from behind his desk. He kept in shape. He didn't let his desk job cost him physically. He put one hand on my shoulder with the other he opened the door.

"The hell with it," he said suddenly. "You've been through enough pain. My report will give you the green light. You're probably in better mental shape than I am. "Congratulation, Tony, on your success. Don't quit. I want you to promise me you'll give me a call when you're back on duty; promise?"

I shook his hand. "Thank you, doctor policeman," I said, "That's a promise."

"Maybe I'll let you take me on ride along. A big piece of me misses the streets."

Mac and I celebrated, we celebrated in style. On the hill in Granada Hills, overlooking the San Fernando Valley is the Odyssey Restaurant. I ate till it hurt. Then we went into the ballroom and danced close, remarkably close. We talked about police work, our future, police work, our future, our future.

"You know, we could save money if we move in together," Mac said out of nowhere.

I liked the idea. I loved the idea. "What makes you think I want to live with you.....in sin?" I teased.

Mac was smiling as she pressed up against me. The hardness she felt wasn't my Glock.

I looked her in the eye, "My long tongue!" I knew without looking at her that Mac was blushing.

"Let's talk about it. Whose place would we move into?"

"Like you said, let's talk about it." The music stopped, "For now, let's go home and see how hard you can get my tongue."

"Whose house are we going to?" We left.

Two weeks later, I took my medical. I was on my way to getting back into uniform. The day after I received the positive medical results in the mail, I received a call from the Chief's secretary. The Chief wanted to see me. A Chief's oral, one on one, would be the last step in my return to duty process. While I didn't have to take a polygraph test again, I guess they wanted a formal sit down with the man himself. Chief Payne was a recent hire.

He came over to APD when our Chief took a less hectic job in a small New Mexico community, near where he grew up. Payne had been an assistant chief in Long Beach for only six years. Given that he wasn't Hispanic, that two of the three finalists were Hispanic, I was surprised that he had gotten the nod from the mostly Hispanic City Council. I had not met the man as he had only formally been with us for ten weeks.

Rolando had been the acting chief in the interim. His secretary told me to have a seat. I waited less than five minutes. When the secretary walked into her bosses' office, I was in a room that was in the middle of the makeover. I held my hand out to a man who couldn't have been more than forty-five years old. He was neatly dressed in a grey suit, white shirt, and blue tie. His face was smooth, his hair black and full. He smiled broadly.

"Tony, have a seat. I apologize for the office, we're getting it ready, but that certainly takes the back burner to APD and all its crime. How are you doing?"

"Except for my nervousness, I'm doing fine, sir. It's been a hurdle, but the worst is behind me. I'm looking forward to getting back to work, sir."

The new Chief walked to his desk and sat in a folding chair. "I've spoken with Assistant Chief Rolando. He says you're doing as well as can be expected under the circumstances."

The Chief's smile was gone. He looked like he was playing poker going after a huge pot with only he and one other player left in the game.

"I'm doing fine, sir. As you probably know, I've passed the battery of tests necessary for me to get back into uniform." This time I smiled. "You're my last stop, sir."

There was still no smile. "What do you expect to do if you come back?"

This caught me off guard. "*If I* come back, sir, I want to get back into the field. I'm perfectly capable. I've passed all my tests."

His head shook from side to side. "We could probably find you a desk job. Would you like to do background investigations?"

The asshole was f*****g with me. He had to be. I didn't go through all this bullshit to sit behind a desk shuffling f*****g papers. Screw that bullshit.

"That's not why I'm here, sir. With all due respect, I passed almost all the tests a raw recruit has to pass. I'm good to go. I'm probably in better shape than most of your new hires."

"Tony, I appreciate your dedication. I more than appreciate your dedication. I admire and respect you, but you're missing half a limb."

And you're missing half a f**g brain.*** "Sir, when I walked in here, did you notice so much of a limp?"

Chief Payne was silent. He rubbed his chin. "Get up, walk to the door, then walk back."

I did. I made certain every step was deliberate, "If you didn't know, would you be able to tell me which leg was the prosthetic leg?"

Chief Payne didn't hesitate. "I don't know."

"It's the left, sir. I'm asking for a shot. I have a damn good track record with this department. I have excellent evals. I'm not asking you to give me bonus points. I'm asking for the same shot anyone would get."

"Let me talk with Assistant Chief Rolando. Tony, I give you credit for what you've done. Understand there are no guarantees in life, nor are there any guarantees here, understood?"

"Yes sir, understood." I reached into my suit jacket pocket. "Before you make a final decision, sir, please read this." I handed him a copy of the newspaper story about CHP Officer Remmel.

"I'll get back to you within forty-eight hours."

"Thank you, sir."

I was out of there faster than passengers would get into a lifeboat after their ship struck an iceberg. F**k this clown. He sure had the right last name. Mac and I discussed the events of my meeting with Chief Payne in the ass. As usual, Mac wasn't as negative as I was.

239

"First of all, he hasn't said no, yet." Mac said, "You can only do the footwork, remember? Secondly, APD isn't the only game in town. You can always become Triple-A with a gun. It'll be a pay raise for you."

We were sitting on my couch. I pinched her left tit through her bra. I was trying to find her nipple to see if it was hard.

"If that's the hardest you can pinch, you better change your workout."

She was trying to get my mind off the Chief, off APD. It was half working.

"I left him the article you gave me. Hopefully, that'll hit home with him."

"All you can do is wait and see." Mac kissed me on the mouth. "Hon, I have to get out of here. I'm working the morning watch tomorrow." Mac looked at her watch, "I've gotta' get a few hours' sleep otherwise I'll look as bad as you in the morning." She stood up. "How about I call you after work? I'll take you to dinner."

I replied, "On your pay, that should be the Beverly Hills Steak House."

"When you get back to work, that's where we'll celebrate."

I walked her to the door, kissed her goodnight, and tried my best to grind my cock between her legs.

"Nice try, sailor, come again tomorrow." She was out the door.

I poured myself a shot of Seagram's, then turned on the television, and tried to find a game show or a decent movie to watch. I got nothing but commercials. I settled for the ten o'clock news. During the commercial, I poured a second shot from the bottle. The edge was coming off. I wanted to go back to APD in the worst way. But if that wasn't to be, Mac was right; there were other departments. She always seemed to have the right answer.

Although I liked the CHP uniform, especially when Mac was in it, even better when she was out of it, I couldn't see myself patrolling California freeways. I wouldn't have long to wait. Payne promised he'd let me know within forty-eight hours. I poured one more shot, downed it, then fell asleep on the couch, thinking about my mentor and best friend, Rocky.

As promised, the Chief's secretary phoned me two days after our initial meeting. She said the Chief, the Assistant Chief, I, and a couple of other 'interested parties' would be part of the meeting.

The meeting was scheduled for 1400 hours, 2:00 o'clock the next afternoon. The meeting would be held on the second floor in the detectives' meeting room. After I thanked her and hung up, I started to analyze the situation. I had a bad habit of doing that. Mac told me to plan but quit projecting. She said projecting is getting into the results department. Planning is doing the footwork then getting out of the way so the results can be directed by someone other than me, a Higher Power. That was more AA talk. It made sense, good sense. I reasoned that if the meeting was to include other than the Chief and me, it had to be positive. A short and succinct NO would necessitate a meeting between Payne and me.

241

I changed into my gym clothes, drove to Marie Kerr Park and ran laps while I mulled over this latest development in my head. I ran fast, and I ran hard. I ran angry. I pretended I was chasing the Chief. I wanted to run his ass into the ground. If I could cause him to have a heart attack while running, I sure as hell wouldn't be the one to give him mouth to mouth. I stepped out of the shower. I started toweling off when the phone rang. I tracked my wet feet from the bathroom floor to the library phone.

"Hello." It was Mac.

"What did you do?"

"I love you too, Triple-A. What do you mean what did I do?'"

"Are your ears gone, too? Why am I part of the meeting with your Chief tomorrow?"

MY FUTURE TO BE DECIDED

We drove eastbound on the 210 freeway to the 2 freeway. I was worried about the meeting and why the hell Mac had been invited. Actually, Mac and her boss had been invited. That made absolutely no sense to me. It made even less sense to Mac. Mac was having fun with it. She was a bit more rambunctious than usual. At one fifteen in the afternoon, there is light traffic on the 2 freeway, which would bring us back to the southbound 5 Freeway and eventually to the surface street exit finally to APD.

"You need to loosen up," Mac said.

"How the hell can I loosen up? My future may well hang on this meeting."

"And as tight as you are, you'll go off like a teenager during his first lovemaking session if you don't lighten up. Whatever the decision is, it's already been made. So, all your worrying in the world isn't going to change anything."

Mac was right again!

"I would say that you're correct about at least one thing. If the decision wasn't in your favor, we all wouldn't be coming together for the meeting."

I loved the way Mac chose her words before she spoke. "Okay, okay. There's a bottle of Seagram's in the glove compartment, get it for me."

I saw the expression on Mac's face turn to a look of horror. She opened the glove box. Then quickly slammed it shut.

"Gotcha."

"You'll pay for that."

"I'm sure I will."

Mac looked behind us. I had no idea what she was looking for.

"I don't think we're being followed," I said.

"Lucky for you." She slid close, undid my zipper, pulled peter out of his hiding place. Mac played slide the sausage while I drove, or tried to drive."

243

I was relaxed when I pulled into the Station's back lot. It was meeting time at the zoo. Mac and I were ushered into the detectives' meeting room.

The oblong mahogany desks were polished to the point of blinding you if the sun hit the desks just right. That was most likely the reason the shades were drawn. We were escorted to our proper place at the table.

The Chief was the first to break the silence, "Let me make the introductions because I'm not certain we all know each other."

The Chief was seated at the head of the table; of course, he had to show his absolute authority. He was also the only one in the room with a nameplate in front of him.

"On my left is CHP Commander Terry Wright. To his left is FBI Agent Michael Sullivan. On Agent Sullivan's left is our own, Detective Julio Jimenez. On the left of Detective Jimenez is Alice Landers, my secretary. Alice will be taking notes in case we want to refer back to something later. On the other side of the table is Dee Mackenzee from the CHP, sitting on Dee Mackenzee's left is our guest of honor, Tony Kano. Finally, on my immediate right is my assistant, Assistant Chief Lee Rolando."

We acknowledged each other. I was certain Mac and I were the ones left in the dark.

 "If anyone wants coffee or soft drinks, the cornerback of the room is your refreshments, help yourself. The reason for this meeting is as follows. You have all now met Officer Kano. I'm sure you all know

Tony lost part of his left leg in a robbery. His partner was killed. Three of the four perpetrators were killed. Aston Martin escaped, however, more about the outstanding suspect later."

The Chief shuffled some papers that were in a folder on the desk in front of him.

"Officer Kano has asked me if he can come back to work, back on patrol. I told Officer Kano I would give him an answer within forty-eight hours. We're here today for that reason. So, let me cut to the chase. We will take Officer Kano back on a sort of probationary period. We want to see how he handles himself, physically and mentally, over the next six to nine months.

"After that, we will reconvene to see whether Officer Kano is fully reinstated, or we put the matter to rest in another manner. So, Officer Kano, congratulations on making the grade, on passing all your arduous tests, on once again being part of the Amity Police Department team."

I looked at Mac and smiled. The smile was tentative. There was more to this, that's why this room had other members added to the meeting. I wasn't sucking on a Kojack's lollipop. I wasn't stupid. The Chief had an ace up his sleeve.

"Next order of business is why we have an FBI representative present, a CHP Commander present, a CHP Officer present and our own detective representative. Here's the answer. After consulting with *all* and I mean all of Officer Kano's doctors, it was decided to phase him back into his initial role of patrol gradually. It was also decided that he have a partner. Here is the bottom line. Officer Kano, it is up to you to accept or reject this proposal.

"But understand, before I spell it out, this is your one and only chance to come back to this department whole, so to speak. And by the way, a game-changer for me was an article Officer Kano gave me. It was a newspaper account of a CHP Officer who lost his legs in an on-duty accident. He is now back, in uniform, and on full patrol."

Payne changed from formal to informal address. He referred to me as "Tony." I didn't know whether or not I liked that. But for now, I had won a victory.

"Tony, we want you to become part of the investigation team to track down the perp who got away; Rocky's killer. We don't want you working alone for various reasons, which I don't want to delve into here publicly. CHP Officer Mackenzee and you will be working as a team. If you accept, following this meeting, you will be briefed on your specific duties and our expectations. You'll be given reports to study; you'll be briefed on our latest intelligence."

Chief Payne smiled. "We are in no hurry for an answer. So, let's take a ninety-minute break. Feel free to help yourself to a beverage or feel free to grab a bite to eat away from the Station. Payne looked at his watch. Let's reconvene at 1615 hours."

 Mac and I were too mystified to eat. *Shock* would be the more appropriate word. There was no discussion in my mind whether or not I would accept the offer, the assignment. Of course I would. I wanted Rocky's cold-blooded murderer more than I wanted my left leg. Catching that asshole would compensate me for the loss of half a limb. I was Italian, Wops were known for making good deals. A killer for a piece of the leg was a good deal to this Italian! The question was, would Mac accept the deal. The look on her face left no room for debate.

CHAPTER 21

BACK TO WORK - INVESTIGATION BEGINS

Rather than eat, we took a walk in the City of Amity. We walked hand in hand. Mac was all smiles, my blue-eyed blonde beamed with joy.

"Ever had sex in a police car?" Mac asked.

I had, on more than one occasion. Women liked men in uniform, especially when they wanted to get out of something. And if a cute gal wanted out of something, it usually meant we could get into something. She'd get out of her clothes, and I get into her pants. So, the answer was yes. In the front seat, back seat, with a cage, without a cage, on the hood, roof, maybe even in the trunk, I thought silently.

Then I responded, "Didn't you ask me that a long time ago?"

"Stop before you kill me," Mac said. "I want to see if I get the same answer again. How many times have you asked a suspect his DOB twice?"

"Nope, I would never do that; have sex in the unit," I lied. "But I suspect you'll change that."

I turned us around. We walked back to the PD. We entered the back parking, looked through the gate, and took an immediate left turn. There were probably one hundred vehicles parked in APD's securely gated parking structure. It boasted cameras 24/7.

Some of the cars in the lot were private cars, some were black and whites, some were unmarked detective units. Mac looked at me. There was beyond mischief in those baby blues.

"I know your balls are big, but are they big enough?" Mac asked me.

We walked to the rear of the structure. I had observed the workings of the cameras from dispatch. I knew they scanned the lot, the entire lot. But this was too exciting, too tempting, and too dangerous to not do. Besides, I was rock hard.

"My balls are big enough. The question is, are your panties wet enough?"

"They're soaked, trust me. If they get any wetter, I'd think I peed myself."

I was looking for a particular unit. Mac's badge number was 96. We had a unit 96. It was sitting in the very last parking space in the very back of the lot. I had a master key to the units on my house key chain. I opened the door. The front seat was going to be difficult with my prosthesis and the f*****g humungous computer. But the back seat would work. This had been a sergeant's car, there was no cage. The rear seat was cloth, not plastic.

I helped Mac onto the back seat. As a kid, I had been "arrested" for throwing snowballs off an overpass at passing cars. It was more like

249

the small-town police wanted to teach this twelve-year-old a lesson. I wasn't handcuffed, but I was put in the back of a police unit. It was uncomfortable, and it scared me, not to mention the belt spanking I got from my father after he picked me up at the police station. Being in the back seat with Mac, on the other hand, was rejuvenating, relaxing, refreshing, and exciting, all at the same time.

She put her feet and her thighs over my back. She slid her yellow panties off, shoved them under my nose and made me sniff them for forty-five seconds then told me to lick them clean. Of course, without the benefit of an attorney and being a cooperative suspect, I did as I was told. She pulled them away from my eager nose then thrust the panties between my legs.

I was in police custody heaven. The main course was better than having your criminal case overturned on a technically. There was no denying this motion, and there was plenty of motion. I could feel the car rocking. I didn't think we'd ever stop. With her legs still over my shoulder, Mac grabbed my neck with both hands. She hung on tight, very tight.

"I'm coming; I'm coming, come with me," Mac said. I did, and we held each other for a long time, a very long time. "I love you; I really, really love you."

"I love you too. As crazy as you are….and that may be why I love you so much, *partner,*" I said.

Mac stuffed her damp panties in my underwear, the case was closed, the file was stamped*: SUBJECT IN CUSTODY!*

We reconvened our meeting in the detectives' meeting room. This time the meeting consisted of the Chief, CHP Commander, APD Detective Jimenez, Chief's secretary, Mac, and me. The Chief was at the head of the table. We all took seats, made a few pleasantries, and waited for the Chief to call the meeting to order. We didn't have long to wait.

"I hope everyone had a healthy lunch?"

I nodded and looked at Mac. I desperately wanted to tell the Chief that we dined at a new restaurant called the **Back-Seat Lounge**.

Second thought, sanity kicked in. I was on a winning streak. I had no reason, no desire to change that.

"Okay then, let's get going. CHP Officer Makenzee, have you decided? Tony, have you made a decision?"

I spoke up. "We accept the terms of the deal, sir. We appreciate the opportunity. I thank you for the chance to return to duty." I then added, "If everything goes well."

"CHP Officer Mac, are you're good with that?"

"Very good with that, sir, I think Officer Kano.....did I pronounce that correctly, Tony?"

I bit my lower lip to keep from laughing. Everyone in the f*****g room had to be aware of what was going on between Mac and me. Neither of us tried to keep it a secret.

"Yes, you pronounced it right." I looked at her blouse, "You have what appears to be a piece of lunch on your shirt."

This time it was Mac's turn to suppress a laugh. "Sir, I do have a question. I realize Officer Kano, and I are partners. Which one of us is the senior partner?"

Everyone in the room chuckled. The Chief hesitated. Mac's comment caught him off guard. It caught me off guard, too. I think the Chief was trying to figure out if Mac was serious or joshing. I was also trying to figure that out. The Chief rubbed his chin, which was starting to show a hint of a beard.

"Since you both bring a different slant of knowledge to this special investigation, I'll leave that up to you. And by the way, this investigation is code-named *GOTCHA.* If there are no further questions, this meeting is adjourned. Tony, tomorrow at 0800 hours, you and your partner will meet with Agent Sullivan and Detective Jimenez next door in the briefing room. Agent Sullivan and Jimenez will be reviewing files with you, lots, and lots of files.

"Before you leave, I want to wish you the best of luck. This case needs to be cleared. It would be great if this team could clear the case. I know Tony, no one wants that more than you. And I know Rocky will be assisting you from on high. The best. Now get out of here. Let's get some police work done."

The Chief really did have a heart. In the morning, we met in another detectives' briefing room. The room was neat, comfortable, boasted oblong tables, television and VCR, and several chalkboards. The walls were decorated with pictures of teams that had "mugged" in the annual Baker to

Vegas run. There were group pictures of the APD officers, the sergeants, the lieutenants, the assistant chief, and the chief.

There was a picture of President Obama with a crudely drawn mustache. There was a picture of Governor Brown with a sidebar that read: "***Once wasn't enough, when will we ever learn!***" Someone drew a black "X" over the exclamation point and corrected the punctuation by adding a question mark. Detective Jimenez and Agent Sullivan stood at the head of the table, looking over a dozen boxes and talking softly.

Jimenez, who stood no more than five feet ten inches tall, looked like he had a few beers too many for his forty-two years. He had more grey hair then he should have had at that age; that hair was thinning.

He wore blue jeans and a grey sports jacket over a polo shirt. Jimenez was not a candidate for GQ. Agent Sullivan was cool, calm, and conceited. He was natty in a five-hundred-dollar double-breasted blue pinstripe suit with solid grey tie knotted into a white on white French cuffed shirt. This man ***could have*** graced the cover of GQ. He must have worked a lot of overtime. In the back corner of the room was a coffee pot, a very large coffee pot with milk, flavored creamers, and sugar sitting next to it.

There were eight boxes of assorted donuts, fruit, celery sticks, and dip and a box of Lipton® tea bags. There was a pitcher with chilled orange juice. The only thing missing was New York steak and eggs. This was going to be fun.

"Okay," Agent Sullivan shouted, "Ladies and gentlemen, let's take a seat so we can get started. This is going to be a long day. We'll take breaks as needed and, of course, will break for lunch or we can all go to lunch together. We'll decide that later. For now, Detective Jimenez is going to brief you on file one, which is deceased suspect number one. We're going to do what we call a matching box score on the large chalkboard to my right.

"Eventually, we will have the names of all three dead perps on the board. We're looking for any commonalities. Once that's done, we'll go to Austin Martin. We'll list all his particulars, which would be things like where he served time, phone calls in and out, people who visited him in prison, who he wrote letters to, hangouts pre-prison, and post-prison. You get the idea. Like throwing a pebble into the water, our list will branch out.

"What we're looking for are names that show up on the board in common. We're convinced Martin is now in the U.S. We want him, and we want the money he stole.

"So, we would like him taken alive because, without Martin's help, we may never find the money. Any questions?"

Detective Jimenez wrote the name Jose Sandino on the chalkboard in large letters, then Jimenez drew a line under the name.

"I'm going to list for us, key characteristics, *and signature factors* or things that would or could link Sandino to Martin. After I've done that, we're going to each take a file and do the same on the board. When that's done, I'll give you the next step."

It took just over two and a half hours to list the characteristics of each subject. When this was accomplished, we were told to look for commonalities between each of the three deceased subjects, and the outstanding suspect Austin Martin. We came up with the following: All did time at San Quentin. Jack Lackey and Austin Martin were cellmates at one time. Morris Moffatt blew up bombs in the army, as did Martin. All four men had criminal records. All four served felony time. Each of the four lived, at one time, within thirty miles of Amity. Jack Lackey and Austin Martin had the same visitor at Q: Mary Duncan.

Agent Sullivan said, "Put an asterisk next to the name Mary Duncan. The latest intelligence says Mary, Mary, who might be very contrary, is still in the southern California area. We have yet to interview little Miss Mary."

Jimenez told us, "We have her under *sometimes* surveillance. We don't have the manpower." Jimenez looked at Mac. "We don't have the people power to keep a tight leash on Mary, at least not as tight as we'd like. Somehow, someway, we are convinced that there is a pipeline to Martin. We believe if we can find that pipeline, we can probably find Martin.

"The money is a different story. We'll talk more about that later. As you heard earlier, we have more sightings of Martin than we've had Elvis sightings. Some appear valid; others, who knows. We've had calls putting Martin out of the country. A couple of these are credible. We know for a fact he's been in Thailand at least half a dozen times over the last couple of years. Whether that was to set up an account for the stolen cash or he likes it there, we don't know, *YET*. We will be checking out each and every lead. And notice I said *WE*.

"We know he had a ***height thing***; he is short, probably about five foot seven or so. He wore shoes or boots with built-up heels to make him appear taller. Item number seven and this gets interesting. Jack Lackey and Martin, the cellmates at Q, the odd couple, were gay. Whether this was just a prison romance or Martin liked backing into Jack's bean stalk, is anyone's guess. If they are faggots, so be it. I mention it because if Martin likes to smoke other men's cigars, we might be able to get a lead on him in a gay hangout.

"Martin has a lengthy record, which goes back to his days as a juvenile. He was busted for everything from GTA to burglary, from petty theft to passing bad checks, from fraud to forgery. This was a major step up into the big leagues for Martin."

I asked Jimenez, "Was Martin pitching or catching?" That drew laughter from everyone but Agent Sullivan.

"In prison, I don't think that matters. What matters is that you're playing the game. But Martin was a rather short individual…..

"Are we talking stature or sausage size?" Mac punched me playfully in the arm.

Jimenez ignored my crude remark. "It's possible, Lackey, who is about six feet tall, forced Martin to comply. Either way, I mention it only because it may be a lead that we can follow up on later. We also have a list of friends and relatives of the deceased and of Martin, who lived in and out of the area. Most have been contacted, we came up empty. We might re-contact later.

"Of note, Martin had a big, loud mouth. He had been picked up twice for 415 fights. He liked to run his mouth but wasn't big enough to back it up. He also may have long hair and a beard. You'll see that in mug shots, but he could have cut both the beard and hair. In the folders you'll review is a wealth of information.

"Some of it may be useful. Some of it is just in the file. Some of it is bullshit. We're going to take a short break, and then we'll reconvene and continue to build our documentation. Are there any questions?"

Okay." Detective Jimenez checked his watch. "Let's get back in here in twenty minutes, please."

When we finally wrapped up for the night, and it was just after eleven o'clock, we knew the following: There were credible sightings, over three years, before and after the robbery and murder of Rocky, of Martin in England, in Thailand and in Italy. How the hell someone of his lack of means had the money to do that left us a lot of unanswered questions unless, of course, he was already spending the stolen cash.

On at least one of those occasions, Jack Lackey accompanied Martin to Thailand. We had the airline confirmation of this. Why had Mary Duncan visited both Jack and Martin in prison? Was there a connection? If so, what was it?

Agent Sullivan explained to us that a Palmdale home was burglarized six months earlier. The burglar(s) started a fire possibly to cover up the break-in. The fire was quickly put out by the homeowner. The house was dusted for prints, and those prints were submitted to the FBI lab for identification. One print lifted from the Palmdale house came back to Austin Martin.

257

Was he part of a residential burglary? With all the stolen money, why would he risk burglarizing a home? Was he a visitor/guest in that home at some time? What was his connection to that home? Why the hell had Martin fallen off the radar? Where the hell was he? Was he out of the country? Where was the money, which seemed to be Agent Sullivan's main concern? Of major concern was Martin's gambling "addiction." Could he have gambled the money away?

Did the Jack, Martin "connection" help us in any way, and if so, how? If someone(s) was assisting Martin, who was it? Our mission was now going to be to follow up on the various leads. At 0930 hours the following morning, we'd have a follow-up meeting. At tomorrow's meeting, we'd answer questions, we'd decide on who would do what, to further the investigation, and what our timeline would be.

Mac and I spent the night at my place. I was hornier than hell, but more than that, I wanted to make slow, sweet love to the woman I loved. Instead, we fell asleep in each other's arms. Waking up next to Mac was almost as good as having two complete limbs. We showered, ate breakfast, then headed to the Station. I was looking forward to getting all the foreplay behind us. I wanted to get this investigation underway. I wanted that prick almost as badly as I wanted to make love to Mac again in a police car.

Agent Sullivan stood at a podium in the Detectives' briefing room. God knows where he found the podium because the only one we had suddenly disappeared.

It was decided by the masses that the podium made briefing too formal. It was less formal, the troops were less afraid of asking questions, when everyone sat at the same level. Tough, big bad cops intimidated by a podium. Figure that one out. We were all seated together, Jimenez on my right and Mac on my left.

"Let's get started," Sullivan's said.

Sullivan had on a solid blue suit jacket; it was buttoned in the middle. His tie was pale blue, his shirt was white. You had to hand it to the man. He dressed with class. Then again, his paycheck was probably fatter than Tommy Lasorda's (sorry Tommy).

"I want to make one thing perfectly clear from out the gate." Sullivan stared at me, and I felt my face flush, "We want Martin alive."

Now my face flushed until I felt it turning red. I'd rather the asshole be killed on contact. No trial; no chance a smart attorney could get him a light sentence or even get him off on a technicality. My way was clean, fast, final, and permanent, and it saved the taxpayers money. Nobody would have to relive the ugly events at a drawn-out trial.

"Are we clear on that?" Sullivan was still staring at me.

The asshole didn't even blink. Mac must have felt me starting to boil. She could see what was going on. Her hand was on my thigh. She reached down putting her other hand over mine.

"Are you talking at me, sir?"

"Your damn right, I'm talking *at you, right at you.* Let's be clear about something, Cannoli..."

I jumped in and spat at Sullivan, "My friends call me Cannoli, sir. You can call me Officer Kano." You could hear a handcuff key fall to the floor.

Sullivan replied, "I was dead set against this from the beginning. I was outvoted. The way I figure it, you've got a vendetta. You've got a score to settle. You're too close to this investigation to be part of it. But since I was outvoted by your buddies, I'll live with it. But so help me, if you screw things up you'll pay dearly, so help me."

Mac took her hand off mine. I'm sure she felt the tension in my body. Like the beginning of an earthquake's rumble, I felt my body shake. Then I exploded. "Listen, Kojack, I have a great big red lollipop you can suck on for starters. And…"

He unbuttoned his fancy suit jacket as if he might be getting ready to fight.

"You listen to me….." Sullivan grabbed a gavel that was on the podium. For a second, I thought he might throw it at me. I didn't give him a chance.

"Shut the f**k up asshole until I'm finished. Unless you'd rather take this out to the parking lot and I'll shove my right foot up your ass until you choke on it. But something tells me you might like the feel of something big and thick going up your ass." I took a deep breath. I was enjoying the shit out of this. "I'm a f*****g professional just like you, Mr. FBI agent. I know my job, and I know how to get it done. Nobody, nobody in this f*****g room, is out for anything but justice. Is that f*****g clear to you?

"So let me make one thing perfectly clear to you, asshole. Keep your professionalism, and I'll keep mine. Step over the line with me, and I'll beat your well-dressed ass into next summer. Now shut the f**k up, and let's get back on task or lets you and I take a walk. When this is over, you and I have a date in the back-parking lot. Is that clear?"

Mr. FBI said, "I wouldn't call it a date; lollipops are not my thing, but I'll be happy to kick your ass in the parking lot."

A few seconds later, Sullivan and I finished playing verbal tennis. We finally got back to work.

"We have two major areas that need further examination. We want to know why Mary Duncan visited both Lackey and Martin in prison. What is the connection? And how are they connected? But, in my opinion, (and your opinion, I thought, is worth a big bucket of chocolate ice cream) our biggest bet is the burglarizing of Myra Williams' house in Palmdale.

"Is it possible he hid the money in the house? Is it possible he and the Williams woman are in some way connected? Is he somehow connected to the house? Does he know anyone in the Palmdale area, or was it a random burglary? If so, and Martin was the perp, what happened to all that money?

"That Kano, should be your starting point. You and CHP Officer Mackenzee should make that priority one. Are we agreed on that?" Sullivan's tone softened.

I nodded.

"Agreed," Mac said, answering for both of us.

261

We revisited several other possible leads. We discussed other interesting facets of the case. Sullivan did a quick review then opened the floor to questions. There were none.

"Kano, you and Mackenzee will report directly to me. Got it?" Sullivan didn't wait for a response. "Detective Jimenez will assist in any department matters. He won't be assigned full time as you two are. Finally, without Martin alive, finding that money is going to be a real pain in the butt. We're done. Let's go to work."

I had a few words for Agent **Sully**. I wasn't done with him yet. I got up and started toward him. Mac grabbed my arm, twisted it behind my back. She whispered in the vicinity of my ear. "Get your red lollipop out of here now, or you'll never again feel my lips licking your candy."

I had mixed emotions about that. That was like watching your hated mother-in-law drive over a cliff in your brand-new Corvette. I grudgingly accompanied Mac out of the room. But first, I managed to toss a comment to Sullivan before I entered the hallway. "Better go to the gym and start training, Kojack. You're going to need to be in better shape to take me on. I'm undefeated."

Mac and I grabbed a couple of files, found an unoccupied room with a telephone and a computer; we went to work. I read up on Mary Duncan while Mac searched for her present address. She didn't have to search for long. She came up with Ms. Duncan's present address. It was a cemetery in Downey, California. She had died in a freeway accident four months earlier.

262

We then went to the Amity City Library adjacent to APD and City Hall. We searched newspapers on their scanner machine. We located the obit for Mary.

We wrote down a few names of relatives then went back to the Station to locate current addresses. Contrary to what you see on television unless you have the absolute latest technology, this work can be long, boring, tiring, and tedious. Ninety minutes later we had a list of three of Mary's relatives who lived within driving distance of APD. We grabbed a bite then drove toward what we hoped would be relative number one. The door was answered by a tall, heavyset black woman dressed in gold slacks and a white t-shirt that clearly showed the outline of her boobs and a bit of her lunch, which stained the white T.

"Ms. Crosley?"

"Yes, I'm Ms. Crosley."

"I'm Investigator Mackenzee, this is Investigator Kano." We flashed our credentials. "We'd like to ask you a few questions about Mary Duncan."

Ms. Crosley stepped outside. She pulled the door closed, then stepped away from the door. "Mary's been gone for months now. What can I do to help you?"

She came off sincere and friendly. "Does the name Jack Lackey mean anything to you?"

Ms. Crosley thought for a moment then shook her head. "No, I don't think so."

Mac showed her a picture.

"No, I'm certain I've never seen him or even heard the name."

"Have you heard the name, Austin Martin?" Mac asked, "Does that name ring a bell?"

Again, the big boobed Black woman thought for several seconds. "No, I haven't heard that name either."

Mac showed her a picture of a black-bearded Austin Martin with long black hair. "Also, try to picture him without the beard and long hair."

"He came over here once with Mary," she said. "I think he said his name was Todd. Yes, Todd. No last name, just Todd. Yes, you can't easily forget that look."

"What was the relationship between the two of them?"

Ms. Crosley laughed. Her boobs bounced. "It sure wasn't sexual, that's for sure."

"Why do you say that?" Mac asked.

"It's because they both preferred the same sex. Mary, God rest her soul, was a lezzy. Todd or Austin, which is what you said his real name is was as queer as a three-dollar bill."

"Did Mary ever talk about Martin?"

Ms. Crosley pulled at her left ear lobe. "Not that I can recall, however, he did telephone a couple of times. But that's because occasionally they'd go to a gay club together."

"Do you know the name of that club?"

She stiffened. "Do I look like I play that way?"

Mac was quick to respond. "Not at all, I thought you may have overheard something….."

"No. Was Mary involved with something she shouldn't have been involved in?"

"No, ma'am, we're trying to track down Martin."

"Did Martin do something wrong?"

Obviously, Ms. Crosley hadn't read a newspaper, or she was lying.

"No," Mac responded. "He came into some money, and we're trying to help locate him, so he can get what's rightfully coming to him, it's that simple. I'm going to leave you my card. If you think of anything else that may help us find Austin or if you hear from him, please give us a call. They'll probably be a reward in it for you."

Ms. Crosley took the card. She went inside the tiny house. Mac and I looked at each other, digested the little we had learned, turned, walked back to our unmarked unit, hopefully for greener pastures. The grass isn't always greener on the other side of town. We struck out at the next two houses. I was disappointed, but that's what I had expected. We weren't really surprised that we had struck out.

If these distant relatives did know anything about Martin, they were keeping hush. I doubted they did know anything. My interest was in Myra Williams and her house. It was curious as to why Martin's fingerprints would be found in her house. Why would Martin break-in? Assuming he did burglarize the place, what was he after? And then, why the hell try to cover it up with fire?

We had a case several years ago where a drug dealer and user burglarized a house. He got caught in the burglary when the homeowner unexpectedly walked in on him. He belted the homeowner, tied him up with some rope he found, finished emptying the house of electronics and jewelry. He then made himself a f*****g ham sandwich with fixings he found in the refrigerator, then set the house on fire. The tied-up homeowner burned to death.

As horrible as this was, the suspect didn't want anyone around to identify him and thought he would cover up signs of burglary, such as pry marks on the door, by burning the place to the ground. It didn't work, the house did burn. It burned enough to kill the homeowner; smoke inhalation. The house didn't burn to the ground. Detectives found the asshole's fingerprints all over the refrigerator door.

When picked up and questioned, asshole denied ever being in that house or close to it. ***Then why were your prints found in the house, dummy?*** Asshole got himself a smart public defender who evidently suggested that he ***plead out. They took a deal offered by the district attorney. Asshole went away*** for twenty-five years to life.

In this case, as stupid as it was to break into the home, steal shit, tie the homeowner up and burn the place to the ground, it made sense from the perps' point of view. What didn't make sense was why Martin was in that house. Mac and I conferred on our next step over a cup of coffee. We agreed before visiting Ms. Williams we'd first talk with the fire department inspector who determined that the cause of the fire was arson.

We'd also want to talk with the sheriff who investigated the burglary and fire, and who wrote the report. We also wanted to meet with the fingerprint expert who dusted for prints. The earliest any of this could be done was the next day.

We went home to romp around between the sheets, on the carpeted living room floor, in the kitchen, and in the shower. Isn't love **GREAT?** On Tuesday, we had two appointments. The first appointment was in the morning, and it was with the battalion investigator who had been part of the investigation of the house break-in at Myra Williams' house out in Palmdale. Palmdale is a middle-class desert community about an hour north of Los Angeles.

It's well known for its poppy fields and its drug dealing. It also has its share of gang problems. Many people who work in the San Fernando Valley and Los Angeles move to Palmdale for the inexpensive housing. Their daily commute can be a nightmare of traffic on the 14 Freeway, which is the only main artery to the Valley and to L.A. short of taking a helicopter. The second appointment was with two of the investigators from the Sheriff's Department, who handled the investigation at Williams' residence.

How and why Martin's fingerprints ended up in Williams' house was eating away at me. The only time I wasn't trying to make sense of that was when I was making love to Mac or thinking of ways I could f**k over Agent Sullivan. The latter came to me in the middle of the night. Sullivan let it be known more than once that he was homophobic.

Aside from the fact that he was an egotistical idiot and full of himself, he had a thing for gays, which was his Achilles heel. Mac and I drove in relative silence to our first appointment.

The silence was broken by me when I took my eyes off the road long enough to ask Mac, "Why do you think Martin's prints were found in the William's house? What do you think he was doing in that house?"

Mac was sitting in the passenger seat, filing her nails. "Good question. It makes no sense that he'd commit a burglary unless that money is tucked away somewhere, and he can't get to it. It's possible, with all those trips made out of the country, that the loot is in an offshore account and he doesn't have the cash to fly out of the country? I don't know; it's as mysterious as that missing Malaysian plane."

"I'm sure wreckage of that jet will be found long before Martin is. But we're going to get Martin. I promised Rocky we'd get the asshole, and I don't make promises I don't intend to keep."

I pulled into a parking space across from Palmdale Fire Station 69, and we walked across the middle of the street. The badge has its privileges. The County investigator was younger than I would have expected. He was tall, thick around the shoulders, and thin at the waist. He kept in shape. He was smiling broadly when we entered.

"You've gotta' be from Amity PD?" He looked more at Mac than at me. He held out his hand.

Mac and I nodded simultaneously, "This is Investigator Mackenzee. My name's Kano. We *are* here from Amity. We're investigating the break-in at the Williams' home. We understand you investigated an attempted arson fire."

"I'm Troy Portmann. Why don't we go into my office, sit down and get comfortable? This could take a while."

The office consisted of a dining room table, that was probably donated, and six chairs that needed reupholstering. We sat and looked at the walls. There were pictures of Palmdale as it looked back in the 50s.

It looked like dirt, sand, more dirt, and more sand. Next to it were pictures of three 1950 American LaFrance fire trucks.

"Can I get you a cup of coffee or something?" He asked.

A shot of Seagram's would have hit the mark, but that probably wasn't such a good idea. "Thanks, but no." Mac also declined.

The inspector had a file in front of him. He opened it. "Okay. On the night in question, we received a call out from the Sheriff's Department who had arrived on the scene of a burglary. When dispatch called, we were told there was a fire in the rear bedroom at 4471 Rose Garden Court. We, of course, responded."

"When you say, 'we responded,' you mean a unit was dispatched?"

"That's correct. At that point, there was no need for me to respond. During the preliminary investigation, deputies established that a bed, in the rear of the house, had intentionally been set on fire, which is when I was notified."

"Is this an area that usually has significant problems, like break-ins, home invasions, auto thefts…?"

"Actually, no, it's normally a quiet area. It's one of the better areas in this decaying city." Troy wiggled in the chair.

He looked at Mac and smiled. I perked up. I looked at Portmann and smiled pleasantly. I knew something the investigator didn't know; Mac was taken.

Mac asked, "Why do you call it a decaying city?"

"We have a state prison in Lancaster. Lancaster is the adjoining city just north of us. About a year ago, they started releasing the prisoners to Palmdale with vouchers to the many low priced motels in the area. Crime has increased. Low-income families, well-intentioned families, have moved from the L.A. area with their gang kids in tow to bring them to a better area, hopefully away from the gang culture.

"They can afford housing here that they otherwise couldn't afford down below. The problem is instead of breaking away from the gangs, more gangs have taken root in Palmdale and Lancaster. This has led to more graffiti, more gangs, more crime, and more drugs. On top of that, Lancaster and Palmdale are spread out. We have a shortage of sheriffs to patrol the area. This makes for a thriving crime area. So, the short answer to your good question is it had been a quiet neighborhood but given what I told you….."

I got the picture. I cut his description of the cities short. "Please tell us what you remember about that investigation."

270

"Okay. It was about 2100 hours when I was called out to the scene. A Deputy told me the house had been entered with the apparent attempt to commit burglary. There was no one home at the time of the burglary. After stealing various items from the home, he apparently went into the back bedroom and poured lighter fluid over a small corner of the bed sheet and the blanket.

"He then threw a match on the bed. Just as it started to get out of control, the homeowner came to the front door. He heard her and ran out the rear door. She ran into the bedroom, observed the bed sheet on fire, and had the presence of mind to grab a deep pot from the kitchen.

"She filled it with water and poured it over the flames. She did this three times, extinguishing the fire. She probably saved the house."

"You're certain it was lighter fluid?"

"Absolutely, and a match. We have the residue from the match."

"Did you talk with the victim?" I asked.

He looked in the file. "Myra Williams. Yes, she was shaken up but friendly. Pretty lady, she was from Australia."

"We know. Was she able to shed any light on the burglary and arson fire?"

"Absolutely not. Before you ask, it was the first arson fire in that area in years. There were a couple of break-ins but no arson. After a preliminary discussion with the on-scene deputies, we decided it was a crime of opportunity. Probably an addict looking for items he could

271

pawn or sell for quick cash for his next fix. Nobody observed a car in the driveway or a vehicle in the area that didn't belong.

"The suspect probably rang the bell. When no one answered, he went around to the side of the house and jimmied the screen. The window was not locked. That's apparently how he entered, but the deputies can give you more information, I'm sure."

"Anything else you can think of that might seem out of the ordinary?" Mac asked.

"Afraid not, however, I know a print was taken from the house that didn't belong to the homeowner or anyone else who frequented the house.

"But to tell you the truth, there was no one hurt and no major damage, so we did a cursory investigation and turned everything over to the deputies. They handled it as a burglary."

I looked at Mac. "Interesting."

"Strange," She said as she looked at the inspector. "Here's our card. If you happen to think of anything else, anything, please give us a call. This is bigger than you think. It might be tied into a homicide, the killing of a police officer." Mac looked at me.

"We thank you for your time. Be safe and be careful."

CHAPTER 22

FOLLOWING A LEAD

When I called to make an appointment to speak with the lead deputy at the scene of the burglary at the Williams' house, I was transferred to Deputy Mitchell. We talked briefly then made an appointment to meet. When my head had free time, I thought about Agent Sullivan. I was formulating a plan to screw with Sullivan. Revenge is sweet!

The Palmdale Sheriff's Station was on the southeast corner of Avenue Q and Sierra Highway. It was a new building and a new site constructed in 2012. It was small, modern, and clean. Immediately inside the building was the front desk.

It was staffed by an older heavy-set gentleman, a volunteer wearing a white shirt with a rectangular identification tag. Before Mac and I could have a seat on the benches against either wall, he asked us if he could be of any help. He kept looking at Mac. Mac, dressed in a black skirt and yellow button-down men's dress shirt, looked back at him. Mac smiled. "We're here to see Deputy Mitchell."

"Can I have your names please?"

Mac flashed her ID. I stepped forward. I showed the fat boy my ID.

"Can I ask the nature of your business?"

He was getting pushy. "We're expected. We have an appointment. It's personal."

"Sorry, sir and ma'am, I have my instructions. I need to know….."

Mac jumped in before I could open my sometimes foul mouth. She looked at his ID tag, took a pen and a small notebook out of her pocketbook, then wrote down his name.

"Mr. Sodajerk….."

"It's Sodaperk, ma'am."

"Whatever. Please get Deputy Mitchell on the phone for us right this minute, or I promise you I'll see to it that you don't work this Station ever again." Mac smiled. "Is that a big 10-4, Soda man?" Mac deliberately split her version of his name into two syllables.

He nodded, reached across the desk, and grabbed the telephone. Deputy Mitchell was a tall, middle-aged man, had ingested too many donuts with his coffee. He was losing his grey-black hair. He greeted us with a smile. The Deputy offered us a chair at a beat-up, oblong table that looked like it spent too many days at the Palmdale Sheriff's Station.

Deputy Mitchell introduced us to a tall, thick shouldered African American named Washington Lincoln. The man might have been in his late twenties. I thought he spent most of that time in the gym. If I had to meet someone in a dark alley, I would prefer it be King Kong to Washington Lincoln.

Deputy Mitchell explained, "This is Reserve Officer Lincoln, Washington Lincoln." Then he added, "His father was a history buff. Reserve Officer Lincoln dusted for prints the night of the break-in at the Williams' house. I thought you might want to speak to him."

"Good call, sir. We appreciate that." We shook hands with the Reserve Officer.

"I have a copy of our report for you. It doesn't say a whole lot. This was your every day, run of the mill residential burglary. The only curious point is why he wanted to burn the place to the ground."

"Deputy, other than that, was there anything that struck you as out of the ordinary?"

Mitchell was quick to shake his head. "By the numbers, so much so that I could have cut and pasted one burglary report to this one. The house was as clean as a hungry tiger's tooth. Nice house, nice lady, just a crime of opportunity."

Some officers did just that. If a previous report seemed to fit the present report, they cut from the former, pasted it to the latter, changed a few dates and names, then turned in the report. I knew one officer who did just that. When he got on the witness stand he was asked by the public defender why the report had an entire paragraph from a former report. The lazy officer was screwed. He had cut and pasted too much without proofreading.

Someone once said, *'Oh, what a tangled web we weave when first we practice to deceive.'* The cop lost his credibility, a few days' pay and a big piece of his reputation over a few minutes of punching keys on a computer keyboard. His only explanation was a possible computer glitch. In my opinion, he should have been fired for trying to lie his way out of the situation he created with his laziness.

If you pull that shit with a go-nowhere report, what might you do in the field in a life and death situation? You would think that would send him a message. In a sense, it did. Now he's more careful when he cuts and pastes. Some people never change.

"How about Ms. Williams, anything strike you about her that might be noteworthy?"

"She's a pretty lady and a nice dresser. She's from Australia and been here forever. We ran a local check. She's, of course, cleaner than a freshly washed dish. Her mortgage payments are up to date. She had nothing to do with this."

"How long has she lived in that house?"

Mitchell scanned the report. "Five and a half years."

Mac turned to face the Reserve. "Officer Lincoln, you dusted for prints, is that correct?"

He was obviously nervous. "Yes, ma'am, I'm still in training. Deputy Mitchell is my second FTO. He is teaching me to lift prints." Mac nodded.

Like a full-time officer, a Level 1 Reserve goes through the same three FTOs that a full-time officer does. He is quizzed, tested, and evaluated at the end of each shift. These records are kept on file for P.O.S.T, Police Officers Standards, and Training. The level 1 Reserve does the same fieldwork a full-time officer does. He wears the same uniform, carries the same gun, and is issued the same badge. The full-time officer draws a salary; the Reserve sometimes is given a uniform allowance. Sometimes he's given a dollar a year. Reserve Officer Lincoln was a dollar a year man.

Mac continued. "Is it SOP to dust for prints at all residential burglaries?"

Deputy Mitchell fielded Mac's question. "Generally yes. Also, I was training Reserve Officer Lincoln in the art of lifting prints. So, this was a teaching moment."

"Got it, and what happened?"

"I found this one useable print. The Williams' place is so clean, it's amazing. But even then, I only found one print I could use; that print came back to a match. That was Martin's print."

"You lifted that print, is that correct?" Mac asked.

"Yes," Lincoln answered.

"And then you ran that print?"

Yes, ma'am." He looked at the Deputy. "My FTO had me run it for training purposes. Normally we wouldn't have bothered."

"And you got a hit?"

"Yes ma'am. It came back to Austin Martin."

Reserve Officer Lincoln was bursting with pride. He should have been, so should his deputy. They both did their respective jobs. They did them well.

"Did you, Deputy Mitchell, do a follow up with the Williams' lady?"

"Actually," the full-time Deputy said, "We met her in the hospital the next day. She attempted to put out the fire on the bed. In so doing, she burned her hands. We called paramedics the night of the burglary. Paramedics applied a soothing cream on her hands, taped a portion of the hand, and suggested she go to the hospital. She arrived at the hospital the next morning. We finished questioning her at the hospital."

"Which hospital would that be?"

"It was Palmdale General Hospital."

"How badly burned were her hands?"

"Bad enough that the doctors told her she'd have scars. One of the doctors thought skin grafting might be in order."

"I see," Mac replied.

"We then notified your office because you had the BOLO, be on the lookout. Then we did a follow-up. We showed Williams the booking photo of Austin Martin."

Mitchell slid a not too recent photo of Martin across the table. Mac and I examined it. It showed the suspect with long, stringy black hair and a full black beard.

"Did you show her any other photos of the asshole? I mean of Martin?"

"No sir. That's all we had."

"What was William's reaction?" Mac asked.

"She said she didn't know him, and had never seen him. She took a long, hard look, nothing."

"Did you buy that?" I asked.

"Yes, sir, there was no reason not to. I'm a good judge of people. I felt that she was telling the truth. Bet my badge on it."

I slid the picture across the table at Lincoln. "Deputy Lincoln…."

"Reserve Deputy Lincoln, sir."

"Reserve Deputy Lincoln. Take a look at this photo of Martin. Study it for a second."

He did as asked. "Now, if you were to cut the hair and remove the beard, do you think you'd recognize the picture?"

He answered instantly, "Probably not. No, I wouldn't."

"I don't think I would either," Mac replied

"Officer Lincoln…" Again, I was corrected. "Reserve Officer, sir."

"Reserve Officer Lincoln, do you happen to remember where you lifted the useable print from? What part of the house?"

279

He thought for several seconds, looked down at the table, then up at me.

He smiled, "Yes, sir. I dusted and lifted the print from the archway between the bedroom and hallway that leads to the living room. It's almost as if someone, without thinking, leaned on it for a quick second, then realized his finger didn't belong there and quickly took it off. Does that help any?"

I shrugged, "It's too early to tell. But it sure can't hurt anything."

I looked at Deputy Mitchell, who looked like he was deep in thought.

Deputy Mitchell asked, "Reserve Officer Lincoln, do you want to do police work full time?"

His face lit up like a fire in a haystack, "Yes, sir, I'm going to complete my training. When there is an opening, hopefully, the department will accept me."

"I'm sure they will. You've done a fine job." Mac stood up. "I want to thank you both for all your help. If you think of anything else, you have our card. Don't hesitate to call us. No matter how slight you think it might be, call any time. You never know what may crack this case."

I got up. We shook hands, thanked Mitchell and Lincoln again and were on our way. We left with little more than we came with, or so it appeared. Mac and I stopped for coffee and to discuss our next move. We hadn't been seated long enough for the waitress to take our order when my cell phone rang. It was Detective Jimenez. He and Agent

Sullivan were in a meeting, and they wanted to know if we had made any progress.

"Yeah," I said. "We've met with the fire inspector then with the investigating deputy, and his Reserve trainee. We've got nothing. Mac and I were just discussing our next move. I think before we meet face to face with the Williams lady, I'd like to stake out her place. The file has a copy of her registration, so we've got a starting point. Mac and I will swing by the Station. We'll grab an unmarked unit. Maybe a stakeout will buy us a break. Do you have anything new?"

Neither Jimenez nor Sullivan was putting in a helluva' lot of time on the case. They were doing some "behind the scenes" investigating but little more than that. I hung up.

I grabbed Mac's hand, "Let's go."

Mac looked at me like I was crazy. "I thought you wanted to have coffee and discuss the case?"

"We'll get it to go. I want a piece of Agent Asshole first."

We walked toward the door. "What are you going to do?"

"I had a bumper sticker made up at the mall. I'm going to put it on Sullivan's private car."

"What does it say?" Mac asked.

"It tells him how much I appreciate his dedication and his help."

We were in the car. "I doubt it. Let me see."

I took the bumper sticker out of my pocket. I thought Mac was going to wet her pink panties laughing. "You wouldn't."

"Watch me. As a matter of fact, you'll be my cover."

I drove. I drove fast. I didn't know how much longer Jimenez and Sullivan were going to be at the station in their meeting. Sullivan, pompous asshole that he was, had a parking space at the Station dedicated to 'Agent Sullivan.' He did half my work for me. When we got to the Station gate, I punched in the access code. Agent Sullivan's personal car, a black Cadillac Allante convertible, was backed into his assigned space.

The car was a couple of feet from the block wall and from the gate that allowed Station foot traffic to egress the Station and walk over to the adjacent park. It was Hollywood script perfect. I found a vacant spot. I parked quickly.

"Let's walk," I said.

Mac and I walked toward the gate. I pretended to drop something. Our not so sophisticated cameras scanned the parking lot. I wasn't worried. Dispatch was probably too busy dealing with calls at this time of day to be paying attention to the parking lot camera.

As Mac watched the Station door that led to the back parking lot, I quickly attached the bumper sticker to the left side of the Allante's bumper. I affixed it quickly but carefully then stepped back to admire my handiwork.

I smiled. "I do good work. Job accomplished. Let's go in the Station and get keys to an unmarked unit."

282

Mac and I sat in an unmarked van in the parking lot of one of the shops on Soto Avenue north of Almador. I knew what city asshole Agent Sullivan lived in, therefore, if he was going home from his meeting with Detective Jimenez at the Station, he would be driving northbound to one of the Freeways. We waited. Mac had one hand on my right thigh and one hand on the video camera I had borrowed from the detective unit at the PD.

"Why are you doing this?" Mac asked.

I smiled broadly. "Because I can and because Sullivan is a pompous asshole who needs to learn a lesson in humility."

"Is it possible you need to feel superior?"

"Not possible, probable. The guy's a jerk," I said.

"You need to learn to accept people for who they are. You need to accept what you can't change.

"The only person you can change is you." Mac looked at me, shook her head, and smiled. "What are you going to do with the video?"

"The jury's still out on that. But you know me well enough. I'll come up with something to embarrass the asshole."

"Is there anything I can say to change your mind? Can I convince you to just *let go of this?"*

I shook my head. "Not a chance, I'm enjoying this."

"So I noticed," Mac replied.

I changed the subject. "On a different note, what is our next move on Ms. Williams?"

"I told you about my thinking. I think we need to stake out the house, see who comes and goes, follow her for a while, to see if she gets herself into anything that interests us."

"You think she's going to lead us to Martin?" Mac asked.

"She's the only card left to play. Can you think of anything else worth trying?"

"No. We're out of chips."

"Almost, that damn print didn't just walk in the house. It didn't just plant itself on the wall." I reasoned, Martin was obviously in that house. The question is was he in the house to burglarize it or was he an invited guest? Is he friends with Ms. Williams or a freakin' idiot looking to get caught? I would take long odds that she is somehow connected to Martin.

"After we get bored watching the house and tailing her, I want to go through her phone records," I told Mac.

"You really don't believe it was a simple break-in?"

"Mac, I am so f*****g confused right now, I don't know what to think. The asshole apparently gets away with a couple of million dollars. We got next to nothing. He isn't heard or seen in this country for months upon months. We have several sightings out of the country then a possible sighting on the east coast. Finally, if all that isn't enough, a Reserve cop lifts his print in a house that was burglarized. Do you make sense of that? I can't."

"Okay, let me try. First, if it were me, I'd check real estate records to see how long Williams has occupied that house," Mac replied.

"According to the investigating deputies, she has lived there five and a half years. But that would be good to verify. You can also go online to a site like Zillow or Realtor.com and check ownership, etc.," I offered.

"Keep going."

"I'd ask her for a list of every repairman, serviceman, and delivery man who's been in that house. A telephone repairman could have been installing a phone in the bedroom. He could have touched the wall."

"You're saying?"

Mac began, "Martin may have bought himself a new identity and could be working a legit job?

"Why not, just shave the beard, the hair, maybe dye it and get contacts. You showed his picture to Lincoln. He said with the beard off and the haircut, he probably couldn't ID Martin. If he's got all this cash and is afraid to spend it because it might draw attention to him or if he's afraid that the serial numbers might be traceable, he could be hard up for dough. Who the hell knows?"

"You've got a good point. You look beautiful as a detective. But I like you better in the chippie uniform. It's tighter. My point is are you wearing panties?" I asked.

"How does your sick mind go from cash to my panties? And I seriously doubt you're going to find out tonight. But let's do this tomorrow. I'll work on the real estate angle and the telephone records. You stay on her." Mac quickly corrected herself. "Stay *with* her."

"Deal…." Then as I looked south on Soto, "I think this is our boy. Get your video in gear."

We watched Sullivan drive passed us. He was in the slow lane trying to figure out why the guy in the fast lane was giving him the finger, and the guy behind him was honking his horn.

"Are you getting this?"

"I'm getting it, I'm getting it. Actually, it's pretty funny," Mac said.

"Do a good job, and I'll give you screen credit."

I pulled out of the lot. I turned north on Soto. I got as close to Sullivan's Allante as I dare.

I sure the hell didn't want him spotting me. Our windows were blacked out. But no matter how irritated the idiot got me, he wasn't totally stupid. He did pass all the exams. He did have the schooling to become an agent. I stayed back a couple of car lengths.

The guy who was on Sullivan's left was now directly in front of him deliberately driving about ten miles an hour under the posted 35 mile an hour limit. His fist was out the window. He was shaking it at Sullivan. You could hear him yelling, "F*****g faggot."

Another car pulled up on Sullivan's left. The driver, a big construction worker wearing a hard hat, blew him a kiss. Sullivan yelled something back at him. Mac captured it all on video. I stayed with Sullivan three and a half miles north on Soto. All the while, drivers were flipping him off, blowing him kisses and cursing him. Sullivan had no idea what was going on.

"I want a close up of the bumper sticker."

Mac seemed to be enjoying herself. "Did I earn screen credit?"

"You get my tongue between your ass cheeks."

"Bumper sticker! Got it." Mac laughed.

"Done?"

Mac said, "It's a wrap."

We broke off the tail when Sullivan turned to get on the northbound 5 Freeway to head to the Valley.

CHAPTER 23

COPS HELPING COPS

I drove Mac home. I parked the car at the curb. It wasn't a nightcap that brought me in the house, although Mac had a fifth of Seagram's in her liquor cabinet for me. If I told you the fresh bottle of Seagram's was wrapped in a not so fresh pair of Mac's lacy white panties, you wouldn't believe me, but it was. I couldn't decide whether I wanted to sniff the panties or take a drink first. Mac stood behind me, loving it. The Seagram's bottle and its contents were the only things I loved that night.

I had an extra razor at Mac's house. I shaved, showered, brushed my teeth, devoured an English muffin, orange juice, and two cups of coffee with Mac before I left her place to drive the forty-five minutes to the Williams' house in Palmdale. Mac, while I was staking out the Williams' house, had her own assignment. She was going to check out the length of time Williams lived in that house. Once Mac developed that list, she would attempt to discover which workmen were in the house. A workman might have left that print.

Fingerprints have been known to remain useable for years, depending on the print and the surface from which it is lifted. Mac's second assignment was to document Ms. Williams' phone calls, both her

288

house phone and her cell phone, to see if she made any calls that could be traced to Martin. Neither task would be easy; both tasks would be time-consuming. As I drove north on the 14 Freeway, my focus was on Martin. I wanted that son of a bitch, and I wanted him bad. I promised Rocky we'd get him. I was going to keep that promise. Rocky would know I'd kept my word.

I couldn't put my finger on what bugged me about this case, but something was not fitting in place. A criminal with the non-traceable money Martin had, would not be breaking into a house, UNLESS that money was hidden in the house. If he and Williams were, at one time, an item, or they still are, he could have hidden the cash in the house. His print in the house could be the result of going into the house to get the money. But if he was gay, he wouldn't be involved with Williams, at least not in a sexual way unless he swung both ways.

Then there was the possibility Williams was somehow tied to the inside person. If so it was an inside job. There were too many possibilities and too many f*****g *ifs.* Another possibility was that the money was still in the house; that he had the money hidden in her house and would "cash-out" what he needed when he needed it. But that left the intentional arson fire, which made no sense.

If he had removed all the cash from the house, it was plausible that he wanted to burn the house to the ground to eliminate any possible evidence he left in the house. If he expected Williams to return to the house and wanted her out of the way, he might have timed the fire so that she would return home when the place was in flames. That made little sense to me and would be too risky, unless he was hiding

289

somewhere waiting for her to come home before he set the fire. That was not high on my list of possibilities.

I was confused. But, if I had money to gamble with, I'd wager that Mac would come up with numerous calls that were made by Williams on her home phone, her cell phone or both that would eventually come back to Martin. That was much more plausible than an intentional arson fire to kill Williams. I exited the 14 Freeway at Palmdale Boulevard, made a left turn, and headed west.

I thought about Rocky as I drove toward Elizabeth Lake Road in Palmdale. I remembered how he would damn near chain smoke cigarettes when he was uptight. I thought about how he would get on my case when I got down on myself. His favorite expression was, "Tony, let it go. Every cop steps on his dick now and then." This was one time I wasn't going to step on my dick.

When I had trouble handcuffing a belligerent suspect who was about six foot three, I got really pissed at myself. Rocky laughed. "What do you expect?" he snickered. "Look at his height and look at yours. Had it been me, I would have pepper-sprayed him. Then I wouldn't have had any trouble handcuffing him." Two weeks later, we responded to a 415 fight in a bar on Pan Am Boulevard. Two drunk idiots, both six foot and built, were slugging it out. Some of the half smashed patrons were betting on the outcome and egging the idiots on.

I didn't hesitate. I said one time, "Freeze, or you get pepper-sprayed." They ignored the order. I reached back, pulled out my pepper spray, shook it up, then sprayed a jet stream in the face of one while Rocky got the other. We had no trouble cuffing either one.

On the way out of the bar, suspects in tow, Rocky threw over his shoulder at the betting patrons, "No winner folks, it's a draw. Go back to your booze. They'll be a rematch later in the week." I was still laughing when we put the perps in the cage in the back of the unit.

I found a convenient and "protected" (the curb was painted red) parking space down the street from the Williams house on Almador Court in West Palmdale. The house was two-story with wrap-around veranda, green grass, neatly trimmed shrubs, and the American Flag flying in the wind off the back-bedroom balcony. The neighborhood appeared quiet, clean, and well above middle income.

I settled in for a long day. About twenty minutes into my surveillance, Mac called a most welcome interruption. She explained to me that when I left for surveillance duty, she pulled up Zillow on her computer. She did her homework. She earned an A+. The Williams house was built in 1991. Williams was the third owner. She had purchased the house seven years earlier. With the market going up, up, up, Williams had a tidy profit until the market crashed. Now the housing market was trying to recoup its losses. While the house was initially a rental, Williams occupied the house when the market took a downturn.

Was it then a possibility a renter had left the print? Martin being the renter or a friend to the individual who had rented the house? Highly unlikely the print would remain clear enough to pull after all those years but possible nonetheless. Mac had yet to delve into Williams' financial background. Was it possible that Williams was behind in her mortgage payments or that when she had equity in her home she borrowed against that equity, and now that the values had dropped, she was upside down in her house and decided to burn it down?

The initial investigators said during digging, they found Williams' mortgage payments to be current. That was highly unlikely. These are the things a cop thinks about when he is alone on surveillance. Part of finding a solution to a case is not only finding the pieces that fit, it's also eliminating those that don't fit. Mac was eliminating possibilities. I went back to surveillance, Mac went back to work.

I watched the house for movement. The wrap-around veranda in front of the house kept me from seeing what was going on inside, even with my high-powered binoculars. I thought about my prosthesis. Most of the time, I didn't even know it was there. It had become second nature. Many nights I fell asleep wearing it, especially if Mac and I spent the night together. I thought about Rocky. I still had guilt about Rocky.

I let him down. I believe he was up there looking out for me, smoking a cigarette, and laughing not at me, but with me; that's the way Rocky was. His great nature was as big as his heart. It's too bad he had to die young. I thought about Mac. I immediately felt the bulge in my blue police pants. I sat for an hour and a half by myself, thinking, thinking, thinking, then finally the front door of the Williams house opened. Out stepped a figure that stood about five foot seven inches tall.

She was dressed in brown slacks that accentuated a "tight" figure for a woman who was in her forties. She had a lighter colored brown sweater pulled tightly across her chest and up around her neck. She was amply endowed. She wore a man's straw hat that was cute and protected her from the sun. On her hands were brown gloves. I grabbed a camera and took photos as she walked to her car, a late model brown Honda four-door that was parked at the curb rather than in her garage. I wondered why. I also decided she liked the color brown.

I took several shots of Ms. Williams and a couple of shots of the Honda. I may have been wasting film, then again, maybe not. I followed Ms. Williams to the Palmdale Mall, where she parked her Honda. Surveillance is an art. Following someone in a vehicle is not what it appears to be on television. It's tricky business to follow or "tail" someone, so they don't see you. Light traffic makes it difficult because you're easy to spot.

Heavy traffic makes it more difficult because you don't want to lose the subject.

In real life, two or three or even four or five vehicles are used to follow a subject. I had one van. Fortunately for me, Ms. Williams was a careful driver. She spent most of her behind the wheel time, on the two and a half-mile trek to the Mall, watching what was in front of her. She gave little attention to the vehicles behind her and specifically no attention to me or, so I thought. She parked her car in row 3A. I parked in row 4B.

Ms. Williams exited her vehicle and walked slowly into the main Mall entrance, enjoying the southern California sunshine. From a safe distance, I watched her walk as I followed Ms. Williams into the Mall. She was cute, and I liked the way she "strolled." I liked her tight ass in those brown slacks. I didn't expect to see any action in the Mall, although one never knew. She could be meeting a friend for a late breakfast. She could be meeting Martin, but that was not likely.

I followed our gal into a woman's clothing store where she spent the better part of an hour, trying on three dresses. She purchased one, paid for it, exited the dress shop, then walked directly to Victoria's Secret, definitely more to my liking. Unfortunately for me, it was too damn conspicuous for me to go into the store, so I waited outside. Ms. Williams seemed to know exactly what she wanted. My male imagination and I only had a few minutes to speculate. From the two stores, it was back to the house. I sat and waited for three hours before my cell rang. Of course, it was Mac reporting in.

I sat on the house, waiting while I talked with Mac. Mac related that Williams, who had been born in Australia, had come over here frequently and finally made her home here. She showed dual citizenship. She was as clean as baby's freshly bathed and diapered ass. We didn't even show a traffic ticket for her in our system. I wanted to question neighbors, but I didn't yet want her to know that we were looking at her, so that would have to wait.

Mac checked Palmdale city records to see if any recent work that would be permitted was done on the house. My thinking was that maybe a worker had entered the house and left the print; maybe that worker was Martin with a new identity. Nice idea but no sale. Williams hadn't had any work done on her house that showed up in city planning records neither recently nor at any time since she took possession of the house.

Mac also ran three credit checks on Williams. Her credit score averaged 733, which was a B plus rating. She owed a few bucks here and there, mostly on credit cards but nothing significant.

I asked Mac if she owed anything on the Honda. She replied, "It's paid for."

"The damn thing isn't worth much anyway," I muttered. "Are there any phone call results?"

"I'm still working on that."

I sighed. "I'm bored. I've got nothing to play with."

Mac laughed that dirty laugh. "I got plenty to play with, but my hands are occupied. If you're good and you ask nicely, maybe beg a little, maybe tonight Mommy's panties will be nice and wet by then."

"Stop, you're driving me nuts." My dick was straining to get out of my pants.

"Let me see how long it takes me to get these phone records. Once I'm done with that, I'm pretty much at a standstill. Maybe I'll come out and join you. I'll check back with you later. Keep your hands where they belong until I tell you otherwise."

I had one major concern about the Williams girl. We showed no record of her working. If she had no job, how was she making the house payments? How was she supporting herself? How was she making her credit card payments? How did she put f*****g gas in the Honda even though it got good mileage? These questions need an answer. Every time I tried to figure this thing out, it came right back to the Williams girl. I was convinced she was somehow tangled into this.

I waited and watched the house. It was quiet until seven fifteen when a 308 Ferrari convertible, red in color, pulled up and into the driveway of the Williams' house. Behind the wheel was a white male. I got excited; this time, it wasn't physical excitement. 308 Ferrari's weren't all that expensive to purchase, but the upkeep was ridiculous. Whoever owned the vehicle, the driver I assumed, had money. This could get interesting in a hot New York minute. I grabbed my binoculars, stepped to the rear of the van, and went to work.

Next to me was a high powered, high dollar camera. Through the binoculars, I watched a middle-aged man, dressed in an expensive black pinstripe suit exit the Ferrari. He looked in the side view mirror, ran a comb through his hair, adjusted his solid red tie against his white shirt, and walked to the front door.

The man had not one bit of facial hair. He did have a head full of thick black hair. He was approximately the same height as Martin, although there was still a bit of confusion concerning Austin Martin's height. I thought he was taller than our records indicated. No matter what, this was a possibility. It fit, it all fit. I watched him take a key chain from his suit jacket pocket. The binoculars were so damn good that I was able to focus in on his Ferrari key chain.

He had a duplicate of his damn 308 on the key chain, right down to the convertible top and the color red. He put the keys in his pocket, walked up the driveway and to the front door. His knock was immediately answered as if he was expected. He entered the house quickly. Un-f*****g fortunately for me, the house had heavy dark drapes. The drapes were pulled tightly shut. I couldn't see shit inside the house. This could be our big break.

I phoned Mac. "We may have our guy." I explained the situation. "I'm gonna' sit on this house till your panties dry.

"We may have Martin. Here's the plate number of his car. Do me a favor and run the damn thing. It's a personalized plate."

"Not a problem. That sounds like Triple-A with a gun work. On those phone records, I won't be able to get them until tomorrow. How about after I run the plate, I drive out there and join you? I have something for you."

"Ooh. I'm sure I'm going to like what you've got for me. It works for me. If they move out before you get here, I'll call you. Keep the phone between your legs on vibrate!"

"The only thing I want vibrating between my legs is your tongue or your cock. Now hang up, quit playing with yourself, and get back to work." There was a brief hesitation. "What you *think* I got for you ain't what you think. So, stop thinking. You'll see it when you're meant to see it. Call me when something exciting happens."

Mac called me at 2015 hours, 8:15 p.m. She parked her vehicle around the corner and walked to the van. I leaned over and opened the door for her. ***This could turn into a working vacation.*** She made her way to the back of the van. I was sitting on a very uncomfortable wooden bench watching the house. Mac sat down next to me. She put her hand on my crotch.

"Did you find a new hiding place for your Glock?"

"Not funny, I'm horny."

Mac handed me a felt-covered red jewelry box. It wasn't wrapped in gift paper. "You were born horny. Don't open it. Not yet. Take it out to the cemetery and open it at Rocky's grave."

"Are you going to tell me what's in it?"

"At the gravesite, trust me."

She gave my *Glock* one quick rub. "Quit taking so many of those little blue pills, and you might not be Glock hard. She squeezed one more time where the Glock wasn't. "What's the action here?"

I had no idea how Mac knew I was taking Viagra and/or Cialis. Perez, at the Station, bought them in bulk and sold them to the guys at the Station. Perez was my supplier. Perez quipped that he took them as a recreational drug. Like a good Boy Scout, we were always prepared.

"The Ferrari in Ms. Williams' driveway belongs to her boyfriend, male friend, husband, or one of the above. He arrived a while ago, and they've been in the house since doing what I wish we were doing.

"Did you come up with anything startling?" I asked Mac.

"Our gal is lily-white. I hate to disagree with you, but if she is involved with Martin, if the guy in the house *is* Martin, she may not know it. I ran her every which way but loose. Myra Williams is from good stock out of Australia. Her folks were legitimate business owners who got healthy on hard work. There is nothing in the family closet that suggests anything sinister.

"I think our lady from down under, if anything, is innocently involved with a soon to be a loser." Mac gave me one more squeeze then asked, "How sure are you that the male who entered the house is Martin?"

I sighed. "I'm not. Even nose to nose with him, I probably couldn't make a positive identification.

"All I've really got to go on is the booking photo. He could have totally changed his appearance, and I'm sure he did. The guy is nobody's fool. The guy who drove up in the 308 matches Martin's general description. That's all I have to go on."

Just then, the door to Williams' house opened. The couple exited the home hand in hand and walked to the Ferrari. He opened the passenger door for her.

"I guess they're not married."

"What makes you say that?" Mac asked.

"He opened the car door for her?" I smirked.

"Any chance you had of getting any tonight buster is ten twenty-two."

Ten twenty-two (1022) was cop code for forget it. A cop in a unit who requested information from dispatch may decide he no longer needs it. He'd radio dispatch and say *ten twenty-two my last request*. The male Caucasian closed the passenger door then walked around to the driver's side of the car. He opened the door, slid in behind the wheel, and started the engine. Mac and I climbed into the front seats of the van. We waited. We didn't have long to wait.

Tailing someone in a van is no easy task. The fact that traffic was moderate and that the male driver of the Ferrari remained on surface streets, made my job easier. The fact that the van is higher than the 308 gave me more visibility. Mac, although a very pleasant distraction, was an extra pair of eyes. We tailed them to a high-end restaurant in Lancaster, about seven miles north of Palmdale.

The restaurant was *The Rainbow Room*. According to the sign outside, steak and shrimp were on the night's menu. I love a good steak. I was hungry and I was horny. Neither appetite was about to be satisfied. The Caucasian male self-parked the Ferrari; I didn't blame him. He exited the sports car, walked around to the passenger side of the car, then opened the door for his lady friend.

She gave him a quick kiss on the cheek as they walked hand in hand into the *Rainbow Room*. The Williams woman had changed into a tight black dress with a white blouse, black leather choke chain around her neck, and black gloves. I had to wonder if she was into B and D.

Mac and I sat. "I'll call in the plate. Let's see what comes back. I didn't get a chance to do that earlier."

Mac called in the Ferrari's California license plate while I watched people entering and exiting the restaurant. There was little else to do but wait.

"They're going to call me when they run a complete check. APD is jumping. Two shots fired calls and an armed 211 on Pan Am Boulevard. The troops are earning their keep."

Police work could be boring as hell for hours, and one hot call could make up for all of it. Or like tonight, nobody even had time to take a piss break. When I was in training, working graveyards, most nights, we'd take code 7 (a meal) next to a big green trash dumpster. When we got that hot call, everything got dumped food, coffee, dessert. Rocky and I dumped enough half-eaten meals to fill two big green trash dumpsters. We lived for that.

"What do you think?" I asked Mac.

"I think Mr. Ferrari is going to come back as clean as Ms. Williams. I think we're in the wrong church. There's something else going on here. I can't put my finger on it, but if I had to bet, my wager would be that Martin was in that house on business, that Williams has no idea who he is."

"I don't want to question her until we have more information about her and her friend, who could still turn out to be Martin. Who did the plate come back to?"

"Jerry Kline, Esquire."

"Who the f**k is Jerry Kline, Esquire?"

"If he's the same Jerry Kline I think he may be he's a high-powered defense attorney out of San Diego. He's defended some real creeps. He either gets them a sweet deal, plea-bargains their sentences to time served or to a couple of years or gets them home free. The guy's good. From what I understand, he's a dirty player. He doesn't care what rock he has to overturn to get a client off, he'll do it.

"If this is the same guy, it's rumored he once had solid information that the married prosecutor was doing his secretary. He zipped his mouth and turned certain pictures he had of the two bumping uglies over to the prosecutor in exchange for a plea deal. Of course, nobody was talking, so Kline and his client scored big time."

"Nice." I thought for several seconds. "If that's the case, he's not our boy. Damn, Damn! Damn! I thought we had him. But I'm still not one hundred percent."

Mac looked at me. A wry smile appeared on Mac's face. "Are you a hundred percent on anything?"

I didn't hesitate. "I'm one hundred and fifty percent on my love for you. How's that?"

"Good answer, mister, keep that up, and you never know what may come your way."

"Would you like to spell *come*?" I asked.

"The fifth, counselor, I plead the fifth."

I bounced my fingers on and off the steering wheel. Normally, during an investigation, you have too many loose ends. Here we didn't have any loose ends except for the suspect and the money. This was making me crazy, or as Mac's AA teaching put it, *I was allowing it to drive me crazy.*

"There's only one answer. You're right, and I hate to admit it. A worker must have left that fingerprint. We'll talk to Williams in the next couple of days. Hopefully, that'll give us a definitive answer."

302

I was quiet for a minute and a half, unusual for me. "I want his fingerprints."

"Whose fingerprints?" Mac asked.

"Kline's."

"How are you going to get them? And what makes you think they're on file?"

"I don't yet know how *we're*," I stressed *we're*, "going to get his prints, but we'll figure something out.

"As far as his prints being on file, if we don't have them, I'm sure the bar association has them. I just want to be sure. I don't want to f**k anything up."

"Is it possible Martin made all those trips out of the country to launder the money? Even if he got twenty or thirty cents on the dollar, he'd be a rich man," Mac reasoned.

"I thought about that. It would explain all the frequent flier miles. If that be the case, we may never find the asshole. But none of that moncy is dirty. The serial numbers are not traceable."

"He doesn't know that. The money truck made bank pickups. If he's cautious, he just might have laundered the money to be on the safe side."

"We'll find him. Even if he is out of the country now, he'll be back."

"The key is the freakin' fingerprint. Figure out why that single print is in Williams' house, and we'll solve the case," I said.

"Dick Tracy is sitting next to me. Can I have your autograph, Dick?"

"Would you settle for the latter instead of the former?" My comment was ignored.

"That print was left in the house by someone who did some work in the house. When we talk with Williams, we'll ask her about workers. Maybe she had a room addition or add-on to her bedroom. After the fire, she may have had someone come in to repair the damage."

"Maybe she and counselor Kline had a bigger bed brought in, so they could roll around on it."

"Speaking of rolling around on beds, what are you going to do with that video you had me make starring Agent Sullivan?" Mac asked.

I chuckled. "I'm still thinking about that one too. I'm thinking about sending it to his wife."

"I hope you're kidding."

"I am. Let me solve one problem at a time here." I placed my very warm hand on Mac's thigh. "Are you wearing panties?"

"Pale blue and damp. But don't get all worked up; we're on duty."

I suddenly shot up straight, looked at Mac, and smiled.

"That's not good."

"That's very good." I punched the key on my cell phone. I waited. "Amity Police Department, Mary speaking, can I help you?"

"It's Kano. Is the WC in his office?"

"Yes, sir."

"Put me through, please."

"Lieutenant Cozen, can I help you?"

"LT, Kano, I need a big favor." I gave the LT my ten-twenty. "I need you to get a hold of the Lancaster Sheriff's Station. We're sitting on a red Ferrari 308 convertible out here that may belong to our guy Martin. It's a long shot, but it's better than no shot.

"The plate is personalized: Ida George Tom Union Ocean Frank Frank. The guy is supposedly an attorney. I want to make sure it's his car. I also want to make sure he's who we think he is. I need a Lancaster Sheriff to get out here and sit on this Ferrari, out of eyesight, until they come out of the restaurant. I want the Deputy to pull the asshole over and get him to sign a citation or whatever. I want his fingerprints. Is that doable?"

"If you weren't f*****g handicapped, I'd say NO. But since it's you and since it's for a good cause, you got it. But you owe me. Remember that."

"And you know I've got you covered."

"Yeah, I'm sure of it. Keep your cell on. I'll call you back."

I had my response ten minutes later. "Tony," the LT began. "Deputy Troutmann is in route to your twenty. Here's his cell. Stay off their channel. It's best all-around if we keep this ten thirty-five."

"Copy that, sir. I'll call Troutmann as soon as I hang up, and LT, that next bottle of Scotch is on me."

305

"Make it an expensive bottle."

I hung up and called Troutmann. "Sir, Kano from APD. We really appreciate your cooperation here. This case involves the murder of one of our own. We're zeroing in on the 187 suspect. We seriously need your assistance." I briefed the Deputy, who was within five minutes of our twenty, on the counselor's car, our location, and what I needed.

"I don't care how you do it; I need the asshole's prints." Then I added, "Watch your back. We're not sure who's who in the zoo."

"That may be easier said than done. The guy's an attorney. We think a defense attorney."

"I'll get it done, don't sweat it," the deputy said.

"He's got a lady with him; she may or may not be tied into this."

"I'm a single man unit, but I really don't see any problem. If anything, being an attorney, he may mouth me to death. Is his plate really, I GET YOU OFF? IDA George Tom Union Ocean Frank Frank. He should be cited, if not arrested just for carrying that plate. He must have had some kind of connection to get it."

"He probably defended some liberal asshole's cousin in return for the rights to the plate. When this is over, our guy or not, I think I'll file a complaint against the plate. See you in court, Perry Mason."

"Where do you want me to set up?"

"We're in the lot in the black van at the northwest corner. If he pulls out of here the way he came in, he'll exit the west exit and go north on Crosley. If you set up anywhere out there, you should be good. You're a slick top plain wrapper so he won't be hinky. He'll be concentrating on getting his lady's panties off."

"Copy that. I'm two out."

"Got it. Mac, my partner, will let you know when they exit the restaurant. I'm going to be joining you if that's not a problem.

I want to see if I can ID the guy."

The rest was waiting and waiting and waiting, any cop's favorite part of police work. Deputy Troutmann was a big dude. He was young, maybe twenty-five with a broad smile and a smooth face. He had blond hair, and hands that could throw a football for a long TD. We shook hands. I briefed Troutmann.

"Sounds like you have your hands full."

"You could make a Hollywood script out of this case," I said with a forced smile. "Nobody's going to believe it. I don't know about my hands but my head's full. This is a tough one. Forget the money the asshole got away with. Rocky was not only a partner, but he was also my closest friend. There's a score to settle here."

"You think this could be your guy?"

"Until my partner told me he came back as an attorney, I thought we might have him. Now I'm not so sure. He could have a phony ID. I want to get his fingerprints so we can run the prints and be sure one way or the other. If we can eliminate him, we can move on. If he's our man, we take him down, and it's over except for the stolen cash."

We didn't have long to wait. Jerry Kline, ESQ., and Myra Williams walked out of the restaurant ten minutes later. Since we were out of eyesight, Mac gave us a running commentary.

"They're arm in arm, giggling, kissing, running hands over each other. They reached the passenger door of the Ferrari. They're hugging." Then, "He pushed her against the car. Now they're making out. Damn guys get a room. They're still kissing. Now she's pushing him away. Hell, I'm getting turned on watching this.

"Now she's looking down at the bulge in his pants. She's giggling. He's opening the car door for her. She's in. He's walking around the car. He's getting in the car. He's starting the engine. He's backing up. Wait, he stopped. He's on his cell, talking. He's backing out. Now he's going forward. He's still on the cell phone. He's coming your way." There was a very brief pause. "He's on the street, and headed your way."

"We got him," I said into my cell. "He's making this easy. We've got our PC for the stop," I said to Mac and to Deputy Troutmann. "23123 (a) of the California Vehicle Code is talking on the cell while driving."

Kline drove the red 308 with one hand and held the phone to his right ear with his right hand. At the corner, the intersection was a two way stop. Kline slowed, looked left then right, and continued driving. He never came to a full stop.

"22450," I said into the phone. "Failure to stop for the stop sign. Now the counselor's going to have some 'splaining to do, Lucy."

"Do you want me to make the stop?"

"Be my guest. I'm going to stay behind the passenger door. I'll watch your back, but I wanna' stay out of sight. I don't yet want him or Williams to see me."

"Got it." Troutmann gave dispatch the address of the stop and the plate on the vehicle.

He exited the unit and approached the car. I stayed behind the unit's passenger door hand on my Glock just in case.

There was still a long-shot possibility that the attorney wasn't an attorney. As Troutmann approached the Ferrari, dispatch came back with a clear plate. Deputy Troutmann stopped just behind the driver's door.

"I'm Deputy Troutmann, LASD, sir. Can I see your license, registration, and proof of insurance, please?" Kline was still on the phone. "Sir, I need you to hang up the phone, please." I could hear it clearly. The fun started.

Kline ignored the Deputy. He kept talking. Deputy Troutmann took his cell phone out of his uniform front pocket. He took a picture of Kline on the phone. Deputy Troutmann held his phone away from the driver. He took his time centering the phone then snapped a second picture of the driver talking on the cell.

"What did you just do?" Kline asked.

"Sir, I took a picture of you talking on your phone after I asked you to hang it up, sir."

"For what purpose, officer?"

"It's Deputy Troutmann, sir. To attach to the citation as evidence, sir."

"Officer, would you tell me why you stopped me?" Kline hung up the phone and placed it on the dash.

"License, registration, and proof of insurance, sir, please!"

"The license is in my suit pocket, the inside pocket I'll get it. Don't shoot me."

The Deputy aimed a pointed finger in the air, cocked his thumb then squeezed a bent finger as if he were firing a weapon. "I won't."

"Honey, in the glove box, is the insurance papers and the registration. Get them for me, please."

I could see Kline handing something to Troutmann. I assumed it was the paperwork.

"Now, will you tell me why you stopped me?"

"Yes, sir. Troutmann examined the insurance papers and handed them back to Kline. "You rolled through a stop sign on the corner back there. You're also on your cell phone. Running a stop sign is a violation of 22450 of the vehicle code. 23123(a) is talking on the phone while driving. That's why I stopped you. Have you been drinking, sir?"

"Deputy, do you know who I am?"

"Yes, sir, I know exactly who you are," The deputy replied.

I started to panic.

"You're the gentleman who ran the stop sign, and was talking on his cell while driving. To top it off, you're **HBD has been drinking.** How many drinks have you had, and in what time period?"

"I don't have to answer that. I'm going to reach in my pocket." He handed Troutmann a business card. "I'm a defense attorney, Officer…" He looked at Troutmann's name tag. "Officer Troutmann."

"It's **Deputy** Trouttmann." The Deputy looked at the business card. It said 'Counselor Kline.'

"You know, Officer, under emergency conditions, it is within the law for me to be on that cell phone."

"Yes, sir, once you pull over and come to a complete stop, sir. Can I ask the nature of that emergency?"

"I was speaking with a client," Kline replied.

"That's fine, sir. Did you run the stop sign because you were speaking to the client, sir?"

"I don't think I'll answer that question either, *Officer.*"

"Deputy, sir."

"Whatever."

Troutmann handled the business card gently. He fingered the corners of the card and tucked the card in his shirt pocket. The Deputy deserved an academy award for lead actor in a reality show.

"Have you been drinking, sir?"

The attorney sighed. "Okay, I had two gin and tonics with dinner."

"Please stand by, sir."

"Officer, you're making a mistake. You're making a blizzard out of a snowflake," Kline replied.

It took an attorney to come up with a line like that. But I had to admit it was a good line. I had to remember that '*A blizzard out of a snowflake.*'

Troutmann walked back to where I was standing, behind the passenger door of the unit.

"I got your prints on the counselor's business card. I'll also have it on the pen he's going to use to sign the citation."

Prick doesn't know the difference between a police officer and a deputy sheriff. He's about to learn. Deputies write tickets to defense attorneys. Trouttmann approached the Ferrari, cite book tucked under his right arm, flashlight under his left arm.

"Sir, I am citing you for failure to stop for a stop sign and for talking on your cell phone, 22450 and 23123 (a) of the California Vehicle Code." Troutmann held the citation book for Kline to sign and handed the attorney his pen. Most likely out of defiance, Kline took out his own pen.

"Sign, sir, to the right of the red "X" in the rectangular box. Signing the citation is not an admission of guilt, sir. It's a promise to take care

312

of the ticket. The court date is under your signature, sir. Please press hard, sir, you're signing three copies."

"You're making a mistake, Deputy. I'll beat this in court."

"That's fine, sir. It will be my pleasure to see you again in court. In the meantime, sir, please drive carefully in the Antelope Valley, and have a great night."

The next morning Mac and I drove to APD to pick up the results of the fingerprint check on Attorney Kline, who I knew wouldn't come back a match for anyone but Attorney Kline. I was correct. On the way to the Station, I fondled the red jewelry box. It wasn't wrapped.

Mac was serious when she spoke, "Don't open this, not here, not yet. Take it to the cemetery; open it at Rocky's gravesite." She swallowed.

I could see a tear in the corner of her eye. "You'll understand when you open it in front of Rocky." She swallowed again. "I love you with all my heart. So did Rocky."

We drove the rest of the way to the Station in silence. We were in time for a second shift briefing. I carried with me a copy of the tape Mac had filmed of Agent Asshole Sullivan and his hypocritical self, driving on the street with the bumper sticker I affixed to his car's rear end. I grabbed the remote just as Mac stuck the CD in the machine. We took a seat near the center back of the room. I waited for the briefing sergeant to take his place seated in the front center of the room. Just before he called the meeting to order, I hit the button on the remote.

The one regret I had was that Sullivan was not in the room. The briefing sergeant turned so that he could see the screen. The first was a close up of the bumper sticker on Sullivan's car. It depicted two men holding hands and said, ***"LOVE ONE ANOTHER. LOVE KNOWS NO BOUNDS!"***

The camera followed the car showing other drivers honking and flipping Sullivan off and one driver throwing Sully a kiss. The film would never win an award, but it was sure funnier than hell; it served the asshole right. Sully had absolutely no idea what was going on, ***YET***.

I turned to Mac and whispered, "I wonder if America's Funniest Videos would run that?" Mac punched me in the arm.

Before we left the Station, we touched base with Detective Jimenez. He had nothing new for us. Jimenez had contacted my buddy, Sullivan. Sullivan had zero to report.

Since Kline's fingerprints matched Kline's fingers, we sat in a local APD coffee shop discussing how we would handle our next day's visit to the Williams house in Palmdale. Myra Williams was our last hope, at this point. We had run out of leads.

Since we had little else to do, we decided to visit the street fair in APD. Every year in April, Amity closes the main street of Pan Am Boulevard. Vendors sale their wares, there are rides for kids and food for the families. While usually quiet, the fair, which runs Friday, Saturday, and Sunday from eleven in the morning to midnight, occasionally sparks gang activity. It's rare, but it has happened.

314

It was early enough, and it was a gorgeous southern California evening, so we took the time to enjoy the festivities. I was relaxed. My leg was not noticeable to those who didn't know I was wearing it. My attitude, save for the annoyance of hitting a brick wall with the case, was better than it had been in months and months. I had a beautiful lady under my arm. Life was worth living. I thought about Rocky and promised Mac I wouldn't open the jewelry box. I was good to my word; however, I was dying to know what was inside the box.

"How about we stop at this bar, and I have a quick shot, then I'll win you a teddy bear shooting hoops?"

"Do you ever think about anything but putting something in a hole?" Mac replied.

There was no reason to respond. Some things are better left unsaid.

We found a bar. It was dim inside the bar. Patrons were few and far between. Most were outside enjoying the festivities.

There was no live music, but believe it or not, the jukebox was playing: *I Fought the Law and the Law Won*. I loved it.

"Right bar, huh?" We found two empty seats and sat down.

"If I didn't know better, I'd swear you paid someone to do that."

"If I didn't know better, I'd swear you were right," Mac replied.

The bartender, a little man with a big stomach and a cowboy hat that looked bigger than him, walked over to us. He smiled, "What can I get you?"

"Give me two shots of Seagram's, please? Mac?"

"I'm good."

"You got it."

The too, big hat cowboy bartender turned. He took a bottle labeled Seagram's off the shelf. He grabbed two shot glasses. Within seconds he poured two shots. He placed one in front of me and one in front of Mac. I grabbed Mac's and put both shot glasses in front of me. I held up my shot glass.

"Here's to you, here's to me, let's hope we never disagree, but if we do, the hell with you here's to me." I downed one shot. I loved the burning as the liquor went down the hatch.

"Does it ever stop with you?" Mac asked.

"Let's hope not. Can you handle one more?"

Mac smiled, "Would it help if I said no?"

I shook my head. "Here goes, Ms. Kojack, what happens if you put the batteries in the Energizer Bunny backward?"

"Kojack only knows how to suck on a big, juicy lollipop. Kojack has no idea what happens if you insert the batteries backward in the Energizer Bunny."

I downed the second shot. "He keeps coming and coming and coming." We left the bar for the street fair.

Between Glaze Avenue and Saturn on Pan Am Boulevard was a guy holding a basketball. "Sink one basket and win your choice of cuddly teddies for the lady. Only one ball through the hoop wins!"

He saw me and threw the basketball at me. Lucky for me, I caught it. Several people in the crowd, who saw the toss, gathered around. I handed the guy three bucks and lined myself up with the basket. I had been a baseball player but was never much for basketball.

"Before you shoot," he yelled in a loud voice, so the crowd could hear. "I'll give you two shots for the price of one because you caught the ball. What a deal!"

"I concentrated on the basket. I aimed and shot. The ball hit the rim and bounced back. I looked at Mac, "Warmup shot."

"Close but no teddy," the hawker said, "You've got one shot left. Give him a hand people. He works hard all week, and the little lady deserves a winner."

He didn't know the half of it. My second shot bounced off the backstop. I handed him another three bucks. The crowd cheered me on. I lined up my body with the basket.

I concentrated as if this were a live shooter threatening my life. I shot, and it was dead on. It bounced around the rim and came back to me. The crowd oohed.

"Last shot, last three bucks."

If I kept this up, I'd be able to buy the f*****g teddy bear. My final shot wasn't close.

317

"Next."

"Let's go."

"Hang on. I played basketball in high school." Mac handed the guy three singles.

The crowd that began to disperse turned around to watch Mac. Mac lined herself up, concentrated on the basket, and shot. NBN, nothing but net, it went in without lubrication.

"Pick your prize."

"Unbelievable," I said.

"The lady's a winner."

The crowd roared and applauded wildly. I was embarrassed. "What do you want?" The barker asked.

"I won it for you. Pick what you want."

"Do I get to carry it?"

"All night, it can even sleep with us. You want a threesome, you got it."

I picked a humongous gorilla.

We walked the boulevard hand in hand. I carried the ape. "We can call him....."

"SAS, Special Agent Sullivan," Mac said before I could finish my sentence.

After the street fair, we drove back to my place. We were both tired but not too tired to make love in the shower then again in the library on the thick dark blue carpet. We went to bed exhausted but fulfilled with the gorilla in the bed. I had my threesome. I couldn't quite get used to having Special Agent Sullivan in bed with us. Those damn little blue pills work!

CHAPTER 24

WORKING A LEAD

The drive to Myra Williams' house was one swift pain in the ass. It was off the 14 Freeway about 45 minutes from my place. That wasn't the problem. The problem was the traffic on the northbound 5 freeway and the assholes that drove the 14 freeway who thought it was a race track. If Mac hadn't been with me, I might have shot a couple of them.

The speed limit on both the 5 and 14 is 65. People liked to drive in the left lane at between 60 and 65. This drove me crazy. Then some want to cut in and out of traffic with and without a directional signal. But nothing pisses me off more than the tailgaters. If I were only in a black and white!

Mac said, "That make of vehicle came without directional signals, they were optional equipment. Obviously, he didn't want them, or he couldn't afford those options. Accept it."

"For one hour, of one day, just one freakin' hour, I'd love to drive a tank on one of these freeways!"

I don't know what I expected when I entered Williams' house. I was pleasantly surprised by what I observed up close. We said our introductions. Myra stood close to five-eight. Her hair was jet black. Her eyes were brown. She wore little makeup. Around her neck was a black choker. On her hands were white gloves. She wore a tight black dress that barely touched the floor. It fit her tight body like a convertible top fits a Mercedes.

A tight white blouse split down the middle, accentuated her ample boobs, showing plenty of cleavages leaving little to the imagination. When Myra Williams dropped the pen, she had in her hand, I didn't dare pick it up. That would have cost me a look at the twins. I think it was Johnny Carson who was interviewing Dolly Parton on his show. Johnny said to her, "I'd give a week's salary to peek at those babies." Mac noticed that I was looking.

While Myra was still picking up the pen, Mac punched me in the arm. I smiled and then shrugged. I was human, and I was male. Couldn't I look as long as I didn't touch?

"Ms. Williams, we'd like to ask you a few questions."

"Why don't you both come in to the living room? We'll be more comfortable."

We followed Ms. Williams into a living room that displayed pictures of what I recognized to be Australia. In the background were probably family members on the beach. One of the women looked a bit like Myra. The living room was small but clean. It was tastefully decorated. The carpet was plush and white. The couch was thick and black. The big-screen television was mounted on a swivel on the wall. Two recliners sat in front of the couch with a glass cocktail table in between the couch and the recliners.

"Have a seat. Can I get either of you something to drink? Coffee, tea, bottled water?" She spoke softly.

We declined the drinks. "We want to talk with you about Austin Martin." I watched her face for a reaction. I was certain Mac was doing the same.

"Who?"

"A man named Austin Martin. Do you recognize that name?" I already knew the answer.

She shook her head. "No."

I handed her a picture. "Take your time. Imagine him without facial hair. Do you recognize him?"

Again, I watched for a reaction. I observed none. Either she didn't know the name of the face or she was one hell of an actress. My bet was that she didn't know him.

Again, she shook her head. "I don't know him with or without a beard. Should I?"

I took a breath. "After the break-in here, the sheriff pulled a print that belongs to that man. Obviously, he was in your house. One possibility is that he was a worker or a delivery person who came into the house." I looked at Mac then at Myra, "Has anyone been in the house before the burglary maybe to do some work?"

She was silent for a moment. "As a matter of fact, there were two people. I had the bedroom closet redone. I also had a phone installed in the bedroom, both before the robbery."

It was a burglary, not a robbery. Most people not in our field mistake one for the other. Robbery is taking by fear or force. I didn't correct her. Burglary was an intent crime. If you went into a store and stole an item, it was shoplifting. If you went into that store wearing a trench coat that had hooks for attaching the items you were "lifting," you had the intent to accomplish your goal prior to entering the store.

The hooks in your coat established the intent to commit the crime. That upped the crime to burglary. If you went into a house that wasn't yours, took items out of the house that didn't belong to you that was burglary.

"Do you have the date the closet was remodeled and the date the phone was installed?"

"Sure. I paid by check, so the date would be in my checkbook register. Let me get it."

I didn't dare look at Myra when she stood up and walked out of the room, although a quick glance at her tight ass would have been a treat. It also would have gotten me into more hot water than I was probably already in with Mac.

"We have two possibilities," I said.

Mac was dubious. "Possible, I suppose, but I don't see our boy working for the phone company or doing carpentry work."

Myra returned. I jotted down the dates and names she gave me. "Now think for a minute. Could either one of these men have been Martin?"

"The telephone installer was a woman."

I gritted my teeth. "Terrific, one down one to go. How about the work on the closet? Could he have been Martin?"

"I suppose. He was clean-shaven. How tall was Martin?"

"He was about five-eight, five-nine, or five-ten. He wore boots or shoes with built-up heels."

"How old was he?"

"He's probably in his forties."

"That's possible."

"I have to ask you a personal question."

"You're going to ask me if it could have been a boyfriend who left the prints, right?"

I stared at her white gloves. "That's correct."

"I suppose."

"This is awkward. I need the names of these gentlemen friends."

"All this is over a robbery?"

"It was a burglary and arson, Ms. Williams."

Mac spoke up. "Austin Martin is a strong suspect in the murder of a police officer, Ms. Williams."

Ms. Williams nodded her pretty head. "I understand. I'll give you the names, but I can promise you not one of the very, very few men who have been in my bedroom fits this Martin's description."

"Can I have the names of those who do?"

"Of course, I'll help in any way I can."

"We sincerely appreciate that." I looked at the white gloves again. Myra caught me staring.

"You're wondering why I'm wearing gloves in the house."

I grinned. "You'd make a good detective."

"I put the fire out and burned my hands. They've been doing skin grafts." She looked down at the carpet, "My hands look ugly. I'm very self-conscious."

Mac said, "I understand, Myra. Can you remember back to the day of the burglary?" Myra nodded. "From the beginning, tell us everything you remember."

"I had come home from shopping." Myra leaned back into the sofa cushions crossed and uncrossed those long, lean legs. "I had two shopping bags. I set them in the kitchen on the countertop."

"Normally, when you go shopping, do you bring your own things home or do you ever have a delivery boy bring them home?"

"I bring them home."

"Okay, please go on."

"I recall that as I set the bags on the countertop, I thought I heard a noise in the bedroom."

"Okay."

"I walked slowly. I was a bit frightened, thinking the worst. I suppose I should have gone out the front door to the neighbors and called the police. But at that point, it was almost like my feet, had a mind of their own."

"I understand," Mac said.

"The bedroom door was opened. I was a few feet from the door when a man ran out of the bedroom to his left then out the back door into the backyard and over the block wall."

"I'm sure deputies asked you this, but did you, at the very second you saw him, think that you knew him?"

"I only saw him for a flash. His face was covered. Then all I saw was his back. It seemed he was dressed in black, all black."

"Then what did you do?"

"I realized something was burning. I didn't know if there was anyone else in the house. I was still frightened and was very cautious. I sort of peeked into the bedroom. That's when I realized he had set the corner of the bed on fire. I ran into the kitchen, filled a deep pan with water, ran back into the bedroom and threw the water on the flames. I did that three times.

"The third time, I slipped on the throw rug next to the bed. The pan of water spilled onto the flames. I started to fall onto the bed. I broke the fall with my hands. I burned my hands badly," Ms. Williams, said as she looked down at her glove covered hands.

"Do you have any kind of video surveillance cameras?"

"No."

How about a security system?" I asked.

"I had one, but I discontinued its use. It seemed like a waste of money. I've never had any trouble here. Never."

"Besides you," Mac asked, "Who has a key to your house?"

"No one, I have the only key."

"Before the burglary, did you take your car in for service?"

"No. I have a friend; he's on your list. He's an attorney. He likes cars. Since I drive very little, I like to walk for the exercise. When my car needs service, Jerry takes care of it for me. He's on the list of names I'll give you." Then Myra added, "I thought of another name to add."

"Is there anything else you can think of that might help us?"

"Nothing, nothing at all. Are you sure I can't at least get you something to drink?"

She uncrossed those legs again, stretched, and gave me a final look at the amply endowed twins, I left Myra's house with the names of four men who we'd investigate, and a hard-on. Mac left Williams' house with an attitude. The minutes I got in the car, Mac said, "Mine are real."

"What?"

"Her tits, I saw you gawking at them."

"I wasn't gawking."

"You were looking," Mac said.

"I'm human, so I looked."

"You looked more than once."

I cracked wise. "She got two tits, so I took two looks." I swallowed. I couldn't win this one. Accept what you can't change. You got caught. "And the point is….?"

"The point is mine are real. Mine won't melt on the beach."

I laughed, "How can you tell hers aren't real?"

"I'm a woman. Trust me, I know."

"Okay, on to bigger and better things. What do you think?"

"You can only wish."

For better or for worse, I ignored Mac's comment.

"Unfortunately, I think she's basically telling the truth. I'd bet her bedroom has seen many more men than she's letting on. But the four on the list will have to do," Mac said.

"Actually, there are only three. Kline's one of the names on the list, and we've already scratched the counselor."

"What's next?"

"The first name on the list has a Lancaster address." I gave Mac the paper on which Myra had written the names, addresses, and phone numbers of her admitted boyfriends.

"Run these addresses on your phone."

We arrived in the 1600 block of Avenue H 1, which was a mile and a half from the 14 freeway. We found the house, and in the driveway was a black Dodge Charger. The house was two-story, painted white. The lawn was recently mowed. The neighborhood was middle class. I would have thought Myra, who made us swear we wouldn't tell her male friends how we got their name, would have gone for guys with more money.

"Let's do a door knock. We've got nothing to lose."

We walked the narrow concrete walkway. I knocked on the door. Within ten seconds, I heard the knob turning. The door opened. Standing in front of us was a middle-aged man dressed in black slacks and a cream colored sport shirt. His hair was short and blond. He was wearing black loafers. He had to be six feet. Myra was a poor judge of height, she rarely saw Franco vertical or this wasn't Franco. I flashed my shield.

"We're looking for Dennis Franco."

The man looked puzzled. "Why?"

I ignored his question. "Can I see some identification, please?"

"Not until you tell me what this is all about."

I nodded. Mac stepped back a foot. "We're investigating a series of armed robberies in this neighborhood. We've been given a general description of a man who fits you to a tee. We can do this here and now, or we can play the game, cuff you, and take you to the station as a suspect. Roll the dice friend." Not one word of that was true.

"That badge says you're an Amity cop. Why are you out here?"

"Cuff him, Dano," I said to Mac. "I had enough."

Mac reached under her blouse. Out came a pair of pink handcuffs, "You think he'll look good in pink?"

I grinned, "Hands-on the wall, feet back, and spread 'em." We were bluffing.

"Okay, okay." Franco reached in his back pocket. He came out of the pocket with his black leather wallet.

Franco pulled out his driver's license. He handed it to me. His license said he was an even six feet. Right age, wrong hair color, although it could have been dyed, and the height was off. I debated with myself if I wanted to try for fingerprints. I quickly decided it wasn't necessary.

To make it look good, I asked, "Where were you last night between eight and ten?"

"I was at the bowling alley on Sierra Highway. I bowl in a men's league. I can give you the names of all the guys we'd bowled with and against. If that's enough, why don't you go back to Amity? You can beat the traffic."

I wanted to knock him on his ass, but the sheriff might not approve. Instead, I dropped his license. When he bent down to pick it up, I fell against him and knocked him on all fours.

330

"I'm sorry, sir. We don't have this much concrete in Amity. I slipped. Not use to walking on concrete." Before he could curse me out, we were halfway down the walkway.

"Let's go back to the station. We can each take one of the two names left on the list and make a few phone calls. If we have to, we can make a house call. And, if you're a really good cop, I just may let you buy me dinner tonight."

"After the way you gawked at those fake tits, you're lucky if I ever let you sniff my dirty panties again," Mac said.

"I didn't gawk. I looked."

"Why are you looking?"

"Because I'm a man and I'm human. Don't you ever look at guys?"

"Not when I'm with you. And even when I'm not with you, I rarely look at another guy. I've got what I want."

I inhaled, "Okay, I'm sorry. No more looking, I promise." I took Mac's hand and kissed it, "How about I buy dinner?"

"You're still not getting my panties until I think you've earned them."

"Fair enough, but I'd still like to know how you can be sure they're fake."

"They're too perfect, and they're too damn big for her size. How can you tell a counterfeit social security card, especially the older ones?"

"The two posts are raised. If you run your thumb over the posts, you can feel the posts," I said.

331

"And by running my eyes over her boobs, I can tell they're bought and paid for."

I was losing an argument I never should have started. Myra had nice titties whether or not they were 'bought and paid for.' Myra also had a nice tight ass, and I'm sure she didn't buy that ass. As for looking, I plead no f*****g contest. I am a man, we men look. I'm sure there are plenty of women out there who check out men's crotches. But the older I get, the wiser I grow.

"So, Angel look, I'm really sorry. I was thoughtless and clueless. I did what I did, and I'm sorry, it won't happen again." I squeezed Mac's hand.

"You can buy me dinner. But you'll sleep with the Gorilla tonight, and you can sniff his panties."

"I think he goes commando." We both laughed.

As I pulled into the Station lot, the first thing my eyes fixed on was Sully's car. This could be the start of more fun than I had since I looked down Myra's blouse. Mac and I managed to not run into Sullivan as we climbed the stairs to the second floor of the Station. We found an empty room with two phones and two computers, and we went to work. Mac took Jose Garcia Chapa. I ended up with the last of the list of names Myra had given us, David Placetow.

Chapa was an easy find. He was also easy to eliminate. He was a Probation Officer at Challenger Memorial Youth Center in Lancaster. Challenger was a lock-up facility for punks arrested for criminal offenses. The place was a self-contained rehabilitation facility for punks after fast money and quick violence. The liberals thought otherwise, but I saw the worst of the worst on the streets. More than three quarters of these kids were the worst of the worst.

Most of these kids were given probation or house arrest the first half dozen times they were caught breaking the law. Then they'd catch a judge who had had enough. He'd sentence them to thirty days, six months or maybe nine months in what the kids called 'Camp Snoopy.' Little known to the honest, hardworking, taxpaying John and Jane Doe, who busted their hump to live in a good neighborhood so they could send their child to a decent school, every one of these camps had a swimming pool. Even the three juvenile halls each had a damn nice pool. Commit a crime, go swimming. Nice, Los Angeles County, very, very nice!

I had arrested enough of these punk kids and had driven enough of them to the Halls and the Camps. I had seen the crap they gave the probation officers. The P.O.s hands were tied. They could do little to these punks. I'd rather be on the streets in the worst of areas then be a PO in a juvenile probation camp. As far as the schools inside these camps were concerned, I had heard from teachers who attempted to teach in these schools that some of these punks were off the chain.

They'd masturbate in front of female staff, they'd smoke grass in class, they would assault other kids and even assault staff. The teachers were afraid to file charges and were even discouraged by the administration from filing charges or even suspending these kids from school. The County Board of Supervisors, who appointed the Board of Education, knew what was going on. They turned a blind eye and a deaf ear to it. I was glad Jose Garcia Chapa was not our man.

David Placetow took a bit more work. I finally tracked him down. He was head of security for the Palmdale Mall. It took an additional fifteen minutes to eliminate Mr. Placetow.

I slammed down the phone. "Shit, we're back to f*****g square one."

"I don't think so," Mac said.

"What does that mean?"

"That means one of two things. It means Myra with her big phony tits either knows more than she is saying or she's telling the truth, the print *was* left by Martin who was burglarizing that house for reasons as yet unknown."

I said, "Either way, its back to square one."

"Not really, we're narrowing it down by process of elimination."

I looked lovingly at Mac. "Are you always that positive?"

"Hell, I'm involved with you. If I weren't optimistic, I'd go crazy."

"Is it possible Martin stashed all or some of the money in that house and was trying to get to it?"

Mac thought for a minute. The tip of her nose twitched, "If he hid the money in her house, then bought and paid for tits is in on it. She has to be."

"Okay. You're saying Martin was trying to get to the money?

Mac shook my head. "I'm saying it is possible that Myra was in on it with him, that she was either somehow involved or that she knowingly let him hide the money in her house. Maybe they had a falling out, and the only way he could get back into the house was to break in. Maybe she took his key away. Maybe, she had the lock changed. Maybe he cut her a piece of the action in exchange for concealing the cash.

"I suggest," Mac offered, "unannounced, we drop by for a visit with Myra again tomorrow. You want to look down her blouse again anyway. The pretext is to find out if she had the locks changed before the burglary. Even though that won't prove anything conclusively, it will point in her direction. We'll even get the name of the locksmith who changed the locks after the break-in."

I sighed, "Anything's worth a try."

Friday morning, we drove back to Palmdale. Traffic on the 5 was heavy. It didn't lighten up till we reached the 14 freeway.

"When this is over…."

I rudely interrupted Mac, "If this is ever over…"

Mac returned the favor, "When this is over, we are going on a weekend getaway."

"Are you asking me or telling me?"

"I'm telling you. We're going away for a three-day weekend on me. And if you're a good boy, will delve into some of those sick fantasies of yours."

I smiled. My eyes lit up like the kid who gets a lollipop after the barber finishes cutting his hair. "Can we also explore some of your sick fantasies?"

This time Mac's face turned red. "Maybe."

"So…you admit you have fantasies?"

"Everybody does."

"Wanna' give me a hint?"

"You're driving. I don't want to excite you too much."

"Where are we going on this all-expenses-paid vacation?"

"It's a mystery run. A friend of mine belongs to a car club. Every so often a member would arrange a mystery run. We'd meet somewhere as a group and caravan to the place that only the car club member who set up the run knew about. For example, once we met at Denny's parking lot in Woodland Hills then caravanned to Santa Barbara for lunch at the Big Yellow House.

"On the route, members would try to guess where we were going, but the only one who knew for sure was the member who arranged the run. So, this will be a mystery run."

"I like mysteries. I like love stories even better."

"You know," Mac began, "They say that partners who ride together every day are closer than husband and wife. I like being your partner."

"Ditto." Boy was I going somewhere I hadn't been before. I sure hope so. "Let's get back to business."

"We know where the print was lifted. Let's check to see if there is a false panel in the wall. It takes a lot of space to conceal that amount of cash. Then again, with his trips out of the country, most of it might be salted away somewhere. He could be keeping 'pocket money' in her house. I'll find a pretext to check the wall. You chat with her. That'll serve two purposes.

"Woman to woman might get you farther than a man to woman. And most importantly, I won't be able to stare at those phony knockers." I smiled and hoped I was racking up points. Keep it up. You're making up for the lost time. You and that ape might have a short relationship." Mac laughed.

When we arrived at the Williams house, we didn't know if Myra would be home. I walked the familiar walkway and knocked on the door. Myra answered. That's one for our side.

Mac said, "We're sorry to barge in without calling, but we were in the area and thought of a couple of questions we hadn't asked."

Myra, attired in all black today except for the white gloves, looked good, very good. I didn't dare look. The blouse covered her neck, so there was no checking out her boobs, which I had already decided had caused me enough trouble.

"C'mon in, I have an appointment," she looked at her watch, "in an hour. Go on into the living room and have a seat. By now, you should know the place pretty well."

I didn't know if she was being friendly or sarcastic. I didn't much care. This case was starting to grate on me. I had made Rocky a promise. I was determined to keep that promise.

"Can I get you a cup of coffee or something?"

We both declined. After Myra was seated on the couch, I asked, "Do you mind if I use your little boy's room?"

"Around the corner, just passed the bedroom on the right."

I nodded, smiled, stood up and walked toward the bedroom, which was out of eyesight from the couch. Instead of turning right, I turned left and stood at the archway to the bedroom. I felt the molding. It seemed solid, so I pressed on it. It was solid. I felt up the wall, down the wall, and all around the wall, solid, solid, solid. "Shit." I took a step into the bedroom and ran my hands over the wall, nothing.

I walked toward the bathroom and felt the wall. Not a damn movement. I walked into the bathroom and flushed the toilet. I returned to the living room. I sat in my favorite stuffed chair. Myra and Mac were deep in conversation.

Mac said, "According to Myra, she's sure no one else, but those on her list had entered her bedroom. And she can't recall anyone else having done any kind of work on the house, not even a locksmith. That leads us to believe that Martin was in this house and committed the burglary, but why?"

I took Martin's picture out of my inside sport jacket pocket along with the pictures of his three deceased buddies. I carefully set the 'four-pack' in front of Myra. "Take a slow, careful look. Remember,

338

Martin may well be clean-shaven. His hair may be dyed or even cut off. Do you recognize any of these men?" I asked.

Myra studied the pictures. She held them up to the light. "I wish I could say I did recognize at least one of them." She shook her head. "I don't, I'm certain."

Mac picked Martin's picture off the table. She looked closely at the picture, very closely. She was studying it like a teenager might study the multiple-choice answers to a pop quiz the teacher had given. Mac decided to play good cop.

"Myra, honey, do me a favor, please. Think back, back to when you first moved in here. Think back to that time. Who was in this house that even remotely fits the description of Martin? Someone who you haven't told us about? Think, Myra."

I looked over at Myra, not her tits, her eyes. She appeared to be concentrating really hard. She closed her eyes. She seemed to be in deep thought.

"Okay, okay. I did have a handyman who lived across the street come over one day about a year ago to fix my clogged sink. But this guy is in his twenties."

We shook our heads. I'm certain the disappointment showed.

"Myra, Myra, there has to be someone. Has to be."

"I guess I just don't get around that much." She pulled off a glove to scratch her hand.

The hand was terribly burned. I could see where they started grafting skin. She was lucky, just like I was really lucky. In Myra's case, it could have been a part of her body that you couldn't cover, like her pretty face. In my case, I could have been killed.....like Rocky. Mac took out her business card. On the back of the APD business card, she wrote a phone number.

"This is my personal phone number, Myra. If you think of anything, or if you just want to talk, even if you want to go out for lunch, just the two of us, call me, Okay?"

Mac didn't actually give Myra her personal number. Most cops carried two cell phones. One was a business number; the other was a "personal number." Obviously, you didn't want to give your personal number to just any asshole. In today's day and electronic age, a phone number is easily traceable to one's address, hence, a 'dummy' phone. The three of us stood up. Mac walked over to Myra. She put her arms around her.

"I know this must be difficult for you, reliving what happened again and again."

Mac looked down at Myra's glove covered hands. She gave Myra a hug, a long hug, too long. She pulled Myra close, a bit too close, then kissed her on the cheek. We got back in the car. I drove away from the house.

"You forgot to tell me you are into women."

Mac didn't hesitate. "I'm not."

"That was some hug. You like pussy?"

340

"You like a dick? I thought most men liked to watch two women go at it?"

"Most of us probably do," I replied.

"Interested in a threesome?" Mac asked.

"I don't know if I want to share you."

"Easy big guy, I'm only kidding, unless, of course, that threesome could be two guys and me."

"What is the matter with you?" I was getting slightly pissed. But I was justified, at least in my mind. "Seriously, what's up?"

Mac laughed. "Trust me, Tony I'm not into women. I've never been with a woman. I have thought about it, almost all women do. But that's as far as that goes. Tell me you've never thought about another guy?"

"When I was younger, I think all kids go through that. I've never been with a guy and have no desire to. I love you so much, Mac, I wouldn't even want to share you with another woman, even if it meant a threesome."

I slowed to let the asshole on my left cut in front of me without signaling.

"So, what was with that hug?"

"I was just checking out your second favorite rack."

"What?"

"I wanted to see if they were real or whether I'm right."

"And you can tell by pressing your body against them?"
"A woman *can*."

"And the verdict is?"

"Fake as charged."

I wasn't sure I believed Mac. That left me very uncomfortable. As I drove, I called Jimenez on my cell. I was in violation of 23123 (a) of the California Vehicle Code, and I didn't give a wet and juicy f**k. If a sheriff pulled me over, he'd have to yank my ass out of the car. I was pissed and frustrated.

"This is bullshit. All this work and where the f**k have we gotten?"

"I told you, we're eliminating possibilities. This narrows it down even more. It was Martin who was either in the house to burgle it or because he was friends, or more, with Myra. I'm beginning to believe Myra."

Then Mac added with a laugh, "Even if she does have big, phony boobs."

"I felt the walls as if they were your beautiful hard body."

"You lie so well, but I'll take it."

"Like your body, nothing that wasn't supposed to move moved. If he wasn't in that house because he hid money there, if he wasn't in that house because he was tight with Myra, why was he there?" I asked.

"Is it possible he saw the house without a car in the driveway, knocked on her door, got no answer, and saw this as an opportunity? Or was he looking for money, jewelry, or both?"

342

I shrugged. "Detective Jimenez, please. It's Kano."

When Jimenez picked up, I got right to the point. "Sir, I think we need to have a meeting. We need to revisit this." I listened for half a minute. "I'd prefer the asshole not be present, but that's not my call. Tomorrow at eleven is fine. The detective bureau works. See you then, sir, thanks."

CHAPTER 25

CANINE TO THE RESCUE

I dropped Mac off at her favorite AA meeting, made one quick stop then drove to the cemetery to see Rocky. I got on my knees. I ran my hand over the grave marker. I reached in my pocket. I placed a box of Marlboro cigarettes and a matchbook on the marker.

"Here you go, buddy, this one's on me."

I took the jewelry box out of my pocket. I opened it and took out the silver wrist band Mac had made. I caressed it lovingly. In the left corner was Rocky's DOB, then his End of Watch date, the date he was killed. Under this was the inscription: *FRIEND, FTO, DAMN GOOD COP.* I placed the band on Rocky's grave marker.

"This wrist band stays in this box, buddy, until I kill the bastard that murdered you. I promised you I'll get him. He won't go to the Station in cuffs; he'll go in the coroner's wagon." I wiped away a tear. "I miss you, buddy. Have a smoke on me."

I stood up, put the wrist band in my pocket then walked to my car. We met at the Station the next day at eleven o'clock. We were five minutes early, but Jimenez and Sullivan were already in the detective's briefing room when Mac and I arrived. I said hello, shook hands with Jimenez and nodded to Sullivan. Mac and I sat down next to each other. Mac had written notes from our various interviews. She placed the notebook on the long, rectangular table. I watched as Sullivan looked at his watch.

"It's show time," the FBI agent said. "How about you tell us why you wanted to meet."

I ran my tongue over my lips. Mac looked hard at me as if to say, don't start anything.

"Okay. First, Mac and I don't have shit. We've done several interviews; all brought us back to square one. Mac will give you an overview."

It took Mac less than fifteen minutes to give Jimenez and Sullivan a rundown of what we had accomplished. When Mac was finished, she asked for questions.

"I have a couple," Jimenez said. "Do you think Williams is telling you the truth?"

"I had my doubts at first," Mac said. "But, yes, I think she's upfront."

"Tony, do you agree with Mac?"

"Yes, sir, like Mac, I had my doubts at first, but after a second visit, I'd bet she is telling the truth."

"Can you take an educated guess as to how Martin's fingerprints got in the house?"

345

"My best judgment tells me he burglarized the place. I'll be damned if I know why, not yet. As Mac told you, I checked for false walls in the area of the fingerprint, nothing, nada. I asked for the meeting because we're out of ideas."

"Does anyone have any suggestions?"

"I have a question," Sullivan said. "Are you two absolutely certain there is no connection between Martin and Williams?"

Mac answered first. "I wouldn't bet a year's salary, but all our questioning, all our training say she's not involved. She's either telling the truth or she's one great actress. It's also possible she knows Martin by another name. She may not recognize him if he's changed his looks."

I spoke up. "I agree with Mac."

Sullivan asked, "Do you ever disagree with her?"

"Sully, you're a real class act, you know that? We're busting our butts trying to solve my partner's murder, and you sit there and make smart ass remarks. If ignorance was money, you'd be a f*****g billionaire."

"I didn't need to drive over here for this. You could have done that over the phone."

"Sully, I thought just maybe if the four of us sat down together and brainstormed, maybe we could come up with another direction. In short, I thought maybe the FBI might have something to offer. I guess I should have known better."

"I'll let that go," Sullivan began, "Only because I haven't walked a mile in your *shoe*!"

"You know asshole when this thing is finally in the history books, I'm going to take that one shoe and shove it so far up your ass you'll choke on shoe leather." I paused to take a breath, "Are your gay buddies out in the parking lot waiting for you?"

"Enough!" Jimenez yelled loudly enough that they could hear him downstairs in dispatch. "Quit the shit. Let's get back on task. "Another outburst like that and I'll personally take you both out into the parking lot."

Everyone in the room snickered at that. Jimenez was out of shape. Mac could probably kick his ass. I wasn't finished with Sully. Jimenez or no Jimenez, Sully had it coming. I opened my mouth to tell him he could f**k a duck in the ass when the desk phone rang. Jimenez stood up. As he walked to the phone, which was on the table next to the podium at the front of the room, Jimenez stared first at me then at Sullivan then back at me as if he was the teacher and Sully and I were misbehaving students.

"Amity Police Department, this is Detective Jimenez."

Jimenez listened to whoever was on the other end of the phone. There was silence in the room. Jimenez took his notebook from his back pants pocket, a pen from his shirt pocket, and put the receiver between his ear and his shoulder. He hurriedly scrawled notes.

Speaking was airport investigator Harry Youngman. "No doubt about it, the vehicle is at the impound yard. I'm absolutely sure, sir."

Jimenez responded, "Thank you for your diligence. We'll be talking, thanks again." Jimenez leaned against the podium. "Okay, class, are you ready for your next assignment, or do you want to continue jerking each other off?" Jimenez didn't wait for an answer. "That call was from the airport police.

"They found a stolen vehicle in one of their long-term parking garages. Because of what's been happening at airports, as you know, security has been tightened. The vehicle was dusted for prints. "Guess whose prints were lifted?"

It came out of my mouth without my telling it to. I swear it did, "Sullivan's!"

Jimenez ignored me, "Martin's."

Four mouths were agape in the room. "You gotta' be shitting me," Sullivan said.

"No shit," said Jimenez, "Martin's prints." Jimenez shook his head.

Mac looked at me and raised her eyebrows. "Unbelievable."

"Un-f*****g believable," I said.

"Maybe now the two of you can put your differences aside, and we can work together to try to make sense of this?"

"Done," I said sincerely.

"Yeah, okay," Sully said.

"Do they think he boarded a plane, or do they think he dumped the car at the airport to make it look like he boarded a flight?"

"They're not sure." Jimenez continued, "Once again, we have more questions than answers. Our best bet is going to be to drive out to the airport. We're going to have to check cameras, interview cops, parking lot employees, witnesses. Everything at the airport is time-stamped, including the stolen. We'll see if we can locate witnesses who dropped their vehicles in that long-time lot when Martin dropped his."

"We're assuming Martin did drop the car, aren't we Jimenez?" Sully asked. "It's possible his prints were in the vehicle but that he didn't drop the car."

"That's a valid point. We'll know more when we question the officer who found it. The car was stolen out of the Van Nuys division. The vehicle is at Van Nuys division with a hold on it for now," Jimenez concluded.

I asked, "Who reported the car?"

"The R/O reported it. It was a legit report. It was taken from in front of the registered owner's house between 0130 hours and 0730 hours two days ago, and nothing was seen or heard. The obvious is he hopped a plane for destinations unknown. Then again, he might be trying to throw us off his trail. He may have taken the car, deliberately left prints in the car, wanting us to believe he boarded a plane. He could be in Amity, laughing his ass off at us."

Jimenez slammed his hand on the table. "I'm getting as bad as you, Kano. This is starting to piss me off."

Mac asked an off the wall question. It was obvious, at least to me that something was rolling around in that pretty head. "What color are Martin's eyes?"

I responded in an instant. "Brown, when I finally catch up to him, they'll both be black." I ran my fingers over my lips. "This guy graduated to the big time. He's grown balls, big balls. He's too smart to steal a car, take it to the airport park it and dump it with his prints in it. It's a ploy, it has to be."

"I hate to say this, but I agree with Kano. The guy didn't play keep away for all this time being stupid. He knows what he's doing. The prints were left intentionally." Sully looked at me and nodded.

Mac said, "I'm going to play devil's advocate. Maybe he figured we'll think just the way you two are thinking, so he deliberately left his prints in the car. Maybe he did hop the jet guessing that we'd think he's still in California."

Jimenez slammed his hand on the table. "F**k all of you, I'm tired!"

Jimenez and Sully drove out to the airport. Mac and I drove to the LAPD impound lot in Van Nuys. Our goal was to see if we could locate any evidence in the car that tied it to Martin. I stopped for a red light on Victory and Van Nuys Boulevard.

"Okay, Mrs. Kojack, what are you thinking?"

350

"Save that question until after we've gone through the vehicle, Mr. Kojack. Let me throw it back at you. What are your thoughts?"

"I'm positive this was planned. As much as I hate f*****g Sullivan, I think he's on to something. Martin *is* devious, and very possibly, he planned this thing, so we'd think he hopped a plane. On the other hand, maybe he did hop the plane. Either way, Martin's worried. But Kojack, here's a better question for you. How the hell does Martin know we're getting closer? How does he know? Someone involved in this case, someone we talked with about this case, somebody is feeding Martin information."

I stopped for another light then made a right turn. I was about a mile from the impound lot.

"If I'm right, that leaves the people we've spoken with personally, the people we've contacted by phone, the people we talked to who might have told other people innocently or otherwise, and us." Then I added, "And there's the possibility of this being an inside job, which leaves one more suspect outstanding in addition to Martin."

Mac looked at me funny.

"It wouldn't be the first time, Kojack. Think about it. How the hell does Martin know we're on to him? I'm going to stick my neck out, way out. I'll bet you a pair of your damp, light blue panties against dinner and box seat Angel tickets that either Myra or Attorney Kline

351

or both are involved in this with Martin. That's the only thing that makes sense to me." I pulled up to the gate at the impound lot. "We're talking millions of dollars here. That would give motive."

The car is in a gated area of the impound lot. It was clearly tagged EVIDENCE, HANDS OFF!!! DO NOT RELEASE!!! The car, blue in color, was a late model, four door Honda Civic. It was clean on the outside. The Airport Police Officer who impounded the stolen was Senior Officer Harry Youngman. He wasn't a young man. He was at least fifty-five years old by my estimation.

He had eaten too many meals that contained too many calories. His stomach was hanging over his Sam Brown. He was maybe five-ten and swung a toothpick between his teeth like yesteryears street cops would swing a baton. This guy was as friendly as a puppy recently adopted from a pound. He rushed toward us with hand extended.

"Lady and gentleman," he said, moving that toothpick from the right side of his lips to the left faster than Nolan Ryan could reach a batter with his fastball. "I understand this Honda I impounded may be a hot baby. I'm Harry Youngman. I am at your service."

I extended my hand. "Good work, impounding this car, sir. We sure as hell appreciate your assistance. This is Investigator Dee Mackenzee. My name's Kano. This car is tied to a cop killer we're trying to apprehend. He was a close friend of mine, my partner. What you found *is* a hot item, a very hot item. We're running second place to this asshole, but we believe we may be closing in on him. That might be why this car is here. He may be trying to throw us off. Tell me all you can about the car. If possible, we'd like to obtain a copy of your report."

"No problem, sir." Youngman hitched up his Sam Brown. "I cruise the lots regularly. Some of our units have license plate scanners on them. The ACLU may be unhappy about these scanners, but with all the terrorists and whackos out there, we need to play catch up too. These scanners can run thousands of plates in seconds. This one came back a stolen.

"I impounded it. I contacted the R/O to confirm it was stolen. It was stolen from in front of the R/O's house in Van Nuys. I drove to the station. I filed my report after dusting the car for prints. Because we're an international airport, we can run prints immediately. I did so, which is SOP for any stolen. The prints came back to your guy. We put out a BOLA. I contacted your office. End of story."

"Hopefully," Mac said, "it's not the end of the story. Hopefully, it's the end of our guy." Then she added, "Any guess as to whether or not he boarded a plane?"

Harry shook his head. "Nope, your guy may be good, but he isn't better or quicker than our cameras." He smiled. "I may be able to help you with that one. We have some pretty sophisticated cameras. Do you have an idea of his destination or an idea of which terminal he may have departed?"

I said quickly, "We're not even certain he departed the airport. This whole thing could be a ruse to throw us off his track. He could be watching us and laughing at us right now."

353

Youngman nodded. "We can look at the cameras, but that's going to be a monumental task unless you can narrow the field to flights or countries."

"Does the parking lot have cameras?" I asked.

The toothpick moved. "Sure does."

"This is a long-term lot. Does it serve specific airlines or destinations?"

Youngman shook his head. "No, it's long term, so anyone has access. But they get a ticket before they enter with time stamp and date of entry. The car and plate are photographed. The lot has cameras throughout."

"I suggest we start by checking those cameras," Mac said.

"I can tell you what time the car entered the lot." Youngman added, biting down on the toothpick. "I've already cross-checked the plate on the Honda to the ticket information."

Youngman was a godsend, now all we had to do was get lucky, real lucky. Mac and I spent the next two days talking with airport personnel, and looking at tape from various cameras. We searched the car. We also had our Reserve staff at the Station cross-reference the registered owners of the car to be certain they had no connection with Martin.

When all was said and done, we had nothing more than we had when we started except for a gentleman in a picture at the Trans World terminal who bore a resemblance to Martin, beard and all. A check

354

with ticket personnel was also a waste of time. Nobody remembered the man. At that time of the evening, the next flight out was to Thailand. Was it a coincidence, maybe? This seemed to be one of Martin's favorite excursions. Did Martin deliberately park in the long term lot knowing the next flight out was to Thailand to throw us off?

We were able to reach the stewardesses by phone who worked that flight. They were unable to remember a man of that description. This was curious. The stewardesses assured us that had someone with a beard, as we described him, boarded their flight, they would have recalled such a man. But had Martin shaved the beard and dyed his hair, odds were he would have boarded the plane undetected. The pilot, copilot, and other crew members could not be reached.

Mac and I huddled in an airport coffee shop. "He didn't board the flight," she said convincingly. "He wanted us to think he did; he didn't. He's still in town."

Mac's cell rang. I got up to go to the men's room. When I got back, Mac was laughing.

"What?" I asked.

"The call.....Myra Williams, she has another name for us. Her neighbors, she told me, from a couple of blocks over, would come over occasionally for a drink. He *somewhat* fits Martin's description. I've got the address."

"Let's give Jimenez and Sullivan a ring to see if they came up with anything, then on the way home, we can check with her friends."

"Sounds like a plan."

I phoned Jimenez. He and Sully, as the voice of Dodger baseball, Vince Scully would say, 'Came up with a handful of empty.'

"All of a sudden, Myra comes up with more names? I don't like this. Out of the blue, a dumped stolen at the airport, then Myra comes up with more names. Something stinks, and it ain't fish that washed up on the shore in the Marina," I said.

"She apologized. She said she hadn't thought about them until she ran into them in the grocery store. I'm sure it's also another dead end."

"Um, somebody, I'm close with told me these things are not dead ends; they're part of the process of elimination."

"A very smart person came to that conclusion," Mac said.

"I don't know about smart, but her tits are real."

"Not at all funny, that might seriously cost you."

"Let's pay a visit to Myra's friends early tomorrow. It's getting kind of late. Before I burn any more bridges, I thought maybe we'd go back to my place. I can use a drink, and I know you can use a cup of coffee."

Mac looked at me like a scolded puppy. "What else can you use?"

We used it all; almost all.

We were on our way to Myra's friends' house, the Patterson's. Mary and John Patterson lived a block east of Myra. It was 0800 hours.

"Let's stop at Myra's house on our way over to the Patterson's. I'd like to talk with Myra before we pay a call on her friends."

356

"Is there anything specific?"

"Yes and no," Mac said.

"Good answer, ever thought about politics after you retire?"

Mac snickered. It was obvious to me she was deep in thought.

My focus point has always been traffic. The only real investigative skills I studied have been in the field of accident investigation. While this is all new to me, and while I'm pushing the envelope doing this, I loved it. I could see myself….. I stopped in midsentence. I looked at Mac. She looked like she was out in left field.

"What's eating you?" I asked.

"Myra. All of a sudden, neighbors who have been at her house who she didn't remember.

"Suddenly, a neighbor who may bear a resemblance to Martin. I don't know, Tony. I just don't like how this smells."

"Okay. You still didn't tell me why we're stopping by her house."

"I didn't tell you because I don't know. My gut says Myra first, Patterson last. Humor me."

"Any day, any time, consider yourself humored."

Mac called Myra, Myra invited us over. "I gotta' play this out; it's so stupid that I don't even want to mention it. After I've taken my shot, I'll tell you about it."

We pulled up to Myra's Palmdale house. I didn't need my GPS anymore to find the house. We walked up to the door. Myra opened the door before we could knock.

"Coffee's on. Come on in. I feel like we're old friends." Myra said.

"Friends, I'll buy but old, not yet."

We walked in. Myra was her usual natty self. She obviously liked solid colors. Her dress was red, her blouse was white. This time the buttons were undone to the point where I could see her white bra. I didn't dare wonder if it was a push-up bra. I sure as shit didn't look. She wore a black and white scarf around her neck and, of course, long white gloves.

"Can I get you coffee?" She asked.

"I'm good."

Mac said, "I'd love a cup if you don't mind."

"How do you take it?"

"Black is fine. Thank you."

"I'll be right back."

The questions started as soon as Myra came back with the coffee which she carried into the living room on a tray.

"Sir, are you sure you won't have coffee?"

"Positive. Call me, Tony, remember, we're old friends."

"I assume you're here to talk about my neighbor?"

"Good assumption, want a job?"

Myra smiled, "I don't know how I didn't think of him sooner. I don't think he'd do anything like that, but you asked for all the names of people who have been in the house, he has."

"Good call, that's exactly what we want."

Myra sipped the coffee. "Do you know how long they've lived in Palmdale?"

"They were here when I moved in."

"Can you describe him?"

Myra closed her eyes momentarily. "He's slightly less than six feet, well built, dark eyes and black hair. He's in his forties, I would say."

"Do you know what kind of work he does?"

"He works on base at Edwards Air Force Base. I think he does computer repair."

That, I thought to myself, would necessitate a security clearance. He was probably not our guy.

Mac set her coffee down then asked, "Can I use the restroom?"

"Of course, you know where it is?"

Mac got up slowly. Just as slowly walked to the bathroom. This gave me a chance to check out those phony titties.

I did. "Have you come up with any other names?"

"No. That's it. This time I'm positive."

"Do you know what kind of car Patterson drives?"

"A Chevy HHR, but it was just recalled, so he's got a rental. That's a Toyota."

I remembered reading that GM recalled more cars than dogs had ticks. "What kind of guy is Patterson?"

"He and his wife are both very pleasant and friendly. Always say hello. He gives me hugs so he can press up against me, but only when Mary is not close by."

I could understand that. "Is he strange or different in any way?"

"Not at all, he's like most men I've met."

I didn't want to know what that meant. "Does Mac have the address for the Patterson's?"

Myra nodded, "Yes, I gave it to her yesterday."

Mac walked back into the room. She smoothed her dress as she sat down. She immediately reached for her coffee. "Did I miss anything?"

"I don't think Patterson is our guy. He works at Edwards Air Force Base. He must have a security clearance. But it's worth a follow-up, I guess."

We left Myra's place and drove two blocks over to the Patterson's house. Nobody was home. Mac asked me to drive her to Home Depot. I found a Home Depot on my phone GPS, off we went. Mac said she needed a new toilet handle, the old one had loosened up.

"You should have said something to me. I would have taken care of it."

"Do I look crippled to you? I also change oil, do tune-ups, and light bodywork."

"I'm impressed," I said.

"There are a lot of good things you don't know about me."

"I'm sure. It gives me…gives us something to look forward to."

We finished Mac's shopping then drove back to the Patterson's house, hoping the second time would be the charm. John Patterson answered the door. He was dressed in black slacks and a white tee shirt. He stood about five feet ten inches tall. He had a bushy mustache, which Myra failed to mention, or he grew it recently. His hair was black and collar length. He did fit the general description.

"I'm Investigator Kano. This is Investigator Mackenzee." I flashed the badge but intentionally did not mention that we were from APD. "We're investigating the break-in at Myra Williams house some time ago." I waited for him to invite us in. He didn't.

"What can I do?"

It seems the suspect jumped over a couple of fences and a wall and may have ended up running through your yard." That was a lie. "On the long-shot chance that you might have seen something or heard something, we're here investigating."

"I remember Myra mentioning that a while back. I was at work when it happened. I work at Edwards, the Air Force Base. My wife, who also works at the base, wasn't home either."

"I see, how long have you worked at Edwards?"

Patterson was quick to answer. He leaned against the door, blocking not only our entrance to the house but clear vision inside the house.

"I don't see what that has to do with your investigation. But the fact is I've worked at Edwards for the last twelve years. I have a high-level security clearance."

He reached into the pocket of his slacks, pulled out his wallet, fumbled through it, took out his license, his Base ID and his clearance card.

"Here. Does this work for you?"

It worked just fine, one more possibility dead in the water. "We don't want to take up any more of your time. Thank you for your assistance.

"Here's a card. If you happen to think of something that might help, no matter how small you think it might be, please call us."

As I slid behind the wheel, I asked Mac to call APD and ask Jimenez to run a quick check on Patterson with Edwards' personnel. "Did you get his horsepower?"

"Ten twelve seventy."

362

"Good eye, Sherlock."

Mac got on her cell while I drove. Myra had given us one more name of a possible. She didn't have an exact address, so we asked dispatch to do a reverse directory check. Dispatch went beyond that and ran the guy for us. He came back dead.

It took two days to get the results back on Patterson. We got exactly what we expected. The guy was as clean as a hungry dog's meat bone. We had nothing in the stolen car. We had no leads on where the hell Martin might be, inside or outside of the country. Both Jimenez and Sullivan were putting pressure on Mac and me. I could handle Jimenez. I didn't want to handle Sullivan. Mac took me to a local APD watering hole.

She sipped black coffee. I downed two shots of Seagram's, then Mac bought me a third.

"What's up?"

"What?" Mac looked at me then quickly looked down at the table.

"You're not plying me with booze for nothing. If you want to get in my pants, just tell me," I kidded. "What's going on?"

"Go suck on a red lollipop, Kojack." Then she said, "I need help but no questions, deal?"

"One more shot buys a deal," I said.

Mac motioned for the waitress, "Give the man a double shot of Seagram's, please."

"You're trying to get me to AA?"

"Not a chance, you don't have an alcohol problem. You don't have a living problem. You've got me. I'm you're problem."

"I love that problem." The waitress set my double shot on the table. I let it sit for a minute. "What do you need?"

"I need back in Myra's house one last time."

"Why?"

"The deal was no questions."

I sighed then downed the double shot. I loved the burning, "Why do you need me for that?"

"I need an excuse that doesn't sound like bullshit. I need something that sounds legit."

"I can't ask why?"

"No."

"Give me a few minutes. I'll come up with something." Mac was sitting close to me.

She reached over and squeezed between my legs. "That might ruin my concentration, but don't stop." She didn't.

I thought about Mac's hand on my crotch. I thought about a good sounding reason for going back to Myra's house. I thought about Mac's hand. I thought about Mac's hand. I thought about Mac's hand…..Mac's hand on my crotch was the prelude for going to Mac's house. We did, and it was fun and games.

When we were finished, Mac asked, "Well, did you come up with a reason for my going back into Myra's house?"

We were stretched out on the bed. I slid my hand under the pillow. I've had all sorts of reactions after sex but never *that* reaction.

"Thanks, Babe."

"It was great. The second best sex I've ever had."

"What was the best?"

"It was the other night with you! Now, if you ever want to have sex with me again, come up with a damn good reason to get back into Myra's house."

"Got it, just ask, and you shall receive. Try this. We borrow a drug-sniffing dog. We tell Myra it's a money sniffing dog that we'd like to run it through the house to see if he'll sniff anything out other than your panties!"

"I love it. You are one sick sorry son of a bitch. I love you for it. That'll work. Can we get the dog?"

"Yeah, Berto works canine. He owes me. I'll call him after…… Mac started working her way down my stomach. I'll call him after…. After…That's feels sooooo good."

I called Myra first thing Monday morning. "Good morning, Myra. I hope it isn't too early to call you."

She giggled, "I'm an early riser."

"Me too, I get up early." If she caught it, I bet she wouldn't bite. I was wrong.

"I bet you get up early. I'm beginning to feel like we're very old friends."

"Me too, can we get better acquainted?"

Mac was standing in my kitchen, taking in every word. She remained quiet. I shrugged my shoulders as if to say, "What do you want me to do?"

"What did you have in mind?" Myra asked.

I smiled at Mac. "I have someone I'd like you to meet."

"You caught the man who was in my house?"

"No. I'd like you to meet Lieutenant."

"Lieutenant?"

"He's the best-looking German Shepherd you'll ever meet."

"Ah, why would I want to meet a dog? I mean I like dogs but......"

"Myra, here's the story. We think there's a chance that money from the robbery, in which my partner and friend was killed, is in your house, somewhere. It can be hidden in the floor, in the walls, in a closet, in the ceiling. Lieutenant is trained to sniff out money."

There was a pause. "I've heard of drug-sniffing dogs but money sniffing dogs...?"

"Yup, we give Lieutenant the scent from the robbery from objects we recovered at the scene, and even after all this time, we think there is an outside chance he can pick up the scent. We'd like your permission to let us bring him to your house. LT will do a walkthrough. Is that good with you?"

There was a pause, then there was a laugh. "I guess so. Do I get something in return?"

"What would that be?"

"Take me out for a drink?"

Mac punched me in the arm, she was getting stronger. I felt that punch. Again, I shrugged as if to say, *what do you expect me to do?*

"That sounds like a winner to me. What would be good for you, Myra? I really appreciate your cooperation."

"Not a problem. What would be good for you as far as bringing Lieutenant over, or what would be good for me as far as our date?"

"I have to check my work calendar as far as the drink. How about meeting this afternoon at about three o'clock?"

"That would be fine."

I had to get with Berto to see if he and Lieutenant were available, but I also wanted a commitment from Myra. All the while, I had absolutely no idea what was in Mac's head. I promised Mac I wouldn't ask. Sometimes cops have hunches. Sometimes these hunches are as far out as finding ice in the California desert in August. Occasionally, these hunches bear fruit. For various reasons, I thought it a great idea to let Triple-A with a gun, play her hunch.

"Myra, I appreciate your willingness to cooperate. We'll see you about three this afternoon."

"Don't forget my reward for cooperating."

I hung up three seconds before Mac punched me in the other arm.

"A word to the wise, Mr. Asshole with a capital ASS, don't mess with Myra. Trust me. If I'm right, you want nothing to do with those phony titties. The only titties you need are mine. Are we clear on that Mr. Asshole with a capital A?"

What can you say to that caveat? "Clear as clean glass, Ms. Kojack."

I called Berto. We arranged to meet at Foxy Roxy's Restaurant just off the 14 freeway at Palmdale Boulevard at two o'clock to go over a game plan and grab a cup of coffee. Berto and Lieutenant arrived at fourteen hundred hours on the money. Mac and I were already seated by the window at Roxy's. We watched Berto drive up in a black and white SUV.

"Is the Lieutenant or Berto driving?"

"I can't tell," Mac said. "For a minute, I thought it was you driving. You and that dog have the same size mouth."

"Same size tongue, maybe."

368

"Do you ever stop?" Mac asked, smiling.

"If I did, would you still love me?"

"Probably, I think I'm infected with a disease called Tonyitis," Mac replied.

"And there ain't no cure for it. So as your program teaches, ***accept that which you cannot change***."

Berto walked in and left Lieutenant in the SUV with the air conditioning running. Berto was only five foot nine. He was dark-skinned with a gut. He was dressed in khakis and was from the Bronx. He never lost the accent. He said hello to Mac then shook hands with me before he sat across the table from us.

"Thanks for coming out," Mac said. "We're stymied by this case. We're grasping at straws. We need your help. We need you to pretend to use LT to search the house for stolen cash."

"This broad really believes Lieutenant can sniff out money?"

"Tony is a lying sack of garbage. He convinced her."

"What are we really after here?"

The waitress took our order, which was iced tea for Mac and me and iced coffee for Berto.

When the waitress walked away, Berto said, "They really don't know how to make iced coffee out here. You take coffee you fill up ice cube trays and put the trays in the freezer.

"You put ice cubes in a large glass then pour freshly made coffee into the cup. That's ice coffee. It's not diluted."

"Makes sense to me. It's like drinking Seagram's with Seven-Up added. It kills the taste, or like putting low octane gasoline in a Ferrari."

"Or like drinking decaf coffee," Mac added. "To answer your question about what we're really after, I can't answer that question, Berto. We're not really sure. We just need it done. Do me a favor, when you and Rin Tin Tin are in the house, don't flirt with the Williams woman; Tony hates competition."

"That hurt."

"So, the Williams broad has approved this assault on her house?"

"Yeah, it's a go for fifteen hundred. We'll go in with you. Of course, we'll stay behind you and the dog. We don't want to kill any scent."

"Okay, how much time do you need?" Berto asked.

"To make it look legit, let's go for thirty or so minutes," Mac said.

The waitress brought our drinks. "On the way-out hon, can I get a large cup with an iced coffee in it for the Lieutenant who's waiting in the car, please?"

"Sure, will there be anything else?"

"A winning lottery ticket," I said.

"If I had one of those, do you think I share it? If I had one of those, I wouldn't even be here."

370

The waitress walked away. It was fifteen hundred hours when we converged on the Williams' house. That meant Mac, Berto, Lieutenant, and I were at the front door. Mac knocked, Williams answered. As usual, Myra was well dressed in tight blue jeans white tank top which accentuated those beauties, white gloves covering the burned hands and black choker. She wore a black straw hat, which was cute but looked out of place.

I took the lead. "Myra, you know Mac, this is Berto, and the good looking one is Lieutenant, who I told you about. LT will attempt to sniff out the money, not Berto."

We all laughed. "Come on in," Myra said softly. I made a pitcher of iced tea."

Myra turned back around to face us. "For the sake of discussion, if that money *had* been in the house and the suspect who broke in did get it, would the dog still sniff it out?"

That was a good question, a question I wouldn't have asked unless I was worried about it.

"That depends on how long the money was in the house and how much money was hidden, Berto bull shitted, Myra.

"In other words, if there is enough scent for the dog to pick up Lieutenant will hit on it." I looked at Mac, and she frowned. She knew exactly what was on my mind.

We stepped inside the house. Mac said, "We're iced tea'd out. We stopped for a cold drink before coming over here, maybe before we leave. We thank you for your thoughtfulness, for your hospitality and for letting us be a pain in the behind."

"It comes with a price," Myra said with a smile as she looked directly into my eyes.

"I need everyone to remain behind LT," Berto said. This way, we don't contaminate the scene."

I was certain Myra didn't understand the mumbo jumbo Berto was laying on her.

Myra surprised me when she asked, "What scent did Lieutenant pick up that he could assimilate it to the money?"

Berto was from the east coast. He studied law before he became a cop. If he didn't know the answer, he could baffle you with his bullshit.

"We recovered a couple of bills at the crime scene. We're hoping enough scent remained on those bills for LT to pick up on."

We stepped into the hallway, which was decorated with pictures, some framed. They appeared to be photos of Australia beaches. The pictures looked inviting. On my salary, I'd never make it to Australia, maybe Tijuana.

"Berto, where do you want to start?" I asked.

"Might as well start right here. Lieutenant, plotz."

I knew 'plotz' meant to sit. That was the extent of my German. Berto said something to LT in German that I didn't understand. He took an envelope out of his pocket. He took two bills out of the envelope, rubbed them together, and then held the bills close to LT's nose. LT's tail wagged vigorously. If this was BS, Berto and LT had me fooled. I looked quickly at Myra. She seemed to be enjoying the show.

Berto gave LT another command in German. LT walked toward the wall and started to sniff. He did this throughout the hallway. My understanding was that when sniffing out drugs, the dog would go wild if he found the scent. LT was broke. We went into the bedroom. Myra excused herself to answer the telephone. Mac went into the bathroom, closed, and locked the door. Berto and LT continued the charade. We were in the living room when Mac returned from the bathroom. Shortly after that, Myra returned from her phone call.

"Any luck?" She asked.

"Nada," Berto responded.

Suddenly LT started pawing at the living room wall. Berto turned ashen. I smiled. Myra stiffened.

"A hit," Berto said. It sounded more like a question than a statement.

"Please stand back and let LT do his thing any damage he does to the wall, APD will cover." LT was now barking at the wall and scratching at it simultaneously.

"Plotz, LT, plotz."

Berto stood looking at LT with a puzzled look on his face. He repeated his earlier command. LT again started to claw at the wall and to bark. That tail was going like wildfire in a desert wind.

"Plotz, LT, plotz."

"Let's dust the wall for prints. I have a print kit in my car," I said.

I retrieved the print kit and dusted the wall. Not a useable print. LT looked at his handler. He was awaiting a command; none came.

"We're going to need to open that wall. Something spooked LT. Let's hope it's the money."

Now Mac and I were the ones wearing the look of surprise. Something sure was inside that wall that got LT's attention. Maybe LT did hit on the money. Berto looked at me, then at Mac, and finally at Myra.

"I'll put LT in the unit. I brought tools with me; they're in the unit. Tony, want to give me a hand?"

"Sure." I smiled at Myra. "Do we have your permission to open the wall?"

Myra nodded, "As long as your PD fixes any damage, be my guest."

LT, Berto, and I walked to the unit. Berto patted LT on the head.

"Good boy, very good boy."

He gave LT a rubber ball. LT took it in his mouth. His tail wagged faster than a helicopter propeller on takeoff. He also gave LT a bowl of ice water he had in an ice chest.

"What the f**k?" I said.

"I don't know either. Something in the wall caught LT's attention," Berto said.

374

"Is it possible…?"

"Doubtful. Those freakin' bills I rubbed under his nose are mine. The only guess I would make is that at some time an animal, a mouse, who knows, but something in that wall or something that left its scent in the wall, got to him.

"If there's money in that wall, it's an unheard of miracle. LT has been trained to do a lot of things, but the only way a dog would sniff out money is if there was the scent of drugs on the money. Was your perp involved with drugs?"

"It's a possibility, remote, but it's possible."

"I hate to open the wall for nothing. We're at the point of no return. If we back away from the wall now, Myra will pitch a bitch and become suspicious."

"You're right. Let's get the shit out of your unit and go to work. The less damage we do, the less will hear about it from the Chief."

I grabbed a black bag that was filled with tools and carried them into the house. "You got bricks in this damn thing?"

"All tools of the trade, my boy, all the tools of the trade, and then some. You never know what you're going to need and when you're going to need it. Be prepared!"

We walked back into Myra's house. Berto bent down. He opened the bag. He rattled tools around. "Here we go." He chiseled a small hole in the wall and then chiseled a wider hole. He stepped back to admire his handy work. "That's should do it."

"That hole is not large enough to get my....my thumb in," I said, looking at Mac.

Mac and Myra were observing with interest. "Oh my God," Myra said. "I forgot when they remodeled my closet, the guy brought his teenage son with him one day.

"The boy replaced the molding around the wall. To do that, he had to pull down a section of the wall. This section."

"Okay."

If it was the carpenter's son, that had no bearing on our case. If Myra was lying, there was a possibility the money was in the wall. My heartbeat increased. Berto did some more rummaging in his black bag of tricks.

"Got it," he said.

He extracted a long metal rod that was flexible and had a mirror on the end and a light. I watched enough television to know what he was going to do with that.

"You're going to insert that in the wall, bend the mirror so you can see three hundred sixty degrees inside that wall."

Berto nodded. "And with any kind of luck, we won't have to do any more cutting."

Berto looked at Myra. Berto smiled, Myra smiled back. Mac looked at me as if daring me to smile at Myra. I didn't dare.

Carefully, Berto fed the camera through the opening in the wall. He was good. It took only minutes for him to begin his search.

"Nothing there, nothing there either." Then, "I'll be a son of a witch."

Everyone stepped forward, "What did you find?"

"Probably what LT was scratching about? Come over here."

I was the first one to look at the picture in the camera. Mac was next, then Myra. I didn't know whether to laugh or to throw something.

"A f*****g beer bottle."

At the bottom of the wall was a beer bottle. Odds are there was still enough beer in the bottle for LT to smell it. The kid was drinking a beer when he was working on the wall. Either he forgot it or dad came out of the closet unexpectedly. Dad spooked the kid. The boy panicked, left the Corona beer in the wall, quickly closed up shop so dad wouldn't have a clue.

"Get the wall fixed," Berto told Myra. "Bill Amity PD. Let me get Lieutenant. We'll finish our work and get out of your hair, providing we don't find any more beer bottles."

We didn't find any more beer bottles. We didn't find anything. We hadn't expected to find anything. Nothing ventured, nothing gained. One more dead end. After we cleaned up the mess we had made, we assured Myra APD would cover the cost of repair to the wall. We then walked out to Berto's unit, where I patted Lieutenant and asked him if he'd like a Corona. LT exercised his right to remain silent. His tail wagged faster than a missile travels immediately after takeoff.

CHAPTER 26

THE DISAPPEARANCE OF MAC

We drove back to the Station. Mac and I had to file a report. Mac was quiet on the drive, which would take a little over an hour if the traffic was light. She seemed to be deep in thought. That frightened me.

"What's going on, Ms. Kojack?"

"I need PC."

"You need probable cause for what?"

"I can't tell you."

Now *I* got quiet. Partners weren't supposed to keep shit from one another. Arguing wasn't going to help. I'd lose out on a professional front. I'd sure the hell lose on a relationship basis. I kept my mouth shut, drove south on the 14 freeway, and tried to figure out why Mac needed probable cause. We had already searched the house with Myra's permission.

We didn't need PC for that. We had opened the wall in Myra's house, with Myra's okay. We didn't need PC for that. I was lost. We hit light traffic. I hit more traffic when I exited the 5 freeway at Soto Street.

The City of Vernon is adjacent to, and north of Amity. It's a city of business with very few residences. The city of Vernon is congested with truck traffic. We hit most of it. It took us eighty-five minutes of mostly silent driving before we turned into the APD parking lot. I parked the unit. Mac and I walked to the Station in silence.

The second the Station door slammed shut, Mac grabbed me by the upper arm.

"I got it," she whispered excitedly, "I got it."

"What do you got?"

"I got the PC." Then she was quiet for half a minute. "Have you ever wanted to be a T-Man?"

T-man was slang for a treasury agent as G-man, in the old days, was slang for government man or agent. There was a twinkle in Mac's eye, a mischievous twinkle that I just knew spelled trouble......for me.

"The courts have held," Mac began, "that someone's trash, put out on the sidewalk, is fair game, correct?"

I didn't answer. I said, "Okay."

"That means we, you are going to become a T-man for a day."

Mac walked upstairs to the Detective Bureau. She said she had some "stuff" to take care of then she had to make a couple of phone calls. I told Mac I'd be in the 'blue room' writing the report that included the rationale for the damage we did to Myra's wall. I was emotionally drained by this case. I had made a graveside promise to Rocky. It was

379

taking its toll on me. An overnighter to San Diego might clear my head. I knew the case was also taking its toll on Mac.

I liked San Diego. If I could afford a decent house in San Diego, I would have moved there a long time ago. But housing there was out of my financial reach. I started the report. It was a straightforward report.

I wrote it, proofed it, spell checked it, then placed it in the Watch Commander's box for approval. I sat, and BS'd with a couple of young cops who had recently been hired by APD.

Mac met me in the blue room thirty-five minutes later. "The report is done?"

I nodded. "Your *stuff is* done?"

Mac nodded. "Signed, sealed, and delivered."

"What's on your agenda for tonight?"

"Nothing tonight, but tomorrow morning, early, is trash pickup, T-man."

"Which to me means what?"

"We'll talk about it later. I'll warm you up for that chore before I tell you about it."

Mac walked me to the corner of the blue room. Out of earshot, she said, "Think lubricant, social lubricant. Think about the panties I've been wearing for two days, the black nylon ones that always get you rock hard. That should loosen you up."

380

I was already beginning to feel the erection in my pants just thinking about those panties, and inside them Mac's wet pussy.

"When I get finished with my *chore,* how about an overnighter to San Diego?" I asked.

"Let's see how things go. That may be a plan, but one step at a time, fair enough?"

"Fair enough, my place, your panties?" I whispered.

It was 0630 hours. The back of the Amity Police Department parking lot was a bit nippy. Mac had a broad smile on her face. I was in the dark, both literally and figuratively. The sun was just starting to come up. I came up last night!

"Are you going to clue me in?"

"You'll see it for yourself soon enough?" Mac said.

I was dressed in jeans and a sweatshirt. Mack told me to grab several pair of nylon gloves from the department closet. They were in my back pocket. A horn honked. At the gate was a green trash truck. Mac accessed her portable radio.

"Investigator one, please open the rear-entry gate."

When I heard open the rear entry gate please, my mind automatically thought other than the station's security. Mac didn't have a clue. It was something else for me to think about. Magically, the trash truck rolled on to the parking lot. His truck rolled to that corner. We followed on foot, and watched as the driver stopped, exited the trash

381

truck, then walked to the rear. He dropped off your standard trash can. Next to the full trash can, the driver placed an empty green container.

"Thank you. If this pans out, I'll let you know. Either way, we appreciate your cooperation."

Mac handed him a couple of folded bills. He got back in the truck and drove toward the exit gate, which opened automatically. I watched the trash truck exit the lot.

I turned to Mac. "Now, will you tell me?"

She shook her head. "Negatory. But let's do this. This is such a long shot that if it pans out, I'll let you eat my……….."

My cell phone rang. It drowned out Mac's next couple of words. It kept ringing.

Mac finished her sentence: "…for one sold hour. If it doesn't, not only will I feel totally stupid, but I'll play out any fantasy you want. Deal?"

I answered my cell. It was Jimenez. He was apparently upstairs in the detective bureau looking down at the parking lot. He wanted to know what the hell was going on.

"We're doing research." I was screwing with Jimenez, but I really didn't know what to tell him. "I'll keep you posted, boss. Relax, enjoy your morning." I hung up.

I smiled at Mac, "Your ass or my fantasy. That means I gotta' cop to another one of my fetishes?"

"You got it," Mac replied.

"And you play it out no matter how weird?"

"Within reason, I know you're sick and weird, but don't go too weirdo on me."

"Deal."

"Good. See how tight those gloves fit. Dig into that trash can. Find me half a dozen items I can pull prints off."

I shook my head but did as I was told. When I was in kindergarten, the one thing I never wanted to be was a T-Man, now I knew why. Garbage is dirty, smelly, and tends to stick together. I had to do some deep digging to get Mac what I hoped she wanted. As I pulled it carefully out of the trash, careful that I only touched it with my gloves, Mac looked it over. When she had eight items she was satisfied with, she called it a morning. That was a good thing because as the temperature increased, so did the stench of the trash.

Mac donned gloves and gingerly placed the "garbage" items in a baggy. "I'm going to the station with this garbage and take care of business. Why don't you take a shower downstairs and change because you *really stink*!" Mac's smile showed love.

That comment would have been funny, but I did smell. "See you back out here in about thirty minutes?" I replied.

"That should work. Because you did such a good job, you can buy me brunch."

"Works for me."

We grabbed brunch then drove south on the 5 freeway to San Diego. A break from the case would help us both. We checked in at the Town and Country Motel at Hotel Circle in San Diego. We took a shower together. We were in a drought, so why not economize on the water. We also saved on the soap. We walked around Old Town in the early evening. For dinner we went to one of my favorite Italian restaurants, "Silverman's," which *is* an Italian Restaurant?

I laughed since I know his parents are from Israel, hers are from Italy. She's the cook, he's the host. It's been working for years. It was a great environment. The food was awesome.

I had made a reservation, so there was no waiting for a table. We were seated. Mr. Silverman came right to our table. "Mr. Kano, how have you been? We haven't seen you in some time."

I smiled. "Unfortunately, I don't get down here nearly often enough, this is Mac."

Mr. Silverman walked over to Mac and extended his hand, "Not only does Mr. Kano have great taste in food, but he also has excellent taste in women."

I wasn't about to touch that with a breadstick.

"What can I get you to drink?"

Mac ordered a black coffee. "I'll have two shots of Seagram's, please."

Mr. Silverman walked away from the table. Mac was taking in the room.

"Interesting, there are pictures of both Israel and Italy on the walls."

"And America," I added, "Too bad we can't all get along, as that scumbag King said."

Mac remained silent.

"We're here to forget about the case," I said.

"Have you?"

I shook my head. "No. I can't get it out of my head either. Can you clue me in on what you've got going?"

"Not yet. If I get anything conclusive, you'll be the first to know. Promise."

Mr. Silverman brought the coffee and my drinks. I immediately picked up one shot glass and held it up. "To solving cases."

Mac picks up her coffee cup. "To solving this case."

We drank. "I love it down here. The weather is beautiful, and the pace is slower. There's more open space. I'd love to live here," I told Mac.

"Why not?"

"Cost of living, and I love Amity PD."

"Two salaries would go a long way down here," Mac said.

Mac was correct. "True. But that would mean leaving APD. Would you leave the Highway Patrol?"

"I wouldn't have to. I could transfer down here. But after working on this case, I may want to become a detective."

I downed my other shot. "Interesting, we do have options. That's a good thing."

Mr. Silverman came back and took our order. In the morning, we drove to Sea World. We had fun but still couldn't forget about the case. That evening we took in a Padres game. The San Diego Padres won. I really didn't care, but I lost a bet on the game to Mac. That meant that at Town and Country, I had to serve her sexual fantasy, which was tying her to the bed and forcibly having my way with her. Cops find strange ways to get release.

We both enjoyed the hell out of that. For forty-five minutes, we forgot about the robbery, burglary, and Rocky's killer. In the morning, we drove north. I dropped Mac off at her place, drove to my house to unpack the little clothing I had taken with me to San Diego, and finally to check messages.

It was still light. I fell asleep on the couch. I woke up to darkness and the Dodger game. I had a headache. It was about to get worse, much worse. I took two shots of Seagram's with three, ibuprofen. I sat back down on the couch, took out my cell phone, and started to speed dial Mac's number. Then I thought she probably needed the rest as much as I did. I hung up.

The Dodgers were playing Philadelphia at the stadium; the game was tied two to two. I watched two innings. The game was still tied when I fell back asleep. This time it was light when I awoke. I showered, shaved, poured some Kellogg's in a bowl, poured milk over the cereal, made a cup of coffee, then sat down at the kitchen table to clear my head of the morning cobwebs over breakfast. It was 0723 hours. I swallowed two bites of cereal and swallowed one big gulp of coffee. My head was starting to come to the reality. Today was the *present* that Mac talked about. It was a new day.

My phone rang. "Hello."

It was Jimenez. "Heard from Mac?"

"Not since yesterday. We got back from San Diego. I fell asleep watching the game. Who won?"

"Philadelphia."

"Did you try Mac's home number?"

"And both cells, Nada."

"What's up?" I asked

"Nothing that I know of, I got a message for her to call back regarding the prints she ran."

"Let me finish breakfast. I'll get a hold of her. I'll have her call you. Anything new with you or Sully on the case?"

"Not a damn thing. How about you?"

"You know if I had anything you would have heard."

"I need you to do me a favor. Back off on Sully. That guy's not wrapped too tight. I don't need any bullshit. Fair enough?"

I laughed. "You got it. I'll get in touch with Mac. She'll get back with you unless you want to give me the number, and I'll give it to her."

"Better you call her. You have her call me."

"You got it, talk at you later." I finished breakfast with two shots.

I got on the computer. I scanned the world news. More bullshit, Still no sign of the missing Malaysian plane or any debris. I thought I had problems trying to locate Martin. How the hell do you lose an entire airplane?

I called Mac at home. No answer. I called her personal cell. No answer. I left a message. I called her back up cell. No answer. I didn't leave a message. I hung up. I had the key to her house. It took me twenty-five minutes to drive to Mac's house. Her Corvette was not in the driveway. I walked up the walkway and knocked at the door. No answer. I unlocked the door, and walked in.

"Police, search warrant," I screamed, expecting to hear Mac shout something nasty back at me. I heard nothing.

I did a quick walkthrough. No Mac. She either went to the station or was en-route when Jimenez and I called. Maybe she went shopping, or God knows where she went. I peeked in the garage. Her car was gone. Everything appeared in order. She hadn't left in too much of a hurry. I left the house being sure to lock the door. I looked on the street for Mac's car. No Vette anywhere. I tried her cell again, still no answer. I got in my car and drove to the Station.

Jimenez was in his upstairs office. "Anything from Mac?" I asked.

"Nothing."

"I didn't see her car in the lot. She may be following up on something. She came up with some hunch that she wanted to play out but wouldn't let me in on it."

Jimenez took a phone call. He did quick work of whoever was on the other end of the line. "The message I took had something to do with a positive ID on prints that Mac sent for comparison."

"Whose prints matched what?" I asked.

"All I was told was that the prints were a match."

"Do you have the message?"

Jimenez swiveled in his chair. I sat on the edge of his desk. He handed me the message. The name on the paper was Sergeant Tarkington. I called the number. Of course, Tarkington was out of the office.

There was no way I could get a number to reach him. I left my cell phone number. I asked that he call me back.

"This case keeps getting weirder and weirder. I'm beginning to think he did flee the country."

"Possible."

"I'm going to take a ride. I'll be back in a couple of hours. If Mac checks in, ask her to give me a call, please. If I hear from her, I'll call you. If Sergeant Tarkington calls, let me know. I left him my cell number."

"If I hear from him, I'll call you. I'd like to know whose prints match what."

I drove to the cemetery to talk to Rocky. I stood at his headstone. There were tears in my eyes.

"Hey, buddy. Once again, I'm sorry I let you down. We should be working this case together. With you here, we would have solved the thing by now."

I was wiping tears from my eyes when my cell rang. It was Jimenez. "Where are you?"

"I'm visiting Rocky."

There was no hesitation in Jimenez's voice, but there was urgency. "Get back to station code three."

"What the f**k is up?"

"Just get back here as fast as you can without killing anyone or yourself."

I looked down. "Sorry, my friend, duty calls. You know how that goes. See you real soon, buddy."

Obviously, something had happened that was related to the case. Maybe Jimenez got a hold of Mac. Maybe she let him in on the deal with the prints. I'm certain Jimenez would have told me or at least hinted that something sinister had happened. Whatever the reason, was that why Jimenez ordered me back to the Station post-haste? It obviously had something to do with the case. I'd bet my last bottle of Seagram's on that.

Weaving in and out of L.A. traffic, both surface street and freeway traffic, was an art. More of an art was not getting pulled over by the CHP or LAPD. As a matter of fact, I didn't see a black and white the entire trip. I arrived at the Station in record time. I parked my vehicle in the Chief's assigned spot. F**k him if he couldn't take a joke. I took the stairs to Jimenez's office three at a time. I knocked on his door. I didn't wait for an answer. I entered.

"Grab a chair."

"What's up?" I asked.

"Sergeant Tarkington called back." Jimenez didn't stop to take a breath. "Where did Mac get the prints?"

"Some of them came out of the trash from in front of Myra Williams' house."

Jimenez said, "She sent in the handle from the flushing lever off a toilet, along with several pieces of trash for printing. The prints came back to Austin Martin."

My mouth fell open. "Son of a bitch. The cunt *is* involved with the asshole."

"It looks like it. Have you heard from Mac?"

"No, you?"

Jimenez shook his head. "Apparently, she doesn't know the prints came back. And she has no way of knowing they're Martin's prints. That makes Mac vulnerable, very vulnerable."

Now I was worried. I took out my cell phone. I hurriedly dialed both her cell numbers. Calmly I left a message on each phone. "Call me. I'm getting hungry and horny." I rubbed my chin. "The lever must have come from the toilet in Williams' house. That's why Mac was hell-bent on getting back into the house; why she bought a new lever.

She took the one from Myra's bathroom. She exchanged it with one she bought. But she had no PC to take that out of the house, so we went dumpster diving for the rest of the prints.

"Do you think we have enough for a search warrant?"

"Probably, you know for a fact where the trash came from, correct?"

"Actually, the trash collector picked up the container from in front of Myra's house. He dropped it off at the station. Mac and I went through it. We picked out the garbage that would print best. One quick phone call could lock up the fact that the container came from Myra's place."

"Go ahead and make the call. I'll find a judge to issue a warrant."

We had the warrant in three hours. What we didn't have was a call from Mac. I liked this less and less. If Mac didn't know the prints had come back, if she didn't know they had come back to Martin, she could be in major danger. Now I *was* worried. When I walked back into Jimenez's office, Sullivan was seated in front of Jimenez's desk.

"It seems you're closing in on Martin."

"Mac made the connection. I don't know how, but Martin is absolutely linked to Williams."

"Where the hell's your girlfriend?"

"It's Investigator Mackenzee to you. If I knew where Mac was, she'd be sitting here right now. I don't know. I'm concerned, seriously concerned. I think the best thing we can do is serve the warrant at Williams' house."

Jimenez said, "I agree. The sooner, the better. I'm assuming no one is at the house, but I'll have SWAT on standby just in case. The three of us will take a run out there. I've already contacted Palmdale Sheriffs. They gave us the green light to handle it and to call them with concerns. If there is anyone at home, I'll bring in SWAT."

"Keep in mind," Sullivan said, "We need Martin alive. I want to know where the f**k the money is."

"I want Mac in one piece." I had no real reason to believe Mac was in any serious trouble but there remained a nagging suspicion in the back of my diseased mind.

It was totally out of character for Mac not to return my phone calls. It was totally out of character for her not to call me several times a day if we weren't together. The drive out to Palmdale from the Station, with traffic the way it would be at this time of day, was ninety minutes. Jimenez made it in seventy minutes flat in an unmarked unit. Slowly and carefully, we walked from the street to the house, watching the windows and the front door for signs of movement inside.

Nothing stirred. We walked up the front steps. I knocked on the door. When I got no answer, Sully rang the bell. He got the same response I got; no response. We tried to look inside. The drapes, the shades, the curtains were drawn tight. Now what? On television, you occasionally

393

see cops picking locks. Most of what you see is based on true life experience.

I carry a pick kit. We were in the house within one minute. We divided up the house among the three of us. We were looking for any sign that Martin had been in the house. This included searching the house for a hidden room or a basement or an attic or any other place where Martin could hide in relative comfort. Contrary to what you see in thirty minutes or one hour of television, this is a daunting task.

It would take us several hours to thoroughly search the house. We needed proof that Williams had knowingly been hiding a fugitive in her house. This would not only give us Martin, but it would also help us build a case against Myra Williams for aiding and abetting a fugitive. We were overly thorough. In police work, that's the only way to do business.

In carpentry, there's an expression, measure twice cut once. In police work, a life can depend on leg work and often does. If nothing else, the three of us were professionals. When JFK was murdered back in November of 1963, Lee Oswald had actually been in the Fed's house, their office. He dropped off a letter.

They wrote it off even though they had had an eye on Oswald. Had someone done the footwork, maybe, Kennedy would not have been assassinated. Who knows? I had always been one to be cautious and careful, except at the scene of the robbery when Rocky was killed. That haunted me. I had to get Martin. I searched the bedroom walls. I crawled into the back of the closet, looking for a recessed wall or door in the ceiling that could lead to the attic or a door on the floor that could hide a basement room.

I was sure that Jimenez and Sully were doing the same. I found zilch. I'm certain Jimenez and Sullivan found the same otherwise I would have heard one of them shout out their find. I crawled under the bed. I lifted the mattress. I checked the bathroom. I moved on to the dresser drawers and went through each damn drawer, painstakingly. I found blouses, scarves, collars, chokers, bras, and panties.

I found neatly folded shorts, jewelry, and some loose change. In other words, I didn't find useable jack shit. Nothing, not one f*****g useable item that said Martin was or had been a resident. I met Sully and Jimenez in the living room.

"Cleaner than a new car," Jimenez said.

Sullivan was downcast, "Same here, nothing, an absolute zero."

"We're going to do it again," Jimenez said dryly. "This time, we'll switch rooms. Be as thorough as you were in round one."

We did this three times. Each time we took different rooms. The final result was not surprising, with no hits, no runs, but apparently one error. Myra and Martin were winning this game. We were rapidly running out of innings. The next move was decided over lunch in Palmdale.

We had no more moves. There was nothing to do at this point but wait, wait to hear from Mac. The only other thing we could do was send out an updated BOLA of Martin to all airports, car rental facilities, and railroad agencies in case he attempted to flee the country. If he somehow had an idea that we were closing in, he'd probably try to get out of the country. I decided when we got back to the Station to go back to Mac's place to do a more thorough search.

I was now worried. It was dark when we arrived back at APD. I walked into the Station to check with dispatch to see if they had heard anything from Mac. Dispatch had nothing. I walked to the lot, to my car and then on to Mac's house. It was 2000 hours. I was in Mac's living room twenty minutes after I left the Station. I looked around. I had only been in Mac's house half a dozen times. I didn't know the house well.

In my few years as a cop, because Amity is such an active city crime wise, I had been in many houses. I had viewed many crime scenes. Some had been "staged" or made to look like something was done in the house that really wasn't. You get a "feel" for this sort of thing. I had no such feeling. I walked each room in Mac's house twice. I was more than careful in searching the house. I couldn't find anything out of order. That didn't mean nothing was awry.

It meant nothing appeared to me to be ***off-center.*** I sat on the couch. I thought I looked, I tried to visualize. Mac and I had made love on that couch. I ran my hand over the cushions. My eyes came to rest on the phone that was sitting on the mahogany table next to the couch. I stood up. I looked down at the phone. There were messages on that phone. I played the messages. There were three from me and one from Jimenez. There was one saved message. I played it. Immediately I recognized the voice.

It was Myra Williams. "Investigator Mac, this is Myra Williams. Please call me when you get this message. It's important. It's six forty-five. Thanks. Talk with you." I played the message a second time, then a third time. I verified the time on the answering machine. I listened again to the message. There was urgency to Myra's voice but not panic in her voice.

CHAPTER 27

ULTIMATE CONCLUSION

I looked at my watch. It was twenty-six hours from the time of that call. A lot could happen in twenty-six hours. The more time that elapses in a missing person's case the less chance you have of finding that person alive. I was now more than concerned. Myra had phoned Mac; undoubtedly, Mac had returned the call. I picked up her phone. I looked. There was no return call to the 661 area, which was the area in which Myra lived. I guessed Mac returned the call on one of her two cell phones. There was no sign of either cell phone in the house.

This was bad news, very bad news. If Myra and Martin were tied together, if Mac didn't know the prints had come back a match, which she didn't know, Mac was in danger. If Myra had any clue that we were slowly starting to piece things together, Mac could be a target. I called Jimenez. I brought him up to date. Then I had a thought and ran it by him.

If Martin was already out of the country, it now appears he wasn't, we now have a need to alert the airports and the hotels and motels around the airports. Chances are he'll be attempting to board a flight.

He could be accompanied by Myra, or they could be traveling alone. Chances are when we find one the other would be close by.

"Let's do this," I said to Jimenez. "Let's get half a dozen of our reserves on the phones. Let's alert airport security, motel and hotel security around LAX, Burbank Airport and John Wayne Airport in Orange County. Make sure they remind security that Martin will be in disguise. The asshole is creative, and he could be incognito as the Pope for all we know.

"Also, Mac's car is gone. She could be with Martin. Have dispatch run the R/O for Mac. Have the reserves also get that out to security. Maybe we'll get lucky. If I had to bet, I'd say Martin would head for a country that has no extradition treaty with the U.S. I know Canada will not extradite any U.S. citizen who faces the death penalty.

"Can we find out which countries have no extradition treaties with us? Also, when the reserves make their phone calls, they need to stress extra security measures for Canada and any country having no extradition with us. Can we get this done?"

"I'm on it. I know Morocco has no extradition treaty." Jimenez said.

"How the hell do you happen to know that?"

"It was a question on my Sergeant's exam."

"You gotta' be kidding."

"And you thought it was easy passing the sergeant's oral," Jimenez said.

"I appreciate it, sir. I owe you one more," I said.

"I'm keeping score."

"I'm going to work my way to Burbank airport. I'm going to check the lots. Then I'll hit LAX and finally Orange County, John Wayne Airport. Keep me posted."

Burbank airport was a piece of cake compared to LAX. I cruised the parking lot. As I cruised, looking for any sign of Mac's car, I thought it possible that she was shacked up with some guy. Hell, I had no lock on her. We were both free to do as we wanted. I didn't want any other woman. I didn't think Mac wanted another guy, yet the possibility did exist. I carefully checked each lot. It was a monotonous task, but it had to be done. It took me three and a half hours to draw a blank.

I needed something to eat. I wanted a couple of shots. Mostly, I wanted to know that the woman I loved was okay. I pulled out of the parking lot. I stopped in a red zone. I took out my cell. I called Mac's cell. It immediately went to recording. I called her private cell. It went to recording. I didn't bother to leave a message.

An airport police officer on a bike pulled up to my car. "Move it, please."

"I will. I'm on the job. Amity PD." I showed him my badge.

"Sorry, sir, anything I can help with?"

"We're looking for a vehicle." I gave him Mac's vehicle's description then the plate number.

"We've been briefed, sir. We have several bicycle officers out looking for it. Do you think it's here?"

"My best guess is LAX, but who the hell knows. The guys a cop killer, so be alert, be damned careful. We don't want to see anyone else go down except this asshole."

"Got it, sir." He got back on his bike and pedaled off.

I drove out of the airport and back onto the southbound 5 freeway. I drove for five minutes. My cell rang. I picked it up, violating the f*****g vehicle code. "Yeah." It was Jimenez.

"You're not going to believe this."

I was ready to believe almost anything about this case. "You found Mac?"

"We located Mac's car."

"You found her car?"

"Hotel security found it at LAX Comfort Corner. We're checking to see if we can pinpoint a room number. A retired sheriff doing part-time security work was briefed by one of our Reserves. The sheriff found it."

"I'm on my way to LAX. What's the sheriff's name and cell number? I'll call him. I want to meet with him ASAP."

We're getting a team together, including myself, Sully, and SWAT. It'll be at least two hours before we're on the scene." Jimenez gave me the sheriff's name.

"Let me pull over so I can write this shit down. I'll never remember the number."

I pulled to the right shoulder and took out my pocket pad. I wrote down LAX OFC Milner, followed by his phone number. I gunned the engine. Without signaling, I pulled into traffic cutting off at least one car. The guy flipped me off. I blew him a kiss.

I called Milner from five miles north of LAX. We agreed to meet at a Denny's a mile or so north of the airport. When I walked into Denny's, I immediately spotted Milner, who was seated in a booth facing the door dressed in airport blue. Milner was at least in his mid-fifties, had thinning black hair on the side of his head. He was overweight by at least thirty-five pounds. His blue airport police shirt was short sleeve showing half a dozen tattoos on both arms. He held out his hand as I slid in the seat across from him.

"You found the car?"

Milner nodded, "Underground parking area."

"How long has the car been there?"

The waitress came over with another menu, "Coffee, please." Milner had an ice tea in front of him.

"Don't know that yet. Only found the car an hour or so ago."

I was trying to think fast, "Can you call your hotel's front desk for me? I want to know if two women and a man checked in within the last two days listing the plate and make of car on your check-in form. I also need to know their room number or numbers."

If Martin did meet up with Myra and Mac it would be in separate cars. Assuming Williams and Mac were in Mac's Vette, Martin would have

402

to be driving a separate car. Milner smiled, gulped down a swallow of tea, and punched two numbers into his cell.

"Milner here, Robert, I'm working with Detective Kano on the security issue we were briefed on earlier. I need this kept 1035." Milner looked at me and nodded.

"We need to know if two women and a man checked in, in the last two days, and listed their vehicle as a ………."

After Milner got off the phone, he briefed me on every last detail.

"I need to know every little thing. Something that might mean little to you might be a game-changer for us."

Unfortunately, Milner had little to tell. The waiting game had begun. What we needed to know was if Myra, Martin and/or Mac checked into the hotel. Milner and I made polite small talk. During the conversation, my thoughts slipped back to Mac, hugging Myra, which was strange, over the top. It grated on me. My phone rang. It was Jimenez. The team was assembled and would be leaving APD within fifteen minutes. That meant they'd arrive by 2230 hours.

"Hold on." Milner looked at me. My guy is with the hotel desk clerk, Eduardo. He says no man, two women checked in with that vehicle. He remembers because one of them was wearing long white gloves, a black choker, black boots, and a black hat. She looked like she belonged on the cover of a B and D magazine."

I had read my share of bondage and discipline magazine. I probably read a large percentage of your share of B and D magazines, too. That was another fantasy. Many cops had B and D fantasies. How many

403

actually played them out, I had little idea. There were reasons for the B and D play. For some, it was a welcome relief from the constant being in control that was mandated by the profession.

Eduardo had a good eye. Myra did fit that bill. "No, guy?"

"Not with them."

"Room number?" I asked.

"5221."

"When did they check-in?"

"It was yesterday about 1500 hours."

I rubbed my hands over my face. No man checked in with them.

"Can Eduardo describe the other woman, and what name they checked in under?" I was worried.

Milner took another swig of iced tea while he waited for Eduardo to come up with the information.

"Myra Williams and Dee Mackenzee, the second woman was a tall, well-built blonde, busty, and serious looking. She tried to strike up a conversation with Eduardo, but the other woman starred her down."

"Let me have the phone. Eduardo, this is investigator Kano. Did Mac, the other woman with Myra, say anything to you, anything at all?"

Eduardo was silent. Then he began, "She looked at the clock and said, "My watch stopped. My watch says its two ten and five seconds. I corrected her and told her the correct time."

404

"That's it." I thought about that for several seconds. Mac was trying to tell us something. "Two ten and five," I muttered to myself. Then it came to me. Two ten point five is the penal code for someone who's being held hostage. Was I reaching, or was Mac a hostage? "Did they have luggage?"

"The B and D lady had a small black luggage bag, small enough to carry on a plane."

"Did either say anything about a destination?"

"No. But you know what. As they were walking away, the blonde said, that's funny, now my watch says five twenty-nine."

Numbers don't lie. I had a two ten-point five and a five twenty-nine. I had it all. It all added up. I handed the phone back to Milner. I laughed. "I'll be a son of a bitch. I'll be a god damned son of a bitch."

Jimenez and Sullivan arrived, followed by a nondescript SWAT van. They staged outside LAX in a closed shopping center lot. We assembled inside the SWAT van. I invited Airport Security Officer Milner to join our meeting. The SWAT van "meeting room" was large enough to accommodate all of us. Some of us were standing. I asked Jimenez if I could head up at least the first part of the meeting. He gave me the green light. I put both hands on the back of a chair then looked at the group. I cleared my throat to get everyone's attention. "Let's get started. A police officer's life might be at stake." You could hear a quarter drop in thick grass.

"My name is Kano for those of you who don't know me, although I think everyone does. Dee Mackenzee, Detective Jimenez, FBI Agent

Sullivan, and I have been involved with the hunt for the killer of Officer Rocky Calhoun for some time now. I think we have located Austin Martin, Rocky's killer, the guy who got away with a small fortune in untraceable cash from the armored car robbery, which cost me one leg.

"It's quite possible Martin is holding Investigator Mackenzee hostage. It's also quite possible Martin has the cash with him. Or maybe stashed close by in an airport locker.

"A couple of seats to my left is retired Sheriff Milner, who is now LAX Airport Security. Sheriff Milner, after a security meeting, located Mac's car in a covered parking area. We have probable information that Martin and Mac are in room 5221 of the LAX Comfort Corner.

"What I need SWAT to do is scout out the room. I want to know the best and least dangerous way of extricating Mac from that room *alive*. I won't pretend to know what you guys know. I'm sure you've forgotten more about this type of extraction thing than I'll ever know. My goal, our goal is to get Mac out alive.

"You may have a clear shot through the window. You may want to pull a ruse to get them out of the room and then take Martin into custody, whatever it takes. I looked at my watch. I have 2355 hours. Take an hour, and then let's reconvene here. I want your very best assessment and intelligence; nothing less. When we reconvene, I'll give you some chilling news."

I had an hour to replay this in my mind time after time. Was I reading more into this than there was to read into it? Mac had said it was two ten and five seconds. Did that really translate to a two ten point five, being held hostage, or was that the last-ditch desperation of a cop with little prior experience as a detective? The five twenty-nine was more obvious. I was convinced I was correct. It is said in police work that there are rarely coincidences.

Too many coincidences usually point to a suspect's guilt. Too many coincidences can make or break your case. It's a matter of following up on those coincidences and not being too lazy to do the footwork. I had too many coincidences. I was sure as hell not too lazy to do the footwork.

I was on duty. But a shot would clear my head. Two shots would make me sharper than a meat cutter's knife. I took a quick walk and wandered into a topless bar. A bit ironic, I thought. Mac gets on me for looking at Myra's titties, and here I am in a topless bar. I walked to the bar and ordered two shots of Seagram's. On stage was a tall thin, ebony beauty. She was wearing the white bottoms of a bikini bathing suit, nothing else, not even pasties.

I downed the first shot. I watched **_ebony_** 'play' with a silver pole. She straddled it, looking over her shoulder at several men who had gathered around to watch. I watched. The dance was sexy as hell. So was she. As I was about to down the second shot, a woman in her thirties walked over to me?

"Want to buy me a drink, handsome?"

She was obviously working, probably for the bar. I downed the second shot. I was already feeling better, my concentration was dead on. I remembered my freshman year in college. I was out of state and

407

on the prowl for a piece of ass. I found my way into a neighborhood bar. In the bar, was one well stacked, young gal. I envisioned her in my bed with my head between her legs. I walked over to her with a shot glass in my hand.

"Buy you a drink?"

She didn't hesitate. I'm a lesbian, you're wasting your time, trust me."

That was the best put down I was ever fed. If true, I was out of luck. If a lie, it was a kind lie. Either way, for me, that ship had sailed.

"I wish I had time, angel, but I'm late for a date with my boyfriend."

I turned and walked out of the bar, hoping she was staring at my tight ass, thinking how can a good looking guy like that waste his organ on a *him!* I walked back to the SWAT van. I was certain I was on the money with my trail of coincidences. I knocked on the van's rear door. It was ten to one in the morning. Everyone was already in the van. I popped a stick of gum in my mouth.

"Sir," I asked the SWAT commander, "Are you ready to report?"

Sergeant Maldonado stepped to the front of the group, "Here's our best intelligence, sir. There are two females in room 5221. That room faces the northeast. From the rooftop directly across the street, we can neutralize either woman. From your description, Mac has been identified as Investigator Mackenzee. We have no male suspect."

I jumped in, "We do. I'll get to that in a minute. Did you observe anything that tells you Mackenzee is being held hostage?"

"The Williams lady has a gun in her right hand. It's not aimed at Investigator Mackenzee. It is at the low ready."

"Given the green light, are you certain you can neutralize Williams?"

"No question, sir. You can bet your retirement on it."

"Wait a damn minute!" Agent Sullivan yelled, "Where the f**k is Martin and my damn money?"

"Second things first," I yelled back. It isn't *your* money. And for your information, Myra and Martin are one and the same." It was suddenly so quiet in the room; you could hear grass growing.

The first mouth to open was, of course, Sullivan's, "Are you going to tell me that Williams is Martin and Martin is Williams?"

"Good Sully, real deep thinking, your teachers would be real proud of you," I said as sarcastically as my brain could conjure. Then I added, mostly for the benefit of SWAT, "This is a strange world we live in today.

"I am saying that all the time Martin spent time, most likely in Thailand, the asshole had a sex change operation. I don't know how complete it is. He/she may still have male plumbing…or not. We can let Sully investigate that." There was muffled laughter from everyone but Sullivan. "Further, Mac is being held hostage by he/she." I took a deep breath. "What's our solution, SWAT?"

Sergeant Maldonado spoke up. "The large window in room 5221 faces the northeast. From a rooftop almost directly across the street, we have a drone's view of that room. My man can open a can of peas without spilling one damn pea from the can with one shot. But my suggestion is we clear the floor and give Martin or Williams or he/she or she/he a chance to surrender. If that fails to do it, we can consider plan B."

"I don't like it," Sullivan said.

Jimenez spoke up for the first time. He was very professional. "What is it that you don't like, Agent Sullivan?"

"The money, if we take Martin out, what about the damn money?"

I spoke up, "Martin is carrying a piece of luggage. I believe some of the cash is in that luggage."

"And if it isn't?"

"We'll all chip in and make your mortgage payment." I wasn't trying to be funny. I was pissed. But with me, the piss builds slowly. "The truth Sully is I don't give a duck's f**k about your f*****g money.

My concern is the life of one of our own. Do you f*****g understand that? How much is a human life worth to you, Sully? Huh? Answer the f*****g question you piece of shit for brains."

Jimenez yelled at me. "Enough. Knock it the f**k off! Tony's right, Agent Sullivan. The money is secondary. We're going out there to save a sister officer. We're going to do just that."

That gave me my opening. "Detective Jimenez, if it's okay with you, sir, I'd like to call the shots on this one. Let me head up the team?"

Jimenez didn't flinch. "It's your ballgame, Tony. Throw high hard ones."

"Thank you, sir," I said.

"Now wait a minute Jimenez."

"It's Detective Jimenez to you, Agent Sullivan. And while we're at it, why *don't you shut the f**k up*?"

It sounded like two in the morning in a small New England hamlet in December. You could hear snowmelt.

Sergeant Maldonado broke a very awkward silence. "I hate to quote an infamous prick, but *we're all in the same canoe*. How about we all paddle in unison?"

Then he continued, "I'll tell you what I tell my team on occasion. We need to put principles before personalities. There is life on the line, a fellow officer's life. If there are differences in this room, settle them after we get our sister home safely. If you can't put your bullshit aside for now, get the f**k out of here because you are going to do us more harm than good. Anyone want to opt-out?" Of course, nobody moved.

I said, "Okay, let's get to work. By my watch, it is 0145 hours. At 0230 hours, everyone is to be in place. Senior SWAT Officer Cusso has a map, an assignment board, and a location directory at the chalkboard to my right. Gather around, and he'll go over that with you. He'll answer any questions. When Senior SWAT Officer Cusso is finished with his briefing, I'll finalize the briefing with the game plan.

"If there are no questions, gather around the chalkboard, please. While we were meeting, hotel security was clearing the fifth floor of the hotel. Everything was going smoothly."

At 0225 hours, we were in place awaiting the signal from SWAT's Sergeant Maldanado.

The radio crackled, "We're making the call," Maldonado said.

The initial plan was for a negotiator to call room 5221. An attempt would be made to contact Williams. I was standing next to one of the two SWAT negotiators when he placed the call. The call was on speaker. It rang several times. No one picked up. Maldanado disconnected.

"We'll give it a couple then try again."

I nodded. I looked at Sullivan, who was standing on the other side of the negotiator. Sully was beyond pissed. Jimenez was allowing me to call the shots. If the phone call didn't work, the next option could be "neutralizing" Williams. This didn't bother me if it meant freeing Mac. I knew SWAT Negotiator Scott Brewer well since we went through the LAPD Academy together. The guy had the body of Arnold Schwarzenegger. He accomplished that with dedication, consistency, and hard work, not with steroids.

Scott looked down at my leg. "How's it going?"

"I don't even know it's not mine half the time."

"You got balls, my friend, big, round, hairy balls. Most guys would have shriveled up and died. You're a fighter, I like that."

412

I nodded my thanks, "You're a fighter, too. I like that." I looked at Sullivan.

"I don't care what it takes. I want Mac out of there unharmed."

"You know we don't make promises. We'll do everything possible to bring her out unharmed, everything."

"I know you will."

Scott made a second call to the room. The phone rang twice. It was picked up.

"This is LAPD Officer Brewer. Who am I speaking with?"

There was a brief hesitation, then, "You know who this is. What do you want?"

Brewer played a long shot. "Listen, Martin, we have this hotel surrounded. You cannot get out. One way or the other, you will be taken into custody. Come on out now and let the process begin. We do not, I stress we do not want to see anyone get hurt, Martin."

Williams or Martin didn't bite. "You done?" The voice on the other end didn't wait for an answer. "Now it's my turn. Nobody is going to give up. You are going to bring a car around the front, and we're walking out of here. Get cute, the bitch dies. I hope you understand Brewer. Put yourself in my shoes. Do I have a damn thing to lose? I don't think so."

"I have to clear that with my superiors. That's not a decision I can make. Give me fifteen minutes, and I'll get back to you. In the meantime, is there anything we can get you?"

413

"Yeah, a new life."

"Let me talk with Mackenzee," I asked.

"When I get my car."

"I want to be certain she's okay."

"She's fine." Then Williams added, "For now."

"Don't hurt her. Give me a couple of minutes to check with my superiors. You know, the way our court system works today, you never know what can happen. If you walk out of there now we'll tell the judge you cooperated, the rest is a crapshoot. You may come out a winner, Brewer told Williams or Martin."

Brewer was doing a helluva' job. But there was no way Williams was going to make a curtain call. This was going to end with us pulling the curtain over Williams all the way. That was the only way it could end.

"Williams continued. "I was a loser that day I was born. Nothing is going to change that. I don't want to hurt Mackenzee, but if I don't get my car, she's going to pay the price. Are we very clear on that score?"

"Perfectly." Williams disconnected.

Brewer stared at the floor. Finally, he looked up at me, "Let's wait fifteen minutes, then I'll give her another call. I was trying to get Williams to bite and confirm she was Martin. She didn't take the bait."

"I got that. Good try, no ten ring. We both know she's not coming out of there on her own. She'll be carried out," I said.

"I've seen more desperate people surrender. Let's play it out. My guess is that you're right. I don't gamble because I'm wrong more than I am on the money. Let's give it the benefit of the doubt," Brewer said.

"Have you heard anything from Rocky's widow?"

"She's back with her folks, at least temporarily. She's taking it hard. They were a hell of a team. They had it going for them. They….." I started to get choked up.

Brewer observed my facial contortions. He changed the subject.

"How are you and Mac doing?" he asked.

I shook my head. "Isn't anything private around here? Does the whole world know about us?"

"Just the entire world of LAPD, Amity PD and the CHP." Then he added, "Probably now the FBI."

Fifteen minutes later, Brewer placed the second call. "No deal," he said when Williams picked up the phone. "The boss says we can't give you the car. Here's what we are willing to do. Let Mackenzee out of there now, then walk out two minutes later. We'll give the judge a written statement that you cooperated."

Williams laughed contemptuously. "That's like marking the price of a new car up thirty percent and giving me twenty-five percent off. I doubt it. I get the car, or Mackenzee becomes the late Mackenzee.

415

You've got five minutes to get back to me with an answer, Brewer. Car for a cop sounds like a good deal to me. Five minutes." Williams hung up.

I whispered in Brewer's ear. He nodded. Brewer keyed the mic. "Presto, this is Team Leader. Do you have a fix?"

"That's affirmative, sir. Dead on and consistent. Give me the word, and we call the game because of rain."

That meant Presto could take Williams out any time the command was given, which is why he had been nicknamed Presto. He could change the outcome of the game on command. One of my favorite lines came out of a Clint Eastwood movie. Clint said, "A good man knows his limitations." Clint was dead on. I knew my limitations. That's why SWAT was by my side. They were the talent.

They were trained to do what I couldn't do. I'd make the call. They'd save the day, I hoped. Losing Rocky, and part of my leg was tough enough. Losing Mac would be a catastrophe I didn't think I could survive. Sully reentered the picture. The call was not going to be Brewers. Jimenez had given me the nod. I just had to give Brewer the go-ahead.

"Remember that god damn money!" Sully yelled. "I want that money."

I reacted. I reacted badly. I reacted very badly. I hit Sullivan with a right cross so hard I lost my balance. He went down. By the time he hit the ground, I said to Brewer, "Do it! Do it now!" I yelled.

Brewer was calm. He simply said, "Presto Chango!"

"My light is green? Confirm?"

"Confirmed," I said emphatically, "F*****g confirmed."

It took less than a split second. Brewer announced over the radio, "Suspect is neutralized. No peas spilled!"

It was almost all over. For Rocky, for myself, I wish I could have been Presto. I wish I could have squeezed the trigger. For Sully, who was getting his suited ass off the floor, I hoped the money was in that damn suitcase. But I had more important things on my mind than money. I ran toward room 5221, toward Mac. Several things occurred just outside room 5221. The most important was Mac running into my open arms. We hugged for a long, long time, or so it seemed.

Williams, who lay dead from one shot to the head, was covered with the white bed sheet. I walked over to the covered body. I uncovered the front of the sheet. I looked down at Martin's face. I said, Gotcha.

Then I spit on his face. I let go of the sheet. I looked up at a cloudy sky. "It's over, Rocky. It's over!" Sully walked over to the piece of luggage that he hoped contained the money. He knelt down. I was on one side of him, Mac, on the other. Brewer stood behind me. I heard Sullivan take a breath. He clicked open one side of the suitcase then the other.

Finally, he opened the case. The first thing I observed was green. It wasn't money. It was panties and things lacy. Sully started tossing underwear and other women's accessories onto the floor. He got to the bottom of the suitcase. Sully found not one freakin' penny. He looked at me.

I shrugged. "Got a panty fetish?" I asked.

Sully didn't need bullets to kill me, his look said it all. I offered him my hand to help him up. He declined.

CHAPTER 28

SAFE AND SOUND

Mac and I were stretched out on the bear rug in front of the fireplace in my living room. She was wearing my second favorite pair of black panties and a matching bra. I was wearing tight white briefs and a tee shirt.

"When did you know about Williams?"

"When the morgue fingerprinted her and the prints came back Martins."

"Okay, smartass, when did you think you knew?" I put my hand inside the waistband of Mac's panties and squeezed her tight ass.

"When I caught you looking at those fake, too good to be real titties. And the one set of prints found in the house. I couldn't get those out of my mind. Remember the hug I gave her that you questioned?

I nodded.

"I pressed up against her trying to feel for a bulge."

"You were feeling for a dick?"

"I thought maybe she was transvestite instead of transgender. But she had the works. Her faucet was fixed. It was most likely those trips to Thailand. That's when I decided to go for the prints. She was always wearing those damn gloves. That was another hint.

"I'm guessing his hands were burnt in the robbery when the money truck blew up. When the house was burglarized and the bed set afire, he saw an opportunity and took it."

"What about the prints?"

"The one place you're not going to wear gloves is in the bathroom. So I decided to see if I could get prints off the lever that you flush on the toilet. That was not a big deal. But I had no PC for that, even if the prints were a match. So, you had to become T-Man for a day."

I took my hand out of Mac's panties and slid my right hand into her bra. I squeezed her nipple playfully. Mac smiled. She was getting turned on, "And then you f****d up big time."

"I did," Mac nodded. "I had given Myra my number. She called me. I had no idea she suspected. She did, and I guess I'm not as good as I thought I was."

I rolled Mac over on her stomach. "You're better than you thought. I can and will attest to that under oath."

I slid her panties off. I sniffed them. Mac grabbed them from me and rubbed them between my legs, or I probably should say *my leg.* Either way, it was game on.

SUCCESS AND WORKING TOGETHER

Three days later, we were in the Chief's office. The *"we"* included Jimenez, Mac, Sullivan, the Chief, the Assistant Chief, and me. The Chief came directly to the point.

"Your team, and SWAT who I met with this morning, did one hell of a job. You'll all receive commendations for your part. Unfortunately, the money is still missing. Sully, Mac, Tony, you are being assigned to track down the missing cash. As of now, Mac is on loan to Amity PD with an invite to come over here permanently. Sully is going to head up the team. Anybody have any questions?"

I looked at Sully, Sully smiled. "Payback's a bitch!" His smile broadened. He stood up. I stood up. We were toe to toe. He extended his hand. I extended my hand.

"The hunt is on. Let's talk about it over lunch. You're buying."

I suspected lunch might be strained, it wasn't. The opposite was true. Sully actually had a likable side to him. I even apologized for punching him in the mouth. I thought Mac was going to choke on the tomato in her salad. Sully bought lunch. The lunch meeting concluded with a decision that we take a three day weekend and reconvene at the same coffee shop Monday morning at ten hundred hours to set a plan of attack for tracking and finding the money. We left lunch laughing. I drove out to the cemetery by myself.

I knelt at Rocky's marker. "First things first," I said aloud, looking down at the grave marker. I placed a carton of Marlboro cigarettes atop the marker with a lighter. "You earned these partner, enjoy. They can't hurt you now." I reached into my jacket pocket. I took out the jewelry box. I opened it. I took out the wrist band. I read aloud, "Rocky Calhone: *FRIEND, FTO, DAMN GOOD COP!*" I put it around my right wrist. "That'll get buried with me, friend. It'll never come off."

Mac and I decided to take two of those three days to drive to Solvang to the Meadow Lark, where Rocky, Paula, Mac, and I never did make it. It took us no time to throw clothing and what not together because we didn't need much in the way of clothing. It also took us only a few minutes to reach the freeway since traffic was light.

The room at the Meadow Lark boasted a fireplace, a fenced back yard, a Jacuzzi, and Mac. It was 2200 hours. It was dark. It was peaceful. It was quiet. You could hear an occasional bird, the croaking of a couple of frogs, and the crackling of the warm fireplace. We were lying on a plush grey carpet, both of us covered only by the same thin blanket. Mac took out a small box from beneath the blanket.

She said softly, "Close your eyes and give me your right arm."

Submissive that I am, I immediately followed Mac's directive. I felt something cold sliding over my wrist. When it was in place, Mac said, "Open."

Mac had slipped a silver bracelet over my wrist. She had adjusted it so it fit firmly, not tightly on my wrist. It read, *One day at a time, I hope this is forever. All my love, always, Mac.*

I looked up. I said out loud, "I love you."

I wiped away a tear and kissed Mac gently. "My turn. Close your eyes." I reached under the sheet. "Give me your left hand." I slipped an engagement ring on Mac's finger. "Open your eyes, angel. We belong together. We were meant to be together. I'll always love you. We're a team. Besides, I can't live without your panties or you. Will you marry me?"

Mac's eyes opened wide. She sighed. It was not a good sigh. "Sit up."

There was something in Mac's voice, an urgent something. I sat up immediately. I looked into Mac's eyes.

UNEXPECTED SURPRISE

Mac looked down at the sheet that covered her. "I want to marry you. I really want to marry you. I want us to be together, *ALWAYS*. I want to spend the rest of my life with you. I want to be with you always. I'll give you another chance to propose after you hear what I have to tell you. You need to know something. I should have told you a long time ago before any of this started, but it happened so fast, so damn fast and I fell so hard, so very hard. I was scared.

"I love you with all my heart and all my soul, you are my everything." Mac looked up into my eyes. I could feel her love for me in those eyes. "I'm no different than Myra," Mac said softly. Many years ago, I was a guy. I had sex reassignment surgery."

My cell phone rang as I got out of the shower. It was Detective Jimenez. "When you're finished with your vacation, I need you to

423

report to the Station. We're going to start hunting down the stolen money."

That was not the end. It was the beginning, a brand new beginning, which included a treasure hunt and major decision. If you don't believe this happened, drive through Amity. I may find a reason to pull you over. We can chat.

THE BEGINNING!

Post Script: The silver bracelet I wear on my right wrist is in memory of Loy D. Cleveland who in real life was my FTO and my partner. Loy and I were the best of friends. The bracelet reads: 08/23/53: Friend. FTO. Damn Good Cop. 08/10/99. I hope you enjoyed this novel, buddy. I'm so sorry I let you down. I'm sorry you're gone. I miss you. Save me that seat in your unit!

Made in the USA
Middletown, DE
07 April 2021